INSIDE
Full-Service
Community Schools

To all the people out there like Sue Maguire who have the dedication, energy, and patience to do this, and to George Dryfoos, whose care and attention have enabled me to continue my work documenting what they do. —JD

For those kids whose lives may be touched by these words, and, of course, for Chris and Kara. —SM

"The horror of September 11 makes the work to build comprehensive full-service community schools more important than ever. The values of democracy are at the heart of a community school. It is a center of learning for the entire community, a center that promotes discussion, tolerance, and collaboration among people of different religions, cultures, races, and ethnicities. It is a place that encourages all children to learn and to develop habits of citizenship and civic responsibility. Community schools, at their best, exemplify democracy in action, as people of all ages and backgrounds learn and work together as neighbors to build a better and more humane community, society, and world."

Ira Harkavy
Vice President, University of Pennsylvania
Chairman, Coalition for Community Schools

INSIDE
Full-Service
Community Schools

Joy Dryfoos • Sue Maguire

Skyhorse Publishing books may be purchased in bulk at special discounts for sales
promotion, corporate gifts, fund-raising, or educational purposes. Special
editions can also be created to specifications. For details, contact the Special
Sales Department, Sky Pony Press, 307 West 36th Street, 11th Floor,
New York, NY 10018 or info@skyhorsepublishing.com.

Skyhorse® and Skyhorse Publishing® are registered trademark of Skyhorse Publishing, Inc.®,
a Delaware corporation.

Visit our website at www.skyhorsepublishing.com.

10 9 8 7 6 5 4 3 2 1

Library of Congress Cataloging-in-Publication Data is available on file.

Cover design by Tracy E. Miller

Print ISBN: 978-1-5107-3697-9
Ebook ISBN: 978-1-5107-3703-7

Printed in the United States of America

Words of praise for
Inside Full-Service Community Schools

Inside Full-Service Community Schools provides a level of helpfulness, as well as necessary steps, to adults and children committed to coordinating the talents of entire communities to serve communities.

> Carole Biskar
> Principal
> Tualatin Elementary School (OR)

The voices of Joy Dryfoos as national policy analyst and Sue Maguire as school principal bring to life in new ways the vision of how full-service community schools can help students learn and families and communities succeed. This book will be of great value to policymakers and practitioners alike.

> Martin J. Blank
> Director for Community Collaboration
> Institute for Educational Leadership
> Washington, D.C.

Inside Full-Service Community Schools offers a lively dialogue between two of our country's leading voices on forging effective school-community partnerships. The book combines solid theoretical grounding with practical advice through a unique point-counterpoint structure. Policymakers, researchers, funders, and practitioners alike will find rich rewards from spending a few engaging hours with this important new book.

> Philip Coltoff
> Executive Director and Chief Executive Officer
> The Children's Aid Society
> New York, NY

Dryfoos and Maguire describe the steps that educators, parents, and community partners must take to establish a full-service school—the "ultimate" in school, family, and community partnerships.

> Joyce L. Epstein
> Director, Center on School, Family, and Community Partnerships
> Johns Hopkins University
> Baltimore, MD

Inside Full-Service Community Schools is a valuable tool for parents, educators, school officials, and elected officials who are interested in looking at innovative ways to improve learning and achievement for our nation's children. Well-run and vibrant community schools are thriving all across America. The authors have compiled a useful, comprehensive guide to what makes the best ones work.

> Sandra Feldman
> President
> American Federation of Teachers
> Washington, D.C.

From the nation's foremost expert on full-service schools, *Inside Full-Service Community Schools* shares information in such a way that both novices to the subject and knowledgeable individuals can learn something.

Donald G. Hackman
Associate Professor
Educational Leadership & Policy Studies
Iowa State University
Ames, IA

Inside Full-Service Community Schools will profoundly shape the national community school movement. Joy Dryfoos and Sue Maguire most ably tell the story of Molly Stark School, and in telling it they teach us what a community school is, how it might be developed, and why it is important to the future of our democracy. It is simply an excellent and important book.

Ira Harkavy
Associate Vice-President and Director
Center for Community Partnerships
Philadelphia, PA

Everyone concerned about the issues of adolescent development and community empowerment will find *Inside Full-Service Community Schools* to be a thoughtful, well-researched, and detailed account of a community school in the context of its community. Using the Molly Stark School in Bennington, Vermont as its focus, the book extends its analysis to similar programs across the country and provides a manual for educators and communities interested in the viability of community schools as a means of public education.

Thomas W. Payzant
Superintendent
Boston Public Schools (MA)

Dryfoos and Maguire have created a "must read" for anyone interested in starting a full-service community school. Their clear-headed analysis and advice will prove indispensable to educators and human service practitioners as they join forces to promote children's learning and development in our nation's schools.

Jane Quinn
Assistant Executive Director for Community Schools
The Children's Aid Society
New York, NY

This important volume cogently captures the potential of community schools not only as a means of providing more effective social and related services to children and families but also as a mechanism that will enhance student learning.

Michael S. Usdan
Senior Fellow
The Institute for Educational Leadership
Washington, D.C.

Dryfoos and Maguire move the concept of a full-service community school from the fringes of public education into the mainstream. [Their book] inspires the belief that the *best* schools are full-service community schools and motivates the reader to seek them out.

Lisa Villarreal
Director, California Center for Community-School Partnerships
Healthy Start Field Office
University of California, Davis

The presentation of the vision, juxtaposed with the practical experience, provides an extremely helpful and well-developed picture of full-service community schools.

Jan Walker
Assistant Professor
Educational Leadership & Policy Studies
Iowa State University
Ames, IA

What a generous book! Giving all their hearts, Dryfoos and Maguire have constructed a generous book about community schools, sharing what they know about community from doing, seeing, studying, and caring. Theory and practice come together in this very articulate book—a model of collaboration in itself that has great value for its specificity, its clarity, and its authenticity. It captures the vibrancy of real, honest, full-service and community schools. Like the best of these programs, this book is infused with energy. In itself, it is a terrific testimonial to partnerships that integrate, comprehend, and help us all to see and do the right thing for all our kids! Thank you!

Margot A. Welch
Director, Collaborative for Integrated School Services
Harvard Graduate School of Education
Cambridge, MA

Contents

Preface

This volume combines the research and observations of Joy Dryfoos, a long-time tracker of youth development programs and a strong advocate for full-service community schools across the country, and the day-to-day experiences of principal Sue Maguire of Molly Stark Elementary School, an emerging full-service community school in Bennington, Vermont. In a unique dialogue from complementary perspectives, the coauthors expose readers to a new approach to educational reform. This book has a strong bias: We hope to convince you to use these community school concepts to create public schools that will be able to meet the demands of our complex 21st-century society.

Community schools differ from traditional schools because they are open all the time as neighborhood hubs, operated through partnerships with community agencies, and designed to provide on-site support services to children and families. Educational enrichment is offered in the context of overcoming social and economic barriers to learning. Youth development and community involvement are important components. Around the country, many different models for incorporating these concepts have been advanced. It is important at the outset to state the basic idea: Remove burdens from schools by building partnerships.

This book begins with some background on the different paths we took to come to the same conclusion: Full-service community schools are an important solution to the problems confronted by many children, families, and their schools today. In Chapter 1, we go into detail about why schools and community agencies need to change the way they operate and bring community stakeholders together. We show that the diverse designs of full-service community schools are responsive to the growing list of barriers confronting children and families. Chapter 2 starts with a brief review of the various models of community schools that have been promulgated largely from the bottom up. The chapter goes on to present some planning concepts used to develop the programs around the country, and Sue Maguire describes how she went about planning the transformation of her school.

In Chapter 3, we present material about the numerous services and programs that can be offered in full-service community schools during the school day, including primary health and mental health services, family resource centers, preschool programs, high school programs, and some one-of-a-kind components that are found in selected community schools. We learn about the Molly Stark Family Center's experience with child care, dental services, parent programs, and other health and social service components within the school. After-school programs are presented in Chapter 4, with particular emphasis on the significant federal program—21st Century Community Learning Centers—which has greatly expanded the field. A number of state and local efforts are described, along with Molly Stark's extensive offerings in after-school enrichment and mentoring.

Chapter 5 looks at the special requirements of community school staffing, with emphasis on the important leadership roles of principals and the new category of community school coordinators. Consideration is also given to the use of youth workers in school settings and the importance of universities in developing more cross-disciplinary curricula to prepare educators, social workers, psychologists, and others to work across domains. In Chapter 6, we turn to a discussion of governance and the challenges that result from mixing school administrations with community-based agencies. How do you organize relationships between stakeholders so that someone is in charge and everyone has a voice in decision making? Many different approaches are reviewed along with the experience at Molly Stark, where the school is the lead agency.

In this book, we emphasize the "people factor" throughout, encouraging broader thinking on roles parents can play in schools. Chapter 7 shows ways that parents can be brought on board and reviews exemplary parent programs around the country. Evaluation research cited in Chapter 8 presents evidence that community schools can positively impact educational, health, and social outcomes. Data from Molly Stark document improvements in educational and behavioral outcomes that may be attributable to the transformation of the school.

We do not downplay the barriers to implementing these models, acknowledging in Chapter 9 that many issues, such as time, space, turf, maintenance, confidentiality, and replication difficulties, must be resolved to create a new and well-functioning school-community institution. At Molly Stark, the greatest concern is sustainability: Where is the financial support going to come from to keep programs like theirs up and running? As we show in Chapter 10, the financial picture is complex. Typically, these kinds of school-community partnerships rely on a mix of national, state, local, public, nonprofit, and private resources that must be combined under one roof. Molly Stark reports tapping 18 different sources of funds in 2000–2001 in addition to the usual public education funding that every school receives. Several bills have been introduced in Congress that would integrate public funds at the federal level and give grants to states and communities to plan and implement comprehensive full-service community schools, but these potential acts are still tied up in committees. Many foundations support this work and intend to continue to do so.

We conclude in Chapter 11 with practical suggestions for advancing the movement toward community schools at the national, state, and local levels. We are upbeat about the future of community schools, given the potential success of these programs, the resources identified here that could be used, and the action building around furthering these models through state and local community school initiatives and the Coalition for Community Schools.

The appendixes contain various survey forms, program materials, and job descriptions from Molly Stark that will be useful to anyone planning or implementing a school-community partnership program. The Resources section has a selected list of organizations, with e-mail addresses and Web sites, that provides a starting point for gathering further information. The many books, articles, and Web sites referenced throughout the book provide a wealth of background on all of the subjects covered. One major caveat: We have tried to present the most recent information available, but in this era of uncertainty, with massive budget cuts and changing political fortunes, we may have failed to capture all the latest news.

We hope the audience for this book is very wide. Of course, we hope to influence educators to consider community school concepts as significant components of school reform. Because one of the authors is a principal herself, principals throughout the country should find some comfort in her experience. We have emphasized the challenges and difficulties, but it should be clear from Sue's story just how rewarding it is to see a school fill up with partners who are willing to help administrators overcome the critical problems they face in this era of testing obsessions and fiscal tightness.

Teachers and other school personnel, as well as school board members and superintendents, will also be interested to learn about how partnerships can benefit their classrooms and their schools. It is essential that they understand that the full services do not come from educational budgets. All kinds of categorical funds—for example, money for prevention of drug abuse, pregnancy, and violence—can be redirected toward more comprehensive programs. Community-based agencies of all kinds also have an enormous stake in the future of education. Health and social agencies will learn how they can relocate their services into school buildings. Youth agencies like Boys and Girls Clubs, Big Brother/Big Sister, Y's, and 4H Clubs will learn how they can become providers of after-school programs in schools.

Mayors and county executives, governors and state commissioners, and public administrators at every level are becoming increasingly involved in school-community planning efforts. United Ways, Local Education Funds, community planning agencies, and youth bureaus are being called upon to lead community-wide planning groups that apply for grants to develop full-service community schools. Universities are being asked to revise their curricula to actively participate in school transformation efforts; this book will be useful in an array of college courses, including educational administration, community relations, and school-community partnerships.

Finally, we hope that this book will be read by the people who should make the decisions: the general public, parents and grandparents, and the youth themselves. Parent demand for responsive schools and strong community involvement is the moving force in school reform.

ACKNOWLEDGMENTS

Joy Dryfoos

I would like to acknowledge the support received from the Carnegie Corporation of New York for my work on this book. This foundation has been supporting me since 1984, first for a long-term youth-at-risk project and, more recently, for tracking the development of full-service community schools. I particularly appreciate the continuing commitment of the "new team" at Carnegie, President Vartan Gregorian and Senior Program Officer Michele Cahill. The foundation's recent program, Schools for a New Society, will give urban communities the opportunity to implement designs for new kinds of schools that bring together school, community, philanthropic, and business leadership. While this book does not necessarily represent the views of the Carnegie Corporation, our goals are consistent with theirs.

Hundreds of people have contributed to this book through their words and their actions. I have tried to reference them throughout the book. I particularly appreciate the help of Marta Acosta, Howard Adelman, Ray Bettancourt, Martin Blank, Carol Calfee, Stenny Hoyer, Dale Lewis, Richard Negron, Jo Nemeth, Jane Quinn, Amy Prentiss, Keith Prior, Eileen Santiago, Denise Shipman, Alan Stein, Richard Tagle, Linda Taylor, Ken Testa, Kathy Turner, Lisa Villarreal, and Margo Welch.

It can be difficult for two people located so far apart with very different lifestyles and schedules to write a book together. We were only able to accomplish this challenge because of our editor, Carol Barkin. She took all our words and reorganized them with logic, patience, and expert editing skills. Without her assistance, there would be no book.

Sue Maguire

It is impossible to credit all of the people who have, in some way or another, contributed to my part of this book. But some people stand out immediately for reading early drafts, talking through ideas and examples, providing insights, and cheering me on. My thanks to Karen Burnell, Judy Cohen, Pat Gibbons, Jim Harwood, and Judy Woodard. And thanks also to Theresa Crosier, who magically got the tables throughout the chapters to look right.

In addition, I'd like to thank all my colleagues at Molly Stark School, past and present, whose dedication and commitment to children and families made it possible to transform our school. It takes courage to do it differently.

Finally, my thanks to Joy Dryfoos and Carol Barkin for their guidance, assistance, and encouragement.

The contributions of the following reviewers are also gratefully acknowledged:

Carole Biskar
Principal
Tualatin Elementary School
Tualatin, Oregon

Michelle Blakesley
Assistant Principal
Round Rock Independent School District
Round Rock, Texas

Martin J. Blank
Director for Community Collaboration
Institute for Educational Leadership
Washington, D.C.

Philip Coltoff
Executive Director and CEO
The Children's Aid Society
New York, New York

Joyce L. Epstein
Director
Center on School, Family, and Community Partnerships
Johns Hopkins University
Baltimore, Maryland

Sandra Feldman
President
American Federation of Teachers
Washington, D.C.

Donald G. Hackman
Associate Professor of Educational Administration
Educational Leadership and Policy Studies
Iowa State University
Ames, Iowa

Ira Harkavy
Associate Vice President and Director
Center for Community Partnerships
University of Pennsylvania
Philadelphia, Pennsylvania

Jane Quinn
Assistant Director for Community Schools
The Children's Aid Society
New York, New York

Michael D. Usdan
Senior Fellow
The Institute for Educational Leadership
Washington, D.C.

Lisa Villarreal
Director
California Center for Community School Partnership
University of California, Davis
Davis, California

Jan Walker
Assistant Professor
Educational Leadership and Policy Studies
Iowa State University
Ames, Iowa

Margot A. Welch
Director
Collaborative for Integrated School Services
Harvard Graduate School of Education
Cambridge, Massachusetts

About the Authors

Joy G. Dryfoos, Hastings-on-Hudson, New York, is an independent consultant and writer partially supported by the Carnegie Corporation. She has written four books and more than 100 articles on programs related to adolescent behavior, prevention programs, school-based health clinics, and full-service community schools. In addition, Joy has served on the National Academy of Science's panels on teen pregnancy, high-risk youth, and comprehensive school health. She is a founding member of the Coalition for Community Schools and a senior consultant to the Public Education Network's Schools and Community Initiative.

Sue Maguire, North Bennington, Vermont, has been an educator since 1977, a teacher for 15 years, and an administrator for 10 years. She is currently the principal at Molly Stark School in Bennington, Vermont, and is an adjunct instructor in graduate administration courses at Massachusetts College of Liberal Arts in North Adams. She lives with her husband, Greg, and their two children, Chris and Kara.

Introduction

HOW I GOT INVOLVED WITH FULL-SERVICE COMMUNITY SCHOOLS: JOY DRYFOOS

For many years, I have been interested in the broad subject of adolescent development, looking first at prevention of teen pregnancy and, over the years, broadening my scope to high-risk behaviors in general. Early on, I realized that problem behaviors were interrelated and that whatever we tried to do to help young people, it had to be comprehensive, holistic, and long term. Most of my work centered on various kinds of community-based programs, primarily in health and recreation areas.

Schools were not in my focus until one day in 1983. I was in Jackson, Mississippi, visiting the local health department to talk about family planning programs, and someone asked if I would like to visit the school-based primary health clinic that the department supported. A clinic in a school? Were they kidding? I was taken to meet the director of the Community Health Center, Dr. Aaron Shirley, one of the first African Americans to graduate from the University of Mississippi medical school and a leader in the struggle for adequate medical care for impoverished families and children. He had received a grant that enabled the Community Health Center to open the clinic in the same high school that he had attended as a boy.

At the school, I observed a fully equipped clinic with a white-capped nurse practitioner. Students were pouring into the space and receiving primary health care that included sports examinations, pregnancy tests, asthma treatments, and whatever else they required. This made so much sense. The students were already in the building. They needed medical attention and received it with little fuss, complete confidentiality, and no bureaucracy. The school's only responsibility was to facilitate access to the clinic.

During the next year, with support from the Rockefeller Foundation, I traveled around the country and discovered at least 10 such school-based clinic programs. The idea was catching on, and an organization in Washington, D.C., then called the Center for Population Options (now Advocates for Youth), took on the job of organizing what was to become a new field. By the early 1990s, the National Assembly on School-Based Health Services was formed, and today there are about 1,400 sites. Although the original models focused on prevention

1

of teen pregnancy, few have such goals today. Many are in elementary schools, and even those in high schools are not permitted to dispense contraception on site (they refer students to local health agencies). The most significant demands for school-based care seem to be for physical examinations, mental health counseling, asthma control, and dental services. I still get a kick out of visiting a school-based clinic and seeing students being treated right there in the school building.

What these new programs established, at least in my mind, was the concept of bringing services into schools to augment the efforts of school staff. I soon discovered other examples. Social workers were being relocated from community-based agencies to act as case managers. Local drug programs provided student assistance workers to focus specifically on students with drug problems. Most notable at the time was the Florida Full-Service Schools Program. In 1991, under the leadership of Governor Lawton Chiles, the Florida legislature passed a law supporting the development of full-service schools. It required the state board of education and the Department of Health and Rehabilitative Services to jointly establish programs in schools to serve high-risk students in need of medical and social services.

Other states were initiating significant school-based programs as well. As early as 1987, the New Jersey Department of Human Services launched the School-Based Youth Services Program (SBYSP), awarding grants to communities in each of its 21 counties (29 programs). Through partnerships between school and community agencies, these programs offered counseling, recreation, educational remediation, employment services, and health services at school sites. In 1991, the California legislature came up with the large-scale Healthy Start Support Services for Children Act, which brought health and social services to hundreds of schools.

As more state programs got under way, it seemed to me that a "revolution" was actually taking place before our eyes. In many localities, the role of community health and other service agencies in helping schools fill their students' growing needs was increasingly accepted. I was inspired to document this phenomenon in my book *Full-Service Schools: A Revolution in Health and Social Services for Children, Youth, and Families* (1994). But more revelations were to follow.

In collecting examples of school-based services, I learned about the Children's Aid Society (CAS) community schools. In 1992, CAS had opened the first of its "settlement house in the school" models, the Salome Urena Middle Academies (IS 218) in the Washington Heights area of New York City. At first I thought of it only as a good example of a full-service school and described it as such in my book, along with the Hanshaw Middle School in Modesto, California, a Healthy Start model. But as I observed IS 218, I saw how the effort extended beyond the "add-on" quality of many school-based services around the country. The CAS approach was aimed at school transformation and reform, the creation of a full-fledged community school. Not only did the CAS model include a primary health clinic (where I had started on this investigation), but it also had so much more.

Focusing on the Salome Urena Middle Academies, I saw how a whole new school had been created to center around the needs of the students. The school was divided into academies, creating smaller, more cohesive learning units and intensive study of specialized areas (math and science, arts, business, and community service). What went on in the classroom was linked to after-school activities to produce a holistic experience for the children. Parents were drawn in through a resource center and exposed to their children's school experience. Demonstrating the value it placed on community well-being, CAS opened the doors of the schoolhouse to all residents and maintained an interest in neighborhood improvement.

As I continued my search for school-community partnerships that addressed the multiple needs of children, families, and schools, I discovered other initiatives whose intent was the transformation of the whole school. This exploration led to another book, *Safe Passage: Making It Through Adolescence in a Risky Society* (1998). Once again I reviewed the current thinking about prevention of high-risk behaviors, but this time I focused much more on the role of schools in changing outcomes for young people, and I concluded that the fields of educational enrichment and youth development services had to be united. For the first time, I could lay out my own vision of what I called a "Safe Passage" school, one that combined quality education with all the necessary support services to help children and families overcome the barriers to successful learning. (It is important to recognize that these were not totally new ideas. A century ago, John Dewey and Jane Addams were talking about the same concepts. In 1935, the C. S. Mott Foundation in Flint, Michigan, launched the community education movement that led over time to thousands of schools offering lifelong learning opportunities.)

By the time *Safe Passage* was published, a number of important "players" who shared this emerging vision of full-service community schools had come forward. Clearly, the people from CAS were potential leaders, as were those from other school-community partnership models around the country, including the University of Pennsylvania's Center for Community Partnerships (university-assisted community schools), Beacons (schools in which community agencies run extensive before- and after-school programs), and United Way's Bridges to Success (schools in which services are brought in by community agencies). Under the auspices of the Fordham Center for School Community Partnerships, we organized an ad hoc gathering of community school advocates from around the country in 1997 and were pleased at the evidence of growing interest.

Around the same time, I invited Pete Moses from CAS and Ira Harkavy, a vice president of the University of Pennsylvania and one of the creators of university-assisted schools, to put on a workshop on community schools at the meeting in Memphis of the New American Schools initiative, a school reform endeavor. Although about 600 people interested in school reform were at the meeting, only four of them managed to come to our workshop (and two of those were from foundations). It was clear that our concept of community schools had no visibility or draw for educators, even though we had achieved some success with other child advocates. Over dinner in Memphis, Pete, Ira, and I decided to actively form a coalition and look for a Washington, D.C., base that could reach out to the educational community.

Within a short time, the Institute for Educational Leadership in Washington put staff member Martin Blank to work organizing the Emerging Coalition for

Community Schools. As of the end of 2001, "Emerging" is no longer part of the title, and the coalition is flourishing, with more than 170 national organizations as partners in the movement.

What Does a Community School Look Like?

Every school is unique, but this is the Coalition for Community Schools' broad vision of a well-developed community school:

• A community school, operating in a public school building, is open to students, families, and the community before, during, and after school, seven days a week, all year long. It is jointly operated through a partnership between the school system and one or more community agencies. Families, youth, principals, teachers, and neighborhood residents help design and implement activities that promote high educational achievement and positive youth development.

• The school is oriented toward the community, encouraging student learning through community service and service learning. A before- and after-school learning component encourages students to build on their classroom experiences, expand their horizons, contribute to their communities, and have fun. A family support center helps families with child rearing, employment, housing, immigration, and other issues and problems. Medical, dental, and mental health services are readily available. College faculty and students, business people, youth workers, neighbors, and family members come together to support and bolster what schools are working hard to accomplish—ensuring young people's academic, interpersonal, and career success.

• Ideally, a full-time community school coordinator works in partnership with the principal. The coordinator is a member of the school's management team and is responsible for administering the services brought into the school by community agencies. Over time, most community schools consciously try to integrate activities in several areas to achieve the desired results: quality education, positive youth development, family support, family and community engagement in decision making, and community development. In this process, the school emerges as a community hub, a one-stop center to meet diverse needs and to achieve the best possible outcomes for each child.

What's in This Book

Every day we learn about new community schools and new forms of community-school partnerships; this book can be viewed as a snapshot of the emerging field as of fall 2001. It is centered on Molly Stark Elementary School in Bennington, Vermont. As Sue Maguire, principal of Molly Stark, points out, the town's image is one of upper-class privilege, with an elite college and ready access to ski slopes and antique shops. Yet, as you will discover, many of the students at Molly Stark School are needy and many are poor, just like those in many of the nation's cities. However, to fill out the picture, we have included comparable material about several other schools. Among them are Quitman Street Community School in Newark, New Jersey, and Thomas Gardner Extended Services School in Boston, adaptation sites of the Children's Aid Society; McCoy Community School in Kansas City, one of the Missouri's Caring Communities Schools; and Thomas Edison Elementary School in Port Chester, New York, supported by a special full-service community school grant arranged through Congresswoman Nita Lowey.

This is not a "researchy" book. Rather, it focuses on experience, some documented, some anecdotal, to present a concept. The research is referenced, but we did not feel it necessary to repeat what can be found in other places. In any case, the context for writing books of this kind has been radically changed by access to the Internet. A good search engine can pull out more than you want to know about any given subject, and some of the most interesting material we have used was located by putting the phrase "full-service schools" into the search mechanism.

I first heard about Molly Stark School at a conference put on by the Harvard School of Education's Collaborative for Integrating School Services. Sue invited me to visit the school, and we have been communicating frequently ever since. This book reflects our ongoing dialogue as each of us has contributed a section of each chapter, written from our complementary perspectives. In the first part of each chapter, I focus on what is going on all over the country; in the second section, Sue provides hands-on information about the various pieces that have been put together to change the whole climate of her school. Together we hope to provide a picture of a well-conceived, functioning, vibrant community school and enough information about the processes and problems of developing a full-service community school to make you want to set out on this journey yourselves.

INTRODUCTION TO MOLLY STARK SCHOOL: SUE MAGUIRE

At first glance, Bennington appears to typify New England life at its best, filled with Vermont images of ski slopes, maple syrup, and breathtaking foliage. Tourists travel through this area to visit Robert Frost's gravesite, view paintings by Grandma Moses, and learn more about how the Green Mountain Boys fought for freedom during the American Revolution.

But there is another part of Bennington. Molly Stark School is in an isolated area of the community not typically seen by tourists driving through town. Its student population of nearly 380 is considered large by Vermont standards. The school is literally located on the other side of the railroad tracks, and until recently, it was also metaphorically viewed as "the school on the other side of the tracks."

Two and a half decades ago, I came to Vermont to teach fifth grade at Molly Stark School. I was ready to change the world for kids. I thought little about poverty or its ramifications because I truly believed it didn't matter; I could make education the ticket for a happy and productive life for all kids, whether rich, middle class, or poor. Through my training, I had learned that teaching consisted of high standards, strong curriculum, and solid instruction delivered by a caring teacher. All these years later, I know that I hadn't learned enough.

One of the most important things I didn't know is something I learned over the years of bringing up my own two children. From the day they were born, they were presented with tremendous opportunity. They were read to incessantly and taken on hundreds of "field trips"—to Disney World, the ocean, the White House, the lake. Without consciously focusing on the educational effects, I prepared them before we went out on our adventures, reviewing vocabulary, practicing social skills and manners, rewarding good observations and answers, and encouraging them all the time. Their part was to enjoy and absorb the information around them. We visited parks and museums, saw movies and plays. They entered school healthy and eager to learn. They knew education was important in our family, and they thrived.

What I slowly came to realize is that not all children have lives filled with these basic supports and opportunities. Far too many kids exist in a world without stimulation. Many live in a constant state of chaos and are isolated from everything beyond their own neighborhood. They don't go to parks and museums and libraries, they don't eat in restaurants, and they don't make regular visits to doctors and dentists.

I am constantly confronted with examples of the struggle and turmoil that families at Molly Stark must face on a regular basis.

• Two days before school starts, Betsy calls to say she and her three children have been evicted and are living in a car. She wants a telephone number to get help, but what she first asks me is whether her children can still come to our school.

• David was excited to join the after-school running program but isn't showing up for daily practices. The instructor questions him, and he finally blurts out that he has no sneakers and he knows his father can't afford them. We dig into our petty cash envelope so our guidance counselor can take him to a local shoe store to pick out a pair.

• Social Services calls to set up a time to interview brothers Tim and Keith, seven and five years old, who nearly burned down their apartment by lighting paper on the stove the night before when their mom wasn't home.

• Jean has had chronic head lice for the last four years, but now the problem is becoming worse. The lice are actually crawling down the part in her hair and onto her face. She and her mom have been seen by our consulting pediatrician, and a home health worker has been to their home to help, but things haven't gotten any better. Now we must consider reporting the family to our local Social and Rehabilitative Services agency for educational and health neglect.

• Josh, a fifth grader, complains that his mouth continuously aches. He can't remember ever going to a dentist. He sees our dentist and, because of the extensive decay, has to have seven extractions. A few days later, I see Josh walking down the hall and ask him how he is feeling. He replies, "Great, I never knew how it was for my mouth not to hurt!"

These situations are a far cry from what I thought teaching was about or even what I thought life was about. They aren't excuses, and they shouldn't be used as reasons why kids can't or shouldn't learn. But they are real stories that block opportunity and every kind of growth—emotional, social, and academic. And these realities can have unrelenting consequences if not addressed. Simply raising the standards bar will not provide the support these children need to succeed in school.

Developing a full-service school was a response to the complex issues facing our school. We began the process long before we had heard the terms *full-service school* or *community school*. The services and opportunities we developed at Molly Stark happened because they make sense for kids and their families. Through collaborative partnerships with a wide range of service providers in our community, we have tried to create the opportunities that most of us would expect and demand for our own children. Along with quality instruction, our school offers extended-day and extended-year services, health and social services, and parent education and support—the things we believe that children need to do well in school and that families need to live productive lives in their community.

Now, as principal at Molly Stark, I still believe that education can be the ticket. I am working with the children of the children I taught years ago, and I continue the search to find what it is that might make the difference for this generation and the next.

Why Full-Service Community Schools?

Wendy Fagerholm

THE NEED IN THE NATION

In the 2000 presidential election, education was the top-ranking issue among voters. Everyone has concerns about the quality of the educational system, and everyone has a different opinion on how to fix it. My own hypothesis is that in many communities, children face significant barriers to learning—barriers that schools acting alone cannot possibly overcome. But I believe that full-service community schools can dramatically reduce many of these barriers. What are some of the areas in which such schools can have an effect?

How Full-Service Community Schools Can Make a Difference

Readiness to Learn

Some children come to school lacking the necessary readiness to sit in the classroom and participate in the learning process. In some cases, the family does not encourage early learning or does not have the basic parenting skills to get the young child off to a good start. Early childhood education and Head Start preschool programs have a proven positive effect on long-term learning outcomes. Community schools can encompass early childhood learning centers and parent education classes. In addition, when the preschool program is located right in the school building, the transition to kindergarten and subsequent grades is easier.

Supportive Adults

Successful youth development is strongly associated with access to caring, supportive adults. Young people in all kinds of communities who are involved in negative behaviors (sex, drugs, violence) often lack any connection to responsible adults. On the other hand, young people who live in very deprived circumstances do much better if they experience consistent and sustained attachment to adults.

Community schools can ensure that such relationships are established. Partner agencies can help supply the large amount of individual attention that many of today's students need. Health care providers, case managers, additional social workers, and volunteer mentors can be brought into the school setting, and their services integrated with existing (and often minimal) pupil personnel services.

Extended Learning Opportunities

There is not enough time in the school day for many children to acquire all the skills they need to succeed in today's educational system. Opening the schools for longer hours and providing creative enrichment programs can help children make significant academic gains. In community schools, after-school activities can be integrated with the classroom curriculum, reinforcing and enriching what children learn each day. After-school programs also help children gain social skills and cultural experiences that lead to strong youth development.

Parent Involvement

Many parents are turned off by their children's schools; they feel rejected by the teachers and do not know how to communicate with them. Community schools develop many avenues for involvement, inviting parents to serve on planning and advisory boards, encouraging them to volunteer in the school, and hiring them as teacher's aides and outreach workers. In community schools, parents can also learn how to monitor their children's school performance and homework and therefore feel better equipped to provide support and help.

Lifelong Learning

Children are not the only ones who need access to extended learning opportunities. Adults can improve their family's status by taking courses to advance their careers or enhance their lives intellectually. English as a Second Language, basic GED, and computer use are among the most sought-after adult education classes. Welfare reform is also increasing the pressure on young mothers to further their education so they can enter the labor force. Community schools, open evenings and weekends, can become accessible and convenient centers for both credit and noncredit courses, and child care can be provided on site.

Opportunity to Perform Community Service

Many children and their families feel alienated from their communities. When they are given a chance to serve the community through volunteer placements in day care centers, senior citizen homes, or community gardening projects, children feel much better about their lives. Community schools can facilitate these service learning placements and ensure that the knowledge gained from the work experience goes back into the classroom. The events of September 11, 2001 brought into focus the importance of developing a sense of community and of teaching children to actively participate in building democratic institutions.

Access to Health Care

Children who are troubled with physical or psychosocial problems cannot perform well in school. Asthma is widespread among the school-age population, as are acne, headaches, and illnesses as minor as colds and as major as tuberculosis. Many children suffer from stress-related symptoms and need mental health services and counseling.

Community schools can encompass on-site primary health and mental health clinics staffed with trained professionals from community agencies. Dental offices can also be set up. These collaborating partners can also assume the responsibility for health education and promotion. For example, they can offer sex education, drug prevention, and conflict resolution classes, freeing teachers to concentrate on their classroom work with students.

Integration of Services

Many families are discouraged from using community services because these services are fragmented and loaded with bureaucratic regulations. Agencies may have widely separated locations, conflicting policies about who can receive services, and little communication with other services used by clients. A well-organized community school can draw these disparate programs together into an integrated package at one site with centralized records and common policies.

Safe Communities

Of the 28 million school-age children whose parents work, an estimated 7 million children aged 5 to 13 return to empty homes after school. Community schools can provide safe and supervised havens from early in the morning to late in the evening.

Positive School Environment

When a traditional school system is confronted with young people who act out and misbehave, it quickly suspends them, adding to the number of high-risk youth in the streets. But being thrown out of school for a time exacerbates the students' problem rather than solving it, because they fall even further behind, both academically and socially. Community schools can create service networks that deal with problem behaviors on site, limiting suspensions and expulsions. When students perceive the school setting as "on their side," they are more likely to become attached to the school community and adopt positive attitudes and actions. When parents feel connected to the school, they are more ready to work with the teachers to improve student outcomes.

Changing Demographics

Throughout the country, schools are experiencing dramatic changes in the makeup of their populations. The largest increases are among Hispanic children, but more and more students from Asia, Africa, and other parts of the world are changing the composition of the student body. Ensuring that children learn English is only one of the challenges resulting from these changes. Often, cultural differences emerge that must be addressed; for example, asking parents to help with homework may be futile if they speak little or no English.

Because partners in community schools often are community-based, culturally indigenous organizations, they can create multicultural environments that celebrate differences and encourage all children to succeed. They may organize music and art activities and family festivals to help people share their cultural heritages with each other.

Basic Needs

Many children come to school hungry; they may also lack clothing and housing. Traditional school systems are not set up to meet these needs. Community schools can institute breakfast, snack, and dinner programs as well as the usual lunch. Community partners can take on the responsibility of making sure that children have warm and suitable clothing and help parents find adequate housing. Such supports can be provided in the context of a family resource center that ensures confidentiality without stigmatization.

Quality Education

Last, but by no means least, too many children are failing in school. Many are left back, and some never complete their high school education. Whether this represents the failure of the students or the failure of the schools to meet the students' needs is a debatable point. In any case, schools are under fire to produce higher test scores. Community schools work to create a more effective school environment, encouraging small classes with well-trained teachers and high standards. With partners from community agencies to address behavioral and social issues, teachers can concentrate on teaching. All the outside programs that are brought into the schoolhouse through such partnerships can be shaped to enhance learning and integrated with the school's classroom curricula.

Observations

In general, community schools call for a balance between educational enrichment and human support mechanisms. However, some initiatives concentrate more on the "full service" part of the equation, while others start with school reform ideas and later add services. No two community schools look exactly alike. As advocates are fond of saying, "No cookie cutters."

In every community, at least some of the children experience barriers to learning. In wealthy suburbs, a handful of young people may live on the margins of society or have troubled relationships with their parents. In more disadvantaged neighborhoods, the majority of the children may come to school unprepared to learn, lacking attention to their basic needs, and suffering from the fragmentation of services endemic in poverty areas. Each community is unique, and although community schools have common overall goals, they address the specific issues differently, depending on the barriers that must be overcome, the environment of the school, the wishes of the parents, the skills of the existing staff, and the resources available in the community to build a stronger institution.

We do not know how many full-service community schools there are in this country. We do know that thousands of schools have instituted relevant pieces, such as extended hours, primary health care centers, or family resource centers. Many of them have evolved into fully realized full-service community schools as the pieces are integrated into a comprehensive model. We know too that of the 85,000 public schools in the United States, about one in four—nearly 22,000—have student populations in which more than half the children are very poor. Given the potential capability of community schools to improve educational outcomes, further healthy youth development, and help disadvantaged families, it would seem wise social policy to consider these emerging models for broad replication and adoption.

THE NEED IN BENNINGTON, VERMONT, IN 1995

We have always been led to believe that a child can rise above his or her bleak life of poverty through a strong education. After all, that is the American dream. But over time, what has become apparent to us at Molly Stark is the difficulty of equalizing the huge imbalance in opportunity between poor children and their more affluent peers. We have found over and over again that many children of poverty lack the fundamental support network necessary to thrive in school. They become "at risk" the minute they are born: at risk for low literacy skills, at risk for school and job failure, and at risk for a continuing life of poverty. Clearly, parents raising a family in poverty love their children, but their dreams and hopes for them seem to diminish over time. Many of these children enter adulthood not ready to participate in a meaningful way as members of their own families and communities. And so the cycle continues.

School problems are not just school problems. That is, the challenges our schools face every day are actually challenges facing our families, our communities, and our country. There is no debating the fact that good instruction, a carefully designed curriculum, high standards, and strong professional development are essential elements of excellent schools. However, even when some of these things are not in place, many middle-class children will learn, progress, and be successful. These are the children who receive much support, experience, and opportunity in their everyday lives.

Conversely, even when excellent curriculum and instruction are present, many children of poverty do poorly in school. No matter how competent the teaching is, how high the standards bar is raised, how dazzling the materials are, how much teachers sincerely want to teach, roadblocks appear. Anyone who has taught in a classroom knows that many ongoing factors affect a child's performance. If a child is chronically ill or lives with daily head lice, it is hard for her to concentrate. If a child has not had positive role models to help him understand the importance of hard work and appropriate social behavior, he has no building blocks for positive and productive behaviors. If a child has not had strong early language development or enriching opportunities before entering kindergarten, she is at a clear disadvantage and may never catch up. What a paradox this is. The greatest amount of academic growth is expected from the children who enter school the least prepared and with the least amount of support.

What We Learned

We started our journey toward a full-service community school because of a large group of staff members who wanted to learn more and wanted to make a difference. Beginning in 1995, for almost a year, we researched and discussed information before we started providing extended services. Here are some things we learned:

More than half the students at Molly Stark live in poverty. Overall, these children, many of whom live in overcrowded subsidized housing, have poorer health, enter school thousands of words behind middle-class peers, are more likely to drop out of school, and are more likely to be abused or neglected. We were especially struck by the rate at which our former students drop out of high school. On average, 15 percent of the students in each high school class in Bennington spent their elementary years at Molly Stark. Yet in 1996, when we first collected dropout data, 28 percent of the dropouts in that year had attended Molly Stark. We knew that something had to change!

These kids have fewer opportunities. The data we collected verified our impression that many poor children come to school with less preschool experience and have fewer after-school opportunities once they start school. We found that many parents (and, unfortunately, some teachers) have lower expectations of what these children are capable of doing.

Some of the existing services are poorly integrated. It is sometimes difficult to develop good communication between school and community service providers. Families with children in need are certainly offered various kinds of help, including home-based therapeutic services (such as occupational therapy, physical therapy, and speech), early intervention for special education services, family advocacy, and adult education and support. But too many families are being served in isolation, with unnecessary duplication of services and duplication of paperwork. Families might have to travel to several individual agencies for categorical services or have their homes invaded by many individual service providers. Often, parents are so confused by the number of providers they work with that they can't identify which agency a worker came from or what the worker's role is. In our experience, agencies would call our school to ask why we weren't communicating with them, only to learn that school personnel didn't even know they were involved in a family's life.

We concluded what we already knew: As hard as we were trying, what we were doing often wasn't working. We needed to look outside our box for different ways to work with the community to serve children and families.

During the 1990s, there was much talk in education circles about national goals. We began to hear phrases like "readiness to learn," "demonstrated competency," "continuous improvement," and "disciplined environment conducive to learning."

To those of us on the front lines at Molly Stark in 1995, those were just words. We knew that we hadn't come close to reaching such goals. If we were to create real change, we couldn't treat this problem as just an education issue. It was time to mobilize our community to promote opportunities for responsible parenthood, guarantee quality child care and preschool experiences, and ensure the healthy development of children. It was time to develop a systematic approach to doing what was simply right and fair for children and families. Only then would real reform take place.

What We Knew When We Began

We compete for funds. Funding is often categorical, and agencies and schools that work with children and families are constantly competing just to provide the minimum. If we can pool our funds, sharing responsibility and skills, the result will be a much more efficient and successful system of care and education.

The earlier the intervention, the better. The first five years of life is a critical time for cognitive and emotional growth. Without enriching and appropriate interventions during those years, children will remain at an extreme disadvantage.

Quality depends on funding. There is a direct correlation between high-quality services and positive student outcomes. Yet though our goal is to always provide high-quality services, we are often put in the position of doing what we can until the money runs out or of diluting what we're doing and not providing all the critical elements necessary to do a quality job.

Services must be intense and over a long period. Quantity does make a difference. Too often, because of a lack of funding or a lack of human resources, we do only a small piece of what is needed with the attitude that it is better than nothing. However, there is no quick fix for the consequences of poverty; that small piece isn't enough.

Services must be comprehensive. Health care, child care, preschool, parent education and support, having caring and competent adults with the children—all these are essentials in the formula for success.

Services must address the whole family. Children live and learn within the context of a family, and a family lives and learns within the context of a community. We need a multigenerational strategy that encourages parents and provides them with the skills they need to help their children do well in school and in life.

We decided our goal was to set the same standard for all children in our school-enriching experiences at an early age, adequate health care, and access to appropriate and nurturing adults. These services would begin to narrow the gaps and, in turn, would strengthen the community of which our school was a part.

2

How Do Full-Service Community Schools Get Started?

Wendy Fagerholm

MODELS AND PLANNING

An essential first step in the development of full-service community schools is going through the planning process. Schools, potential community partners, and parents must come together to try to figure out how to meet the needs of their constituents and how to overcome the barriers to quality education. As Sue's narrative makes clear, this is a continuous process, first visioning and then revisioning to constantly redesign the school so it fulfills its goals. And along with planning and visioning comes the necessity to learn about alternative approaches. Although creativity is important, no one should have to reinvent the wheel. In recent years, practitioners have produced a body of knowledge about building new kinds of institutional relationships that have improved educational and social outcomes. What follows is a short presentation of current concepts and models, preceding an overview of the planning process.

Although we speak of a community school in the singular, it is certainly possible that a cluster of schools or an entire school system could be transformed into community schools as the result of the planning process. Because Molly Stark School, the continuing example considered in this book, is a single site, many of the comparisons and contrasts will be with other single-site operations, though we will also pay attention to systemwide changes here and in subsequent chapters.

Community School Models

The introduction to this book presented a definition of *community school* that included certain elements: open all the time, run by a partnership, providing access to an array of services, responsive to the family and the community, and focused on overcoming barriers to learning. A number of different models have sprung up around the country that fit roughly into this definition. While we don't know how many community schools currently exist, we do know that the concepts are spreading rapidly through replications, adaptations, and spontaneous generations. Each formal model is backed by an organization that offers technical assistance and training.

The forerunner of these various models was the "lighted schoolhouse." Pioneered by the C. S. Mott Foundation in Flint, Michigan, this model spread throughout the country, bringing extended-hour learning, recreation, and social activities into the school building. These schools are usually called community education sites and are strongly oriented toward addressing community needs and facilitating lifelong learning for people of all ages. The National Center for Community Education (NCCE), also in Flint, provides extensive training for those who work in the community education field, focusing on such issues as how to maintain high standards in adult education programs. NCCE also trains school and community agency staff to plan and implement after-school programs.

Beacons, introduced in New York City through the Department of Youth and Community Development, bring public or nonprofit community-based organizations (CBOs) into schools to make use of before- and after-school hours for youth development and community enrichment. Each Beacon program is unique, based on the capabilities of the provider agencies and the particular cultural and socioeconomic needs of the community. Beacons are heavily involved with neighborhood enhancement through community service projects and the arts. The Fund for the City of New York's Youth Development Institute provides technical assistance. In San Francisco, the city government supports a substantial number of Beacons.

A "settlement house in the school" approach has been created by the Children's Aid Society, also in New York City. This model is actually called a community school. It is built on a close relationship between the school system and the provider agency (or agencies) and addresses both school restructuring and the provision of one-stop services. The Children's Aid Society has also organized a technical assistance center.

In university-assisted schools, universities or, more likely, departments of universities establish formal relationships with schools and sponsor a range of activities. University faculty work with teachers on curriculum and with administrators on school restructuring; university students practice-teach in schools and offer after-school activities. In some cases, the result is a full-fledged community school, open all the time with a wide range of one-stop services. The University of Pennsylvania's West Philadelphia Improvement Corps serves as the technical assistance center for university-assisted community schools across the country.

Bridges to Success is a community school program sponsored by the United Way and pioneered in Indianapolis. The United Way forms a consortium with other community agencies to bring an array of services into schools. The national United Way office works with its local agencies to replicate this model.

Caring Communities is Missouri's version of community schools. State dollars from seven state agencies are pooled and administered through the foundation-supported Family and Community Investment Trust. The schools form local community partnerships with social service agencies and health and mental health providers.

The concept of full-service schools comes from Florida's innovative legislation in 1991 that called for integration of educational, medical, and social and/or human services in a manner designed to meet the needs of children and youth and their families on school grounds or in easily accessible locations. It was expected that full-service schools would provide "the types of prevention, treatment, and support services children and families needed to succeed . . . services built on interagency partnerships which would evolve from cooperative ventures to intensive collaborative arrangements among state and local and public and private entities" (Florida Department of Health and Rehabilitative Services, 1991). The collaborating agencies included education, health care, transportation, job training, child care, housing, employment, and social services.

Other community schools, like Molly Stark, are school generated; they work from the schoolhouse out and develop partnerships with community agencies that contribute or contract services. Most community schools are open extended hours, over weekends, and over the summer. Some alternative, magnet, and charter schools share these characteristics.

Although these brief descriptions suggest that a firm delineation exists between various kinds of school-based programs, in reality the situation is not quite that clear. The latest versions of school-community partnerships have been labeled extended schools by one foundation and successful schools by another. In this book, we call these entities full-service community schools or just community schools.

Different Components of Full-Service Community Schools

All the community school models previously described are directed toward bringing a package of different services into school buildings and giving children, youth, and families access to the supports they need. The following paragraphs describe some of the discrete pieces of the package that may be put together to develop a full-service community school.

Case Management. Communities-in-Schools (formerly Cities-in-Schools) is a national organization that works with local communities (businesses, social service agencies) as a broker to bring five basic kinds of services into schools: mentoring, after-school programs, mental health counseling, career counseling and employment programs, and community service opportunities. Communities-in-Schools is very successful at relocating social workers and other community agency staff into schools so they can act as case managers and mentors to specific high-risk kids who need a lot of individual attention and guidance.

Primary Health Clinics. These facilities are operated in school buildings by outside health agencies. They are staffed by medical personnel and provide primary health care, emergency care, dental examinations, mental health counseling, and health education. They may also provide social services for students and families. In 2001, about 1,400 school based primary health clinics were in operation, largely in disadvantaged communities.

Youth Development Programs. Some community schools put together a number of different youth activities, such as mentoring, substance abuse counseling, sports and recreation, community service learning, and preemployment services. The New Jersey School-Based Youth Services Program exemplifies this approach, allowing schools to contract with CBOs to enhance their ability to help students succeed. Beacons are also particularly oriented toward youth development.

Family Resource Centers. Facilities in schools or community sites are designed to offer services for parents, such as parenting education, literacy, employment assistance, immigration information, housing help, food, clothing, case management, health services, and early child care. Programs specifically for teen parents are frequently located in these kinds of centers.

Early Childhood Development. Another forerunner of community schools, a program called Schools of the 21st Century, is aimed at linking child care with family support centers in schools. Created in 1987 by Edward Zigler, director of the Bush Center in Child Development and Social Policy at Yale University and a founder of the nation's Head Start program, this effort brings together school-based, year-round, all-day child care for children three to five years old; after-school and vacation care for school-age children; family support and guidance through a home visitation program for new parents; and other support services to increase access to child care. In some communities, Head Start programs are being relocated into school buildings to provide continuity with the later school experience.

Referrals. While the main function of school-based health centers and family resource centers is to provide services at the school site, some programs focus more on linking needy students and families with community agencies. The Kentucky Family Resource and Youth Service Centers are staffed mainly by coordinators who create a bridge between schools and CBOs to ensure that health and social needs are met—if not on the school site, then elsewhere.

After-School Programs. The most rapidly growing school-based enterprise is after-school programs, stimulated by the significant federal 21st Century Community Learning Centers program and many state efforts (see Chapter 4). Schools with intensive after-school programs are considered open to further development in the process of becoming full-service community schools.

School Reform. As part of the school transformation process, some community schools look for school reform models that can be readily adapted. The School Development Program created by James Comer of the Yale Child Study Center is one such program. Everyone in the school is mobilized to help children succeed. Three approaches are basic to this effort: a very inclusive planning and management team (parents, teachers, administrators, support staff, and students); a mental health team for counseling children and parents and linking them to outside resources; and a strong parent participation program that brings them into the school as both volunteers and paid workers. The Comer program has been combined with the Zigler program to produce Cozi schools, based on a full-service community school model that is very comprehensive, covering children's needs from birth to age 12.

The Planning Process

A key concept from the beginning of the planning process is inclusiveness: The more people and groups involved at the outset, the firmer the foundation for a comprehensive program. California's after-school program guide recommends that "although integrating [large numbers of stakeholders] into a common vision may be very difficult, they must be harmonized for a program to be successful.... What is it that community members want to accomplish? ... How much of a commitment of resources are community organizations prepared to make?" (Fletcher, n.d., p. 5).

Convening a Planning Group

Where does this process start? Almost anywhere, depending on which groups or individuals in a community get fired up to do something about a school or a group of schools. Clearly, at Molly Stark, the principal took the initiative. In many places, social service agencies, mental health agencies, or youth development agencies initiate the process and invite schools to enter collaborative discussions. Often, funding agencies stimulate the development of community schools by issuing requests for proposals that require the participation of certain groups or individuals.

A recent example is the School and Community Initiative of the Public Education Network (PEN), funded in part by the Annenberg Foundation. PEN's constituent organizations (called Local Education Funds) were invited to compete for grants that would allow them to plan their community's infrastructure for school-community partnerships and linkages. When creating their plans, Local Education Funds were encouraged to include policymakers, such as mayors, councils, school boards, superintendents; organized stakeholder groups, such as business roundtables, PTAs, community-based organizations; and individuals, such as parents, teachers, and community leaders.

However the initiative gets under way, those groups and individuals identified as important to the planning process should be invited to join a formal group responsible for creating a plan.

Components of Planning

In general, a comprehensive plan for one or more full-service community schools should include

- Results of a needs assessment
- A list of agreed-on goals
- Delineation of activities required to fill those goals
- Identification of roles of school and community agencies in carrying out those activities, specifying lead agency functions in governance structure
- Details about required staff with job descriptions and salary
- Timelines for each proposed activity
- Available and needed resources to accomplish goals
- Available and needed space for setting up programs
- Access to transportation
- Monitoring and evaluation processes
- Ongoing training and technical assistance
- Reflection on sustainability and continuity of programs

Many of these subjects are covered in subsequent chapters, but we review needs assessment, goal setting, and selection of the lead agency in the following sections.

Conducting a Needs Assessment

The first step in planning anything is to figure out what the current situation is and what the potential is for improving it. As the old adage says, "If you don't know where you are going, any road will lead you there." Based on its extensive experience working with communities that want to adapt its school model, the Children's Aid Society suggests including the following six steps in a needs assessment. Answering the questions that accompany each step should help you determine where you are going as you think about developing a full-service community school.

1. *Gather the data: "What are our community's overall needs?"* Use government and census data that describe the community's health, economic, and educational profile; pay special attention to "key indicators" on the status of children and families, such as median income, unemployment rates, housing data, crime statistics, and child immunization rates. School performance measures available from school districts include dropout and graduation rates, attendance, test scores, discipline problems, and suspensions. Demographic data are important for understanding the ethnic, cultural, and age distribution of the neighborhood.

2. *Reach out to families: "What are some individual needs?"* Use formal and informal interviews, surveys, and meetings to understand residents' perceptions of the community's needs. Which needs are most critical? How effective are current services? What barriers prevent access to services? One suburban school was astounded to discover that the most critical family need expressed to outreach workers during home visits was for food.

3. *Call on the experts: "What do professionals and community leaders think?"* Talk to community leaders, school administrators, teachers, health professionals, and heads of social service agencies, as well as police officers and business and religious leaders, about specific service needs and gaps.

4. *Learn what services already exist: "Where do we stand now?"* Do an inventory of services currently in place in the school and in the community, including youth programming, health services, family supports, and education. How accessible are these programs? Which are stretched too thin? Are any underused? The Coalition for Community Schools has created a useful checklist of programs and services for this purpose (Blank & Langford, 2000; see Appendix A).

5. *Look at your strengths: "What can we build on?"* Think about tangible resources, like a community health center or a nearby university, as well as intangible resources, like high parent involvement or strong teacher commitment. Both kinds are important building blocks for success.

6. *Look to the future: "What might be ahead?"* Thinking about what could be coming in the next three to five years will give you a better chance of solving problems early and of recognizing opportunities. For example, one fledgling

community school was located in an area where old public housing was being razed (lowering the school population and displacing their families), but new housing was expected to replace it within two years.

Who conducts the needs assessment? Some of the work can be done by a team from a local university or an existing community planning group. It is also desirable to involve young people in this stage of the planning process; they can be very effective in "mapping" the community. Focus groups may be conducted to gain insights into the opinions of parents, school staff, and community people.

The result of the needs assessment should be a detailed document that spells out who needs to do what. In the second part of this chapter, Sue describes one approach to this outcome, specifying what activities or services are needed, and when, to fulfill the different goals of the program, who is responsible, what sources of funding can be tapped, and how the impact can be assessed. The chart in that section includes a column for resources needed to start up the activity.

Carol Calfee and her colleagues in Florida have created a step-by-step guide, *Building a Full-Service School* (1998), that includes many helpful charts for collecting data and turning that information into a planning tool.

Setting the Goals

It is very important that the stakeholders—policymakers, service providers, and committed individuals—who participated in the planning process arrive at a consensus about the specific goals of the program. This is necessary for setting priorities, for clarifying the purpose of the effort to the public, and for short- and long-term accountability and evaluation. The Coalition for Community Schools has promulgated a list of goals that are common to many plans for community schools:

- Children are ready to learn when they enter school and every day thereafter.
- All students learn and achieve to high standards.
- Young people are well prepared for adult roles in the workplace, as parents, and as citizens.
- Families and neighborhoods are safe, supportive, and engaged.
- Parents and community members are involved with the school and their own lifelong learning. (Blank & Samberg, 2000)

The guide to organizing full-service schools based on Florida's experience lists goals similar to the coalition's but adds three more:

- School boards provide a learning environment conducive to teaching and learning.
- The school, district, and state ensure professionalism of teachers and staff.
- Communities provide an environment that is drug free and protects students' health, safety, and civil rights. (Calfee, Wittwer, & Meredith, 1998)

Note that two of these goals focus on the classroom, connecting the provision of services with the school climate and with effectiveness in the classroom. The Florida guide spells out each goal in terms of relevant services that can be brought into the school. For example, the guide mentions 20 services that can help achieve a drug-free environment, from mental health counseling to youth gang intervention. The guide also includes a chart that presents possible evaluation measures for each goal.

The plan should carefully outline the goals and put them into a framework that leads to identifying the appropriate services. Accountability issues should be addressed when the planning process begins so the community school can demonstrate its effectiveness in achieving its goals.

Identifying Leaders and the Governance Structure

Perhaps the most difficult question to answer at the very beginning of the planning process is, what agency should be the "lead"? In other words, who gets the grant and who does the work? Answering this question helps set up a structure that enhances collaboration.

Obviously, the school is always a primary player in collaborations to develop full-service community schools. In addition, the collaborative body will include representatives from various community agencies, as well as individuals such as parents and community leaders. Out of this group, a lead agency often emerges, usually a CBO designated to work with the school to extend the hours and the scope of services.

Various relationships are possible between the school and the lead agency. The school principal may act as the leader, as in the case of Molly Stark School, or may share the leadership with a full-time coordinator who actually works for another agency, as in the case of the Children's Aid Society or the Beacon schools.

One view of how to decide whether the school or a community agency should take the lead comes from the Florida full-service school experience. One might assume that the school or the agency that initiated the planning process would lead at the outset. However, in many full-service school programs, a school is designated the program's lead partner as a requirement of a state grant (as was the case in Florida). Calfee et al. (1998) cite reasons why the school should be the lead partner: (a) Schools are where the children are, and school systems own the facilities; (b) schools often initiate collaboration because they recognize the dramatic need for family support services; and (c) schools are already required to collect extensive data about children. In addition, Calfee et al. spell out some problems that can occur if the school dominates the interagency effort: (a) difficulty in attracting dollars from agencies that have not traditionally collaborated with schools; (b) overcrowding and demands for space; and (c) the (incorrectly) perceived burden of adding health and social services to the school's responsibility for academic programs.

Melaville and Blank (1998), in their study of school-community partnerships, also offer some advice about the advantages and disadvantages of different kinds of lead agencies. They agree that school districts may have more clout and better access to certain resources like Title I federal education funds for disadvantaged children (see Chapter 10). But Melaville and Blank are concerned that school districts may not place a high enough priority on the full-service program and may have difficulty administering some outside grants, given the complex bureaucracy in which school districts must function and the union regulations regarding hiring and salaries.

Melaville and Blank see community collaboratives like Caring Communities in Missouri as more broad based and consumer oriented, but these collaboratives may have difficulty running programs because of time constraints and the demands of relationships with schools, such as turf issues and confidentiality (see Chapter 9). Nonprofit CBOs, such as United Way agencies or recipients of Beacon grants, may have the advantages of clear vision, flexibility, responsiveness, commitment, and neighborhood ties, for example. But they may have limited management capability and financial resources and may have to operate within a tight budget.

Clearly, the selection of the lead agency is an important and complex challenge. Once a leader is chosen, the governance structure can be put in place (see Chapter 6).

Systemwide Planning

Some of the important work on community schools has occurred at one or two schools at a time. Molly Stark is just one school, the Children's Aid Society started in two schools in New York City, and United Way's Bridges to Success began in six Indianapolis schools. The question now being raised is, could an entire school system develop a plan for full-service community schools?

Boston

In Boston, a large number of school and community people are working together to try to further the cause of community schools. This group grew out of a challenge by the superintendent, Tom Payzant, who showed an interest in "going to scale" in Boston, but only if the stakeholders there got together and came back to him with recommendations about how to accomplish this goal. A group, Community Schools in Boston (CSIB), was first called together by the Coalition for Community Schools but soon took off under its own steam. At one point in its evolution (it is still evolving), this preliminary statement emerged:

> The future of all Boston children depends on schools, families and communities working together in partnership. Community Schools in Boston envisions the school as the hub of a community—a home where caring for kids is understood to synthesize quality education, family support, health and human services, and youth and community development initiatives. The effective school weaves all these strands together to improve student learning, strengthen families, and build healthy neighborhoods. (N. Katz, notes from CSIB meeting, July 23, 2001)

According to an observer, the CSIB planning "process" is valuable in bringing a number of visible community partners and the Boston public schools together as a group to think and work collaboratively; the goal is to build a systemic approach to furthering and sustaining school-community ties and building strong partnerships within specific schools, communities, and clusters (groups of schools). CSIB acknowledges the difficulty of balancing centralized planning with decentralized relationship building. Its members believe they must continue to diversify their own group and simultaneously encourage the central administration of the Boston public schools to build policies from the top that promote and support bottom-up efforts. One proposal is to create a kind of representative roundtable where top-down efforts can be integrated with the many deeply rooted bottom-up local projects. This planning process, based on fitting many small school-community partnerships into a cohesive whole, has been challenging and time-consuming.

Portland

In Portland, Oregon, a unique, collaborative, countywide community school venture is being undertaken by public officials and school people. The Schools Uniting Neighborhoods (SUN) initiative was launched in 1999 jointly by Portland's commissioner Jim Francesconi and Multnomah County's chairperson Beverly Stein in collaboration with school districts in Portland and elsewhere in the county. The goals that emerged from the planning process are not only to help children and families academically and socially but also to leverage the sharing of public assets through the expanded use of schools and to build partnerships to achieve coordinated service delivery. Participants hope that opening the schools to a wide range of programs will result in a "seamless" offering of services to communities and their youth.

The planning process was inclusive and intensive. Over an extended period, SUN's objectives were hashed out by a group of concerned citizens, educators, and local government officials. They reviewed full-service school models from around the country and came up with their own conceptualization of a SUN community-centered school and an innovative governance structure.

Observations

Whether for a single school or a systemwide program, planning is essential to the successful development of multiagency, multicomponent efforts. At the outset, the stage must be set for everyone involved to come together and address at least some of their differences. We know that if a school opens its doors to outsiders, turf problems can follow. We know that to extend the school day, custodians' hours have to be extended as well. Insurance coverage, confidentiality, eligibility regulations, transportation—all these issues should be considered and plans should be formulated up front, before the doors even open.

Community school practitioners will attest to the amount of time this can take. But the time spent at planning meetings is very well spent if the result is a workable planning document on which everyone agrees. This document is also crucial in the all-important public relations campaign that should accompany the grand opening of the community school. Everyone in the community needs to know what is going on and feel that he or she has a voice in the process.

One group that often feels the most left out during the planning stages is the classroom teachers. The school principal and support staff are usually the ones tapped to attend meetings with the outside stakeholders and help make decisions. Yet if the goal of the program is to increase academic achievement, the plan will be useless without teachers' input. Considerable effort needs to go into integrating what will take place outside the classroom with what is going on in the classroom. In a well-planned, comprehensive community school, students should not be aware of whether it is school time or after-school time in terms of the quality and enrichment they receive.

Finally, you don't have to reinvent the wheel. Books, journals, and Web sites provide a wealth of information (see the References and Resources sections at the end of the book), and they will lead you to other useful documents on topics you wish to pursue.

MAKING THE PLAN AT MOLLY STARK

One fall afternoon in 1995, after an exceedingly stressful day, a small group of us began to talk about life at Molly Stark. It was evident that even the strongest and most dedicated staff members often felt frustrated and discouraged. Students seemed increasingly aggressive and disrespectful. Many parents appeared less focused on their children and less supportive of education. More parents than usual weren't showing up for parent conferences, and it was more difficult to get parents to support the school on discipline issues. It was during this conversation that we made the decision to talk about doing things differently. I had already taught fifth and sixth grades at Molly Stark for 15 years and had served as the assistant principal for 2 years. Now, as principal, I knew I was in a position to make change.

In his book *Parental Involvement and the Political Principle*, Seymour Sarason (1995) talks about people who continue to "ride a dead horse." When confronted with a dead horse, he says, people will try any or all of these responses: buy a stronger whip, try a new bridle, switch riders, move the horse to a new location, ride the horse for longer periods, say things like "this is the way we've always ridden this horse," appoint a committee to study the horse, arrange a visit to other sites where dead horses are ridden efficiently, increase the standards for riding dead horses, create a test for measuring riding abilities, compare how dead horses are ridden now with how they were ridden 10 years ago, complain about the state of horses these days, blame the horse's parents, or have a metaphysical discussion about the meaning of death. Instead of doing any of these, we decided it would be best to dismount. We began to look at what we needed to do for kids and their families to help them help themselves.

The First Step: Important Conversations and Information Gathering

We began in the fall of 1995 by developing a focus group, inviting participation from anyone on the staff who had an interest in making positive change. I decided to also invite three community members—a pediatrician and a psychologist with whom we had worked on many occasions, and a police detective who had been at our school far too many times for the wrong reasons. We knew all three had worked successfully with children and their families, as well as with our school staff.

The first meeting was in October on a Thursday morning before school. I remember this so vividly because at the time I felt that this meeting was a disaster. About 15 people were there, and it turned into a session of venting complaints. We talked about out-of-control kids, apathetic parents, and disillusioned staff. One staff member told us how unsafe she felt with volatile students and parents. Another said she had basically given up on the apathetic kids who just weren't ever going to learn. Another asked, "Why do we work so hard when it doesn't make a difference?" Many issues were laid out on the table, but at this point, we had no answers. What we did decide was to start gathering information and sharing it with one another.

As we continued to meet, we asked ourselves some crucial questions about pivotal and sometimes controversial issues: What is our job as a public school? What does our school need to create in order to provide opportunities for success for children and families? What are our beliefs regarding our school's role in the lives of families? These were complex questions that not just this group but our entire staff needed to consider. By spring 1996, one thing we had all agreed on was that we were ready to look outside the box for ways to help our children find success.

An important thing to remember is that we spent that first year (1995–1996) planning before we proceeded with implementation. We discussed the fact that the issue of quality was crucial, and quality would only come with good planning. Planning meant figuring out what was needed for children and families, how to provide these services and programs, the order in which to implement them, and how to get the necessary funding.

Once the focus group had gathered information from various sources, the next step was using that information as a basis for defining the most crucial needs of our school population. This would help us determine what resources to tap and what programs to provide and would help us match needs to the available resources. Our goal as a school and a community was to determine the most efficient way of delivering services to families—services that were accessible and affordable to all.

We looked at community statistics, state data, individual school information, and surveys and suggestions from teachers, parents, and students. For example, data from the community showed a lack of dental services for Medicaid-eligible children; state statistics informed us that our county had the highest dropout rate and the second highest teen pregnancy rate in the state; school data told us that physical and verbal aggression as well as absenteeism were well above local and state averages; teachers voiced concern that far too many students were entering our kindergarten without the skills and social experiences they needed to do well; parents were worried about their children's health needs and their safety during the summer months; and some students said they didn't want to be at the school because they didn't feel safe.

To help us define the needs of our school and community, we tried to focus on what would have the biggest impact on the lives of children and families. This is a list of what we discussed and continue to discuss over time; these questions help direct our work:

- What are the most critical needs that prevent our children from learning?
- What needs are somewhat but not fully met? How do we know this?
- What are we doing to connect in a positive way with families?
- What services are currently accessible to children and families at our school, even if they don't have transportation?
- What services, if any, are being duplicated in our community?
- What services are provided in the community but are not easily accessible and therefore might be provided at the school site?
- What agencies and providers are involved with our school now?
- What agencies and providers might be involved in the future? (We considered local health and mental health services, social service providers, libraries, hospital.)
- Which of the available services are working in a positive way for our students and their families?
- What safe, enriching activities, if any, are our students participating in before and after school?
- What parent support and education programs are available? What programs and services do our parents wish we offered?
- Are sufficient child care and preschool services available? What measures will we use to determine if they are of high quality?
- What do we know we need to accomplish our goals: money, human resources, materials, staff development, and so on?
- What can we learn from site visits, written material, practitioners, and other outside sources?
- What will be the critical elements of support necessary from the school district's central office and board of education?
- How will we collect data? What outcomes are we looking for? What will be some indicators of progress?
- What barriers to success do we foresee?

In spring 1996, we made a connection that helped us move forward: We became affiliated with the Yale Schools of the 21st Century program. This model, from the Yale Bush Center in Child Development and Social Policy, promotes access to year-round child care, family outreach, nutrition and health services, early preventive support and intervention for children and parents of young children, and collaboration with community services. We attended a conference in New Haven, Connecticut, participated in site visits to schools that had successfully implemented this child and family service model, and talked to as many practitioners as possible to learn through their experiences. Although this model was not specifically presented as a "full-service community school" model, everything we learned about it focused us in that direction.

The Plan Takes Shape

In the 1996–1997 school year, we developed a five-year plan, encompassing what could be provided immediately, what could be provided over the next several months, and what would take a year or more to develop. This sounds overwhelming, but we needed to develop a framework, always with the understanding that it would change many times. One important task was to talk about what *was* working. Molly Stark already had many dedicated staff members and some good programs. We divided the existing programs and services into four categories: health and wellness, curriculum and instruction, family involvement, and social responsibility. As we discussed what we already had, we also talked about what we planned to implement over the next five years.

For each category, we developed a service plan grid that showed both present and future services and included information about needed staff, funding, and other resources (see Tables 2.1 through 2.4). This gave us a starting point and showed us what issues to consider and discuss as the process unfolded.

These grids were just a starting point. We found that our plans continuously changed. For instance, in our health category, we had developed a model for dental care in which a dental hygienist would refer students to local dentists who had agreed to see our students on Medicaid. We never imagined that a retired dentist would approach us in 1998, one year into this model, and begin a dental practice in our school. When we started a homework club, we didn't foresee that within two years we would have four homework clubs, two at the school and two off site. When we began our reading club, we didn't know that three years later we would begin a math club.

Our summer programs provide another example of our changing plans. Although we have begun to offer academic programs in the summer, we have not yet been open for child care or recreational and enrichment programs. For a variety of reasons, including staffing and funding, we have not successfully met this goal. However, we are hoping to do so in the near future.

Some programs that worked well were expanded. When our family outreach worker started, she was employed for 10 hours per week. Because of the needs of our families and the success of this program, two years later we expanded the time to 15 hours per week.

Many of our programs weren't part of the original plan. Throughout the process, new ideas came from a variety of staff members. For example, the mentoring component in our original plan, the PALS program, paired high school students with Molly Stark students. We didn't consider looking for community mentors until a staff member applied for and received a three-year grant to hire a mentoring coordinator. This expanded our program way beyond our original vision.

Table 2.1   Health and Wellness Service Plan Grid, 1996 to 2001

Present Service	Location/Time	Who Is Responsible?	Funding	Implementation Date	Factor Determining Success (Assessment)	What Is Needed to Sustain Service?
Healthy snack cart	Hallway/Mornings	Classroom teachers, students	None needed	September 1993	Increase in number of students using snack cart	N/A
Clinical psychologist	Any available space/Two hours per week	Requests through Educational Support Team, nurse makes schedule	EPSDT*/Medicaid funds, funds from Vermont Agency of Human Services	September 1996	Decrease in number of absences and discipline referrals among students receiving services	Secure funding, determine consultant
Pediatrician	Any available space/Two hours per week	Requests through Educational Support Team, nurse makes schedule	EPSDT*/Medicaid funds, funds from Vermont Agency of Human Services	September 1996	All children have access to medical care and are referred to specialists as needed	Secure funding
Physicals and inoculations for third and sixth graders with no primary care physician	Nurse's office/One time each year	Survey sent to all parents to determine eligible children	Funds from Vermont Agency of Human Services	1996–1997 school year	Decrease in number of students without access to well-child physicals and inoculations	Secure funding

Table 2.1   Continued

Future Service	Location	Who Is Responsible?	Funding	Planned Implementation Date	Factor Determining Success (Assessment)	What Is Needed for Start-Up?
Dental program	Screening in nurse's office, dental work at dentist's office	Dental hygienist	EPSDT*/Medicaid funds, Medicaid for dental work done	September 1998	Decrease in number of students without dental care	Hire dental hygienist to work with local dentists interested in this program, secure funding
Staff wellness program	Molly Stark	School nurse	Grant money, fees from staff when necessary	September 1999	Increase in number of staff in program	School nurse to check into different programs
Eye care	To be determined	School nurse	Medicaid	September 2000	Decrease in number of students without needed glasses	Find optometrist who will participate

*Early Periodic Screening Diagnosis and Treatment

Table 2.2 Curriculum and Instruction Service Plan Grid, 1996 to 2001

Present Service	Location	Who Is Responsible?	Funding	Implementation Date	Factor Determining Success (Assessment)	What Is Needed to Sustain Service?
Golden Pencil, Artist-in-Residence	Throughout the school in classrooms	Molly Stark staff, Golden Pencil Committee	Title VI, local grants	1990	Increase in writing motivation and skills	Secure funding
Math Olympics	Molly Stark	Fifth-grade teacher	Local funds	1991	Increase in problem-solving skills	N/A
Phonological awareness for all kindergarteners	Molly Stark	Title I teacher	Title I	September 1996	Increase in number of first graders on grade level in reading	N/A
Future Service	Location/Time	Who Is Responsible?	Funding	Planned Implementation Date	Factor Determining Success (Assessment)	What Is Needed for Start-Up?
Professional development in reading, math, and writing	Molly Stark/During school hours	Consultants hired by principal	Title II, local funds, grants	Reading: 1999–2000 Math: 2000–2001 Writing: 2001–2002	Increase in number of students meeting or exceeding state standards	Determine consultants, secure funding
More pre-K programs	Molly Stark/During school hours	Staff employed by school, partners in community	Child care subsidies, grants, special education/Medicaid funds	Unsure due to lack of space	Increase in social and academic skills of kindergarteners	Secure funding, find space, become licensed child care facility

Table 2.2 Continued

Future Service	Location/Time	Who Is Responsible?	Funding	Planned Implementation Date	Factor Determining Success (Assessment)	What Is Needed for Start-Up?
After-school enrichment programs	Molly Stark/ After school	Person hired to set up logistics	Grants	September 1997	Students who attend reflect demographics of Molly Stark population	Secure funding, hire organizers, get program facilitators
Homework club	Molly Stark/ After school	Homework club facilitators	Grants	September 1997	Students who participate complete homework and improve work habits	Secure funding, hire facilitators
Reading club	Molly Stark/ After school	Molly Stark staff member organizes adult volunteers to facilitate	Grants	September 1997	Students who participate improve reading skills	Secure funding, determine program organizers
Academic summer programs	Molly Stark/ Summer months	Molly Stark staff	Local grant, Title I	Summer 1999	Increase in students meeting or exceeding state standards	Secure funding
Extended-day kindergarten	Molly Stark/ Throughout school year	Molly Stark staff	Grants, child care subsidies	September 1999	Increase in social and academic skills of kindergarteners	Secure funding, find space, become licensed child care facility
Summer vacation programs	Molly Stark/ Summer months	Molly Stark staff	Grants, child care subsidies	Summer 2001	Increase in activities available to students	Secure funding, find space, become licensed child care facility

Table 2.3   Family Involvement Service Plan Grid, 1996 to 2001

Present Service	Location/Time	Who Is Responsible?	Funding	Implementation Date	Factor Determining Success (Assessment)	What Is Needed to Sustain Service?
Recreational and educational family nights	Molly Stark/Designated evenings	Molly Stark staff	Local funds (for materials)	September 1996	Number of participating families	Staff coming to consensus on when, where, and the theme
Open house, first-day picnic	Molly Stark/First day of school	Committee	Parent-teacher group funds	September 1996	Number of participating families	Small amount of money, staff to participate
Future Service	Location/Time	Who Is Responsible?	Funding	Planned Implementation Date	Factor Determining Success (Assessment)	What Is Needed for Start-Up?
School-age child care	Molly Stark	Staff hired for child care	Subsidies, fee for services, grants	September 1998	Number of students participating	Secure funding, hire staff, determine space
Family outreach worker	Molly Stark/10 hours per week	Referrals made through Educational Support Team	Grants, special education/Medicaid funds	September 1998	Increase in number of children focused on learning and parents supporting education	Secure funding, determine possible employees
Adult education programs	Molly Stark/Various times	Tutorial Center employee	Tutorial Center	September 1997	Increase in number of adults in Molly Stark community completing their GED	Determine space, determine employee

Table 2.4   Social Responsibility Service Plan Grid, 1996 to 2001

Present Service	Location/Time	Who Is Responsible?	Funding	Implementation Date	Factor Determining Success (Assessment)	What Is Needed to Sustain Service?
PRIDE social skills program	Throughout Molly Stark	Entire Molly Stark staff	N/A	September 1996	Number of students showing appropriate social behavior	Staff commitment
PALS high school/Molly Stark mentoring program	In community/ Outside school time	Guidance counselor, high school community service person	Title VI	September 1988	At-risk elementary students gain social skills and their discipline referrals decrease	N/A
School Store	Molly Stark/ Before school one day per week	Classroom; oversight by scholarship committee member	N/A	September 1993	Scholarship given each year to graduating senior who went to Molly Stark	Staff commitment
Primary Project school adjustment program	Molly Stark/ During school hours	Trained paraprofessional supervised by guidance counselor	Local funds	September 1988	Students show improvement in adjustment to school	Funding for position

Table 2.4 Continued

Future Service	Location/Time	Who Is Responsible?	Funding	Planned Implementation Date	Factor Determining Success (Assessment)	What Is Needed for Start-Up?
Adventure-based counseling	At Molly Stark/ During school hours	Guidance counselor, special educator	Title VI for equipment	September 1997	Students apply co-operation skills throughout school day	Training for facilitators, secure funds for course, equipment
Conflict management program	Molly Stark playground/ During recess	Guidance counselor facilitates training and maintains the program	Local funds for incentive program	September 1998	Decrease in number of conflicts on playground	Training for students, secure funding for incentive program
Mentoring programs	Molly Stark/ During lunch or recess	Guidance counselor, mentoring coordinator	Grants	September 1999	Increase in students' interest in educational success and decrease in discipline referrals	Funds for mentoring coordinator, interested community members
Community Pride Program	Molly Stark/ During school hours	Classroom students supervised by their teachers	N/A	September 1999	Students involved in giving something positive back to the school community	Commitment from staff

Getting Parents on Board

A key question was when to bring parents into the planning process. Parents are important stakeholders and should have a role in making decisions that will affect their children. However, it is also important that the people who work together in a school community have time to talk candidly about the concerns, needs, apprehensions, and beliefs that they bring to the process. Initially, this kind of discussion was uncomfortable with parents present.

However, we wanted parents to be involved from the start, so we decided to send them a questionnaire to get some pertinent baseline information. While creating the survey, we considered carefully whether the questions were respectful, clearly worded, easy to understand, and without educational jargon and acronyms.

After our survey went out to parents in spring 1996, we gave the same questions to students and staff. We asked questions based on what was currently happening, trying to get a sense of the perception of all three groups. Some examples follow:

- Do you know what the bottom-line behaviors are for our school?
- Do you think Molly Stark is a happy place to be?
- Do you think parents and teachers work well together?
- Do you think students treat teachers with respect?
- Do you think students treat each other with respect?
- Do you think the planning room helps to improve student behaviors?
- Do you feel safe at Molly Stark School?
- Do you like the Artist-in-Residence program?
- Do you like the Molly Stark TV show on Friday mornings?
- Is Molly Stark a clean, comfortable place to learn in?
- Do you feel that students with discipline problems get more attention from adults?
- Would you be interested in after-school programs?
- What programs would you like to see for your children?

We also had all three groups rate (by choosing Thumbs Up, O.K., or Thumbs Down) the traditional activities we offered, such as field trips, Family Fun Nights, special arts programs, and Monday Morning Celebrations.

The survey results validated our discussions and gave us some baseline information. The parents, staff, and students all felt positive about our traditional programs. They enjoyed our schoolwide writing program (Golden Pencil) and the artist-in-residence who came to work with the kids each year. Not surprisingly, field trips, special programs, and Family Fun Nights were popular, and so were our Monday Morning Celebrations and the Molly Stark TV show on Friday mornings.

The results of the questions around behavior and discipline were more problematic. Many staff and students didn't feel particularly safe at school, and some parents expressed concerns for their children's safety. Surprisingly, in spite of this, most kids, staff, and parents felt that Molly Stark was a happy place to be.

Written surveys could not give us all the information we needed because some parents did not have the skills or comfort level to fill them out. As another way to get parent input, we invited groups of four to six parents (a representative mix) to meet with one or two school personnel to answer specific questions, such as what services they would like to see offered, what concerns they had about their children, and what they liked about what the school already provided. We also held "bagel bashes" in the community room at one of Bennington's housing projects. We did this throughout the 1996–1997 school year, permitting communication in both formal and informal ways on a continuous basis. During this information-gathering time, we found that some parents required support, encouragement, and personal attention to be willing and able to lend their voices.

As parents felt more and more welcome, they became comfortable approaching school staff and sharing information about what they thought was and wasn't working, what children and parents felt good about, and where the gaps were. One concern expressed by many parents, especially poorer ones, involved their children's free time after school as well as during the summer. This was a concern we knew we had to address in our plan.

Keeping Everyone on Board

A crucial task was to regularly bring all information and plans discussed back to the school staff. What happens in a full-service community school goes far beyond what is traditionally expected in a public school, and it was important to keep all our staff members informed along the way. Teachers had varying degrees of comfort at first, and some feared that providing more services at the school would overburden their already very stressful and busy days. Jim Harwood, a kindergarten teacher at Molly Stark at the time, expressed his uneasiness about implementing the full-service school model:

> I felt three issues would impact my classroom and school in negative ways. The first issue was money. I wanted to continue to provide a quality educational experience for the children in my classroom. I could not give up any money from my budget. I wondered how much money each classroom teacher would lose to support these new activities. The taxpayer would not be willing to give the school more money. The second issue was time. I had a full plate and could not take on any new tasks. I was sure the principal would never have any time for my classroom issues. I was sure the guidance counselor and nurse would never get to my classroom again. The third issue was the focus of the school. I wondered if our academic focus would change as we added more non-academic programs. How would our school be viewed in our community? I wondered if we were spreading our time and money too thin with so many new services.

These were all common and valid concerns shared by other classroom teachers. Their fears showed how important it was for staff members to have a clear understanding of what their role would be in a full-service school and what they, too, would gain from the support such a school provides. Teachers in any school have two very important and difficult roles: to provide excellent instruction and to be kind and welcoming to children and families. Services should not take from teachers' budgets, time, or support but should actually give teachers more of a chance to do what they were hired to do: educate children.

A year later, Jim Harwood became the assistant principal of Molly Stark. He describes the contrast between what he thought would happen and what actually happened:

> I began to change my perspective about full-service schools when I brought the idea of a Kindercamp to my administration. As a kindergarten teacher, I felt that children would enter school more comfortable and confident by coming to school for an orientation program a few days shortly before school began. I presented my plan, and the administration approached it seriously. We applied for and received a grant to fund Kindercamp, and I soon realized that money did not need to be a blocker for programs that were good for kids and parents. As our school developed its vision, I also saw that time for quality instruction wasn't going to suffer but in fact was going to be enhanced. I now had a whole system of support for my students. If a child or family needed help, we looked at our menu of services to see what was needed. This only made my job as classroom teacher easier. The school, in fact, did have a strong academic focus. Now the situations that often hurt a child's chance to do well in school were beginning to be rectified. My concerns faded because I was given information and support and allowed time to move at a comfortable pace toward a full-service school model.

Jim's Kindercamp idea is a good example of how we incorporated new ideas that were not in our original plan.

Teachers must play an important role in the process and know that their ideas are valued. We continue to discuss all the steps of the plan along the way. We share articles and information about site visits, and we regularly ask any additional interested staff to join in the journey at whatever level they feel comfortable. Some staff members were at the forefront of making change. They rolled up their sleeves and helped to make things happen. Others stayed in the background, quietly observing yet not blocking the process.

There were other important stakeholders to keep informed besides parents, staff, and students. It was important that the community know what was happening at our school. Early on, in spring 1996, I invited the directors of every family-oriented agency in our community to a meeting. I called each personally, and they all attended. We discussed the work of the focus group and the direction we felt we were going. We invited them to collaborate with us to help children and their families. Some came on board immediately with excitement and great ideas; others politely listened. Within a few weeks I had met with Sunrise Family Resource Center and the Tutorial Center (our local adult basic education facility). We had found our first partners.

Two other important stakeholders were the superintendent and the school board. Their understanding and acceptance of this model was essential, and their lack of support could easily have blocked the plan. A continuous flow of information from the outset helped ensure their support.

Spreading the Word

Public relations concerning our school and all the new programs and services came about without much effort on our part. The governor and lieutenant governor became interested in our efforts, and with their visits came many newspaper articles with great headlines like "When a School Is a Community," "School of the Future Focuses on Families/Kids from Birth," "At the Heart of Community," "Breaking the Mold," and "Molly Stark Adds Day Care." Organizations and schools began to ask us to speak about our mission, and the news traveled fast. Visitor after visitor from Vermont, across New England, and even the Netherlands came to talk and learn more about full-service schools. With the talents of Cheryl Edwards, our computer room supervisor, a Web site was developed—http://www.svsu.org/schools/MollyStark/.

We didn't spend much formal time promoting our school or the idea of full-service community schools. We were doing good things for kids, and the momentum grew on its own.

The Professional Development Component

In conjunction with all the changes happening at Molly Stark, we have offered an array of professional development opportunities for our staff. Quality instruction and kind and caring teachers are at the core of a school that is doing right by its students. Continuous, worthwhile professional development presented by facilitators with expertise and credibility is a crucial aspect of a sound plan.

To begin the school year in 1996, I hired Robert Brooks to speak with the teachers. I had heard him speak at a conference the year before and immediately knew that his message was an important one. He spoke about finding children's "islands of competency" and about empathy, respect, and the critical influence that a good teacher can have. He helped us focus on the idea that if we were to earn the trust and respect of the members of our school community, we would need to be consistently considerate and trustworthy.

Because one of the concerns of our staff was the amount of conflict and aggression the students exhibited, in spring 1997 I hired the Educators for Social Responsibility, conflict resolution trainers from Boston. Our entire staff was trained in conflict resolution, and in turn, the following school year, our guidance counselor trained fifth and sixth graders as conflict managers to help resolve issues on the primary playground.

Much of our professional development has been academically oriented. When I heard Marjorie Lipson, a professor at the University of Vermont, speak about reading instruction at a state meeting in fall 1998, I invited her to Molly Stark. During the 1999–2000 school year, she worked with us regularly, helping us establish a common language in reading instruction and teaching and discussing strategies and materials. In addition, she taught a graduate-level reading course at our school that 13 of our staff members chose to take. The following school year, we worked with a teacher from the Vermont Science and Math Institute, Jean Ward. She came to Molly Stark twice a month to model-teach math problem solving. She, too, taught a course (in math problem-solving instruction), and this time 20 teachers chose to participate. More and more staff members were becoming comfortable reflecting on and enhancing their skills.

The Governance Structure

There are many levels of governance at Molly Stark School. We needed to be aware of them all as we developed policies, managed day-to-day operations, and generated money for programs. Our school site governance was somewhat determined by the fact that the services were driven by our school, not by an outside agency, and therefore came under the jurisdiction of the school district and the board of education, each of which had their own set of policies. However, there were still daily governance issues to be considered.

In 1999, we appointed an advisory council that included some key school staff (principal, site coordinator, teacher, nurse, guidance counselor), as well as many community members. The role of this council would be to hear what was happening, add ideas, research problems, brainstorm solutions, promote community collaboration, and provide expertise in their individual areas. To be honest, we were only active about meeting with the advisory council when we first set up the Family Center programs. However, each time I fret about this, I take comfort from realizing that we often contact council members individually for advice and assistance.

A School-Tailored Plan

We began with programming where it made sense for our particular school within our particular community. We knew it was essential to do a quality job from the start, because as positive responses get around, enthusiasm and commitment to the process spread rapidly. On the other hand, one program or activity implemented poorly can result in generalizations that "full-service schools aren't good." We tried to find needs to address that seemed manageable, that didn't exceed our monetary and human resources, and that would show immediate benefits to our students and families. For example, after-school programs benefit both children and parents. We started small (four activities that lasted for four weeks), found four volunteers willing to be facilitators, used already available classroom space, and watched things happen. As interest soared and the momentum increased, this small beginning grew into a multifaceted program in which facilitators are paid and children have an array of choices.

Many full-service schools we have read about or visited do not provide all the services at the school site but refer children and families to community agencies. At Molly Stark, we have found that creating successful partnerships and providing an array of services at our school location allows our staff to do their primary jobs.

Why is it important to provide services at the school? First, because everyone is expected to go to school to learn, so there is no stigma to going to school for other services. For example, it is often much easier for parents to bring their child to a preschool at their local elementary school than to a preschool that requires the child to fit into a low-income or special-needs category. Second, providing services at the school can be a more respectful way to work with parents. To get the help they need, parents don't have to visit multiple community agencies or, worse, have multiple providers invade their home. A dad who would not let a provider into his house was questioned about his "resistance to help"; his eye-opening reply was "I've had seven people in my home this week. No more!" How many of us would want seven people showing up on our doorstep and asking questions about our family life?

Finally, because we are a school, we *do* have an academic focus. Our primary job is to educate children with the goal of having our students finish school and move into a community to live in a productive way. When children don't learn to read, write, and understand math concepts, they will have a much harder time reaching that goal. The services in a full-service community school provide children with the support they need to be more successful academically.

Our plan is dynamic. It continues to evolve over time. Although we don't always know what each day will bring, we have a shared belief that the direction we are heading is right for kids.

About two years into our journey, Vermont's Lieutenant Governor Doug Racine called me at school. He had just been at a full-service school conference at Harvard, and when he came back to Vermont, someone told him that we had developed a full-service school at Molly Stark. He asked if he could come down to visit and, of course, I said sure. Then I went out into the office to ask if anyone knew what a full-service school was because the lieutenant governor was coming down to see ours. I looked up "full-service school" on the Internet and promptly ordered Joy's book on the topic. In retrospect, it does seem surprising that we had never heard the term before. To me this shows that it was an idea whose time had come and that what we had started to do made sense, whatever it was called. We just decided to take a serious look at doing what was right and good for kids and families and planned accordingly.

3

What Kinds of Services Can Schools Provide?

Judy Cohen

OVERVIEW OF SERVICES AND COMPONENTS

What goes into a full-service community school? As you will see from Sue's descriptions in this chapter and the next, many different kinds of programs can be put together. I am always amazed at the ingenuity of practitioners at the local level who find interesting and innovative services to bring into schools. Every community school has a different configuration, depending on what is needed and what is available in the community that can or should be relocated into the school.

After-school programs have become such a large subject that they have been assigned to their own chapter in this book. This chapter looks at support services for children and families that are usually provided during the school day as well as during extended hours. School-based primary health care clinics and family resource centers are highlighted.

Overview

Our information about community schools derives from a variety of sources, including publications, unpublished reports, site visits, and anecdotal information. A study conducted in 1998 by Tia Melaville and Martin Blank provides insights into some of the characteristics of 20 diverse school-community programs, ranging in size at that time from four school sites (Children's Aid Society) to over 1,500 (Communities-in-Schools). For each program, the study asked what activities were provided at an average site. All of the programs offered some form of parent education and tutoring of students, and almost all mentioned referral to agencies not at the school site. Almost all (80 to 90 percent) offered case management, primary health care, before- and after-school child care, mentoring, community service opportunities, recreation, leadership and career development, employment counseling and job training, and community organizing. About 75 percent had an infant and toddler program or preschool-age child care. More than half provided housing assistance. While primary health care was high up on the list, many reported that their programs were limited and could not meet demand.

A do-it-yourself manual, *Building a Full-Service School* (Calfee, Wittwer, & Meredith, 1998), gives an idea of the number of different services that can be tapped to attain certain goals. To achieve the goal of readiness to learn, 18 services are listed, and about the same number to enhance school performance, increase school safety, encourage adult literacy, and so forth. Calfee et al. propose more than 100 varied program components, strongly emphasizing health care and mental health counseling.

School-Based Health and Mental Health Services

Several major categories of services are particularly significant. I start here with school-based primary health care clinics because that was the first component that grabbed my attention. It is also an excellent "foot in the door" for outsiders who want to penetrate the walls of the school. Imagine a clinic inside a school. As you enter a small waiting room, you see children waiting their turns, perhaps playing with stuffed toys, reading books, or watching a film on drug-abuse prevention or conflict resolution. The walls are covered with educational materials and posters. A child is called into an examining room and stretches out on a gurney for a medical examination by a pediatric nurse practitioner. The child's medical history is on file, just as it would be at any other clinic. A parental consent slip is also on file, and the parents can be called if necessary.

This little scene makes so much sense. The problem is addressed immediately, and the child usually is able to return to class. If medications are necessary, they can be supplied and administered by clinic personnel.

Almost all primary health clinics now employ social workers or counselors as well as medical personnel, responding to the increasing demand for mental health services. Because almost all the sources of funds for school-based health and mental health care are not from education resources, school authorities generally welcome clinics that offer to help children overcome the barriers to learning.

Schools incorporate health services in many ways. In traditional schools, school nurses provide assistance to millions of children, often checking for immunizations and attendance and administering medications. But in some places, more than the usual amount of health care is necessary. At Molly Stark, a "traditional" school nurse conducts basic screening and offers health education, but additional health services are offered by a full-time dentist as well as a pediatrician and a psychologist who are on call to see individual students and conduct physical examinations for third and sixth graders.

McCoy Community School in Kansas City, Missouri, is one of the most comprehensive models of Missouri's Caring Communities program. Its fully equipped clinic, called the Panda Place Wellness Center, has been carved into the old school building. It has an examining room and offices, and the staff, provided by the Samuel Rodgers Community Health Center, includes a family nurse practitioner, a medical assistant/receptionist, a community health outreach worker, and a pediatrician. The clinic offers free primary care services, routine physicals, vision and hearing screenings, immunization, and laboratory services to all neighborhood residents aged 18 and younger. McCoy opened a dental clinic in 2001 in partnership with the Smile Team, a statewide dental collaborative. According to Jennifer Santiago, a registered nurse who works at Panda Place, "We expanded this year [2001] to include adults, and we serve them on a sliding scale. The biggest benefit [to them] is the convenience because of family work schedules and lack of transportation" (Gray, 2000).

At McCoy, a licensed clinical social worker is provided by another agency, the Don Bosco Community Center. Psychiatric and psychological services are provided by still another local medical facility, Truman Behavioral Health. Counseling groups are offered during the school day for children of divorce and for other specific issues; individual counseling is readily available for at-risk students and their families to work on improving peer and family relationships. Anger management counseling is offered by the Rose Brooks Center, a local shelter for battered women.

The Health Place at Quitman Street Community School, an adaptation of the Children's Aid Society (CAS) model in Newark, New Jersey, is where health, dental, and mental health services are provided by the Newark Beth Israel Hospital. A nurse practitioner, social worker, and medical clerk are on site at all times. The offices—an examining room, dental suite, private offices, and waiting room—have attractive décor and professional-looking furnishings.

At another CAS adaptation site, the Thomas Gardner Extended Services School in Boston's Allston-Brighton neighborhood, primary health care is provided by St. Elizabeth's Medical Center, dental care by the Joseph Smith Health Center, and mental health care by the Allston-Brighton Mental Health Clinic. Bilingual social workers provide individual, family, and group therapy using a case management approach. They respond to emotional and behavioral issues that students bring into the classroom, such as depression or acting out, and they address family relationships and carry out crisis intervention in situations that may include abuse, neglect, and domestic violence. The social workers also supervise interns from Boston College who provide the same services as part of their training.

Family Resource Centers

At the national level, Family Support America is working to encourage the creation of family-supportive community schools. It is estimated that the number of schools housing family support programs may already be as high as 5,000 (Blank & Melaville, 1999).

The family resource centers at CAS schools are operated by staff, parents, and other volunteers. Parents can learn what is going on in the school and how they can become involved. They also can obtain support services such as emergency assistance, food, housing, legal aid, and assistance with employment, benefits, and immigration. Parents are welcome to socialize and "hang out" together, either informally or through planned events. The centers offer parenting workshops that include information about family life and sex education, entrepreneurial skills, nutrition, and child rearing, as well as courses to improve parents' ability to assist their children with schoolwork. Adult education classes are held every afternoon and evening, including higher education courses through partnerships with colleges. At one CAS community school in New York City, the University of Santo Domingo offers graduate courses that enable professionals who have emigrated from the Dominican Republic to obtain licenses and accreditation in their fields.

The center at Quitman Street Community School in Newark is called the Parent Academy. A large, well-equipped room is the locus for GED classes, parenting classes, and parent workshops in subjects like computer technology. Parents can also review examples of tests that their children will take during the year. Parents at Quitman are required to sign a "contract" to give six hours of volunteer services a month to the community school. They have responded enthusiastically and welcome the opportunity to participate in their children's education as aides in the classroom and cafeteria, on the playground, on field trips, and in the after-school program.

School-Based Clinics Around the Country

In 2001, the 1,400 school-based health centers in 45 states served an estimated 1.1 million children, a tenfold increase over a decade (*Access,* 2001,
p. 1). A survey of 806 centers provided insights into the characteristics of
the programs (National Assembly on School-Based Health Care, 2000).
Some 56 percent are in urban areas, 30 percent rural, and 14 percent suburban. Some 30 percent are elementary, 19 percent middle school, and 51
percent high school. The average enrollment for these schools was about
1,000 students, and 64 percent were reported to be enrolled in the clinics.
Nearly two-thirds were minority (29 percent African American, 26 percent
Hispanic, 4 percent Asian, and 3 percent Native American).

Who administers the school-based health centers? Mostly hospitals,
health departments, and community health centers (73 percent), but also
university medical centers (5 percent) and nonprofit health care agencies
(9 percent). About 10 percent of primary care school-based clinics are
operated directly by school districts. Most centers employ nurse practitioners, physicians, and physician's assistants. Mental health professionals
are part of the clinic team at 57 percent of the sites. Most of the clinics are
open 30 or more hours a week, and half operate during summer months.
Most have prearranged backup care for emergencies.

Most school-based clinics provide health screenings, treatment of
acute illnesses, immunizations, lab tests, and prescriptions. More than half
conduct dental screenings. Among middle and high schools with clinics,
most provide some form of reproductive health care, but 77 percent are
prohibited from dispensing contraceptives. For students seeking birth control, most school-based clinics make referrals to other facilities but conduct
follow-ups on site to make sure the students have actually acquired and are
using birth control. Over 80 percent conduct pregnancy testing on site, and
most do treatment for sexually transmitted diseases.

At the Thomas Gardner Extended Services School in Boston, parents can
gather in the multipurpose room to attend special workshops or receive assistance in accessing social services such as housing, immigration, entitlements,
and emergency food and clothing. In the evening, parents and other adults can
take classes in ESL, GED preparation, and computers.

Parent involvement at McCoy Community School in Kansas City has
increased dramatically, with almost 88 percent attendance at parent-teacher
conferences in 2001. In partnership with the Kansas City Community Church
Organization, school staff were trained to make home visits, during which parents talk about their child and share their expectations for the teachers and the
school. A parent volunteer coordinates this effort, which is reported to be very
well received.

Several states have rather extensive family center programs; examples are
Rhode Island's Child Opportunity Zone (COZ), Kentucky's Family Resource and

Youth Service Centers, Connecticut's Family Resource Centers, and Minnesota's Family Service Program.

Preschool Programs

Molly Stark's Family Center houses a preschool component, and the community's Early Education Program is also located in two classrooms in the school building. A growing number of community schools include preschool child care as part of the package. PS 5, the CAS model elementary school in New York City, focuses on early childhood development and incorporates Head Start, Early Head Start, and other preschool programs. Neighborhood outreach workers from the school recruit families from the giant housing projects nearby to come to PS 5 to arrange for prenatal care and learn about parenting. Fathers are encouraged to attend with their partners. A psychologist conducts classes in infant stimulation, and parents learn about child development, creative play, and nutrition. The parents have the opportunity to bring babies and toddlers into the school for hands-on experience. As their children's first teachers, parents learn to read, talk, and listen to their kids, a basic step in creating readiness to learn that is especially important for these immigrant families.

The Quitman Street Community School in Newark has a partnership with the Bank Street College of Education's Project New Beginnings. Project staff provide intensive professional development to teachers, paraprofessionals, administrators, and parents in pre-K, kindergarten, and Grade 1 classrooms. The goal is to enhance early childhood learning, particularly in language development and communication skills.

Services in Community High Schools

Compared with elementary and middle schools, high schools present a different challenge to developers of community school programs. Students are, of course, older, and any previously unaddressed problems are more deeply rooted. Parents are less accessible. And students are in constant motion, changing or cutting classes and sometimes getting lost in the halls of large, overcrowded buildings. Yet the principles of community schools—extended hours, partnerships, individual attention, community focus, and integration of support services and classroom experiences—make sense when applied to reforming high schools. Several interesting examples demonstrate how this can be accomplished.

University City High School in Philadelphia

Built in 1971 as a technological center/magnet to attract white middle-class students to the inner city, University City High School (UCHS) has had a tortuous history. When it failed to achieve its original goal, the school was rescued by a former principal who reorganized it entirely. In the late 1990s, with another new principal, Florence Johnson, and in partnership with University of Pennsylvania's West Philadelphia Improvement Corps, UCHS became a rich and varied learning community with a special emphasis on school-to-work initiatives. The school is organized around nine "charters"—small units of 150 to 200 students who stay with the same teachers for four years. The charters focus on different areas, such as health careers, law, science, and computers. One charter is for students who need more motivation, another is for high achievers, and one, called Twilight School, is held from 3:00 to 6:00 p.m. for returning dropouts who have jobs.

Several hundred University of Pennsylvania (Penn) students and faculty come daily to UCHS from disciplines as diverse as English, education, classical studies, city planning, theater arts, and social work. The Law Charter students have internships in local law firms through Penn's law school. A full-time community school coordinator is provided by the university. In 1999, 10 different university courses were offered at UCHS directly by Penn faculty, involving both university and UCHS students. One joint project focused on the history of Black Bottom, a community displaced by urban renewal near the high school. Penn students collaborated with high school students and faculty in designing research and mounting an intergenerational community performance.

Half (16) of Penn's student teachers from the graduate school of education are placed at UCHS, where they work with small learning communities within the charters on designing new thematic curricula. An exemplary project resulted in greenhousing, where the students learned basic biology, produced plants to sell, and worked in arboretums. The University of Pennsylvania Medical Center and its hospital provide paid apprenticeships to students from the Health Charter, who attend classes at UCHS designed and taught by Penn faculty and graduate students. In the Technology Charter, Penn graduate students in urban planning teach UCHS students to do community work, looking at issues such as job creation and crime prevention.

Elizabeth Learning Center

One of the few examples of a pre-K through Grade 12 community school, the Elizabeth Learning Center in Cudahy, California, is a collaborative effort of the Los Angeles Unified School District, the teachers' union, a variety of community partners, and the New American Schools Development Corporation. It has been recognized as an Urban Learning Center Model by the U.S. Department of Education.

According to Howard Adelman and Linda Taylor, codirectors of the Center for Mental Health in Schools at the University of California at Los Angeles (UCLA) and important stakeholders in the Elizabeth Learning Center, this example goes beyond the concept of full-service schools by defining the components necessary for overcoming the barriers to learning and promoting healthy development. The model encompasses reform of curriculum and instruction, efficient governance, and integrated child and family supports. Services are not just added on, they are carefully integrated into the educational restructuring.

At Elizabeth, school readiness is addressed through an on-site Head Start. A family center serves as a focal point, where parents can come in for counseling and groups can meet. In addition to a school psychologist, the program brings in a social worker and two interns for family counseling. More than 1,000 adults each week attend classes held from 7:30 a.m. to 9:00 p.m. Two cooperative child care centers staffed by parent volunteers are available at all times to allow parents to take courses in ESL, GED, and citizenship preparation, computers, parenting, and parent leadership training. The school hired a full-time coordinator for the family center, as well as five part-time "community representatives" for outreach and coordination.

The family center offers "transition support" services: A community representative welcomes new parents and students (this neighborhood has rapid turnover), designating "peer buddies" to act as special friends for newcomers. New parents receive packets of maps, schedules, and other information in English and Spanish.

A school-based health clinic with support from a local medical center and hospital provides extensive free services to all students, with small charges for parents and siblings who want to obtain medical services there as well. For students in Grades 10 through 12, the Health Academy features service learning and community service opportunities through partnerships with community agencies. Nearby colleges provide instructors in health-related subjects, and Kaiser Hospital and St. Francis Medical Center offer internships.

Elizabeth Learning Center is highly organized, with teams managing programs in each of the six "enabling" components. For example, Student and Family Assistance has 18 different programs under way, including tutoring, counseling for students and families, case management, conflict resolution, health services, teen pregnancy prevention, and attendance. UCLA's Center for Mental Health in Schools (2000) has published detailed documentation of this unique pre-K through Grade 12 community effort.

Unusual Program Components

As noted in Chapter 2, most community schools are made up of certain discrete components, such as health clinics, family resource centers, youth development programs, and educational enrichment. The activities they engage in are fairly consistent across models. But the unusual program components described here demonstrate how imaginative people can address old problems in new ways.

Laundry

One school had difficulty overcoming parents' resistance to visiting the school. When someone commented that the parents had no access to a self-service laundry in that community, several washers and dryers were placed in the school basement. Not only did parents flock to the school to do their laundry, but the teachers used the facility as well. Communication between the parents and the staff started over a common need, and the parents began to trust the school.

Housing

A school was located in a neighborhood with many substandard housing units (not unusual for community schools). The family center provided instruction in housing repair, lent tools, and offered help in acquiring materials for home improvement. These efforts improved both the quality of life in the area and the parents' perception of the community school as a positive source of support.

Police

In a Hispanic community, families felt threatened by the presence of "big white cops." The local precinct was interested in improving relationships with their constituents, so the police officers were invited to the school to learn Spanish. A parent and a middle-school child teamed up to be the teachers. As the police began to learn Spanish, they built on their relationships with these families to encourage visits to the precinct headquarters. Everyone enjoyed the experience. The crime rate in the area subsequently decreased, which was attributed partly to the trusting relationships that had developed between the school, police, and residents.

Violence Prevention

The Santa Rosa County, Florida, Full-Service Schools Program expanded in recent years to encompass the goal of violence prevention. Probation officers were moved onto two high school campuses, along with the officer in charge of the sheriff's department's juvenile division. Delinquency decreased as high-risk students began to see the officers as supportive rather than threatening.

Community Development

In Kansas City, Blenheim Elementary School, one of Missouri's Caring Communities sites, held a neighborhood summit in collaboration with the East Meyer Community Association. Topics included street lighting, curb repair, safety and crime, housing rehabilitation, energy issues, and how to communicate with the city over neighborhood problems. The Blenheim advisory council is working to coordinate improvements for families and children in that neighborhood.

Power Lunch

Every month in Kansas City, McCoy Community School parents, district administrators, and local business and community leaders, as well as school staff, are invited into the school for the Power Lunch. Participants read to students and share their life experiences. In Read-Ins sponsored by the school, families can participate in literacy activities, receive free books, and share a dinner. Neighborhood cleanups are organized periodically to bring together school and family.

Peacekeepers

At the George Washington Middle School in Indianapolis, Americorps members lead a peacekeepers program featuring conflict resolution, a peace club, and peer mediators.

Gardens

The children in one Philadelphia community rarely have an opportunity to see anything grow. With the help of an ecologically oriented professor at a nearby university, the cement surrounding the school has been removed and a garden planted right on the grounds. Students learn to grow vegetables, which they later sell at an on-site market. In a neighboring high school, students learn how to grow herbs hydroponically and sell them at a health food emporium.

The St. Helena Unified School District in California developed a comprehensive nutrition program in conjunction with a local culinary institute, the California Foundation for Agriculture in the Classroom, the U.S. Department of Agriculture, and local businesses. Middle school students work with teachers and volunteers to design, create, and maintain a garden in a deserted lot. This has become an on-campus display of native California plants and ecosystems and is used as a focal point for the study of geology, ecology, and agriculture.

The Rigler SUN school in Portland, Oregon, received a grant from the Portland Bureau of Housing and Community Development for its Green Space project, a mix of gardens and park space. Half the community garden plots are used by the neighborhood, 35 percent by students doing class work, and 15 percent by senior citizen clients from the adjacent health center.

Dogs

The Mayor's Community Schools Project in Buffalo has a working relationship with more than 100 different organizations. As part of the after-school program at one site, the local Society for Prevention of Cruelty to Animals (SPCA) provides instruction and supervision to students who want to learn how to train undisciplined "dogs at risk" and prepare them for adoption. In addition to training the dogs, the students receive instruction in conflict resolution, peer relationships, and nonviolent problem solving. The program director has observed

---

Bank to Open Full-Service Branch in School

In Milwaukee, the state's first full-service bank housed in a school will try to do more than just teach students. Mitchell Bank's newest branch, Cardinal Bank, will try to attract members of the growing Latino community on the south side. "Even though many of the students work and their families work, many don't use banks because they come from Mexico and don't trust banks," said the business careers coordinator at South Division High School, site of the bank. Other schools in the state have classroom banks or credit unions, but South Division will have the first full-service, in-school bank. Cardinal will offer savings and checking accounts, safe deposit boxes, and loans. Five student volunteers were trained on the bank's computer system and will work as tellers.

SOURCE: Associated Press, August 14, 2000.

that this program increases students' feelings of empathy, kindness, and respect for all living things.

Putting It All Together

Community schools package these components in many different ways. In some cases, like Missouri's Caring Communities, certain components are required to get state funding. At other sites, like Molly Stark, components are added as needed or as resources become available. As these programs grow, management and administration can become quite complex, which is one reason every full-service community school needs a full-time coordinator to partner with the principal. All these different pieces have to fit together if the program is to be comprehensive.

Like Molly Stark, McCoy in Kansas City has entered into partnerships with an array of community agencies. McCoy's partners include 20 neighborhood organizations and area agencies that connect students, parents, and neighborhood residents to the school and community resources.

At Thomas Edison Elementary School in Port Chester, New York, Principal Eileen Santiago described the transition in her school as a slow and incremental process realized through partnerships with parents and members of the community. Parents, especially among the large number of Hispanic immigrants in the area, wanted child care and homework assistance. Other concerns included affordable housing and medical care. "Necessity was the mother of invention as we reached out for help from local community-based organizations, a nearby college, government representatives, and the business sector" (Santiago, 2000).

As of mid-2001, Edison is contracting with a range of public and private agencies: The Westchester and United Hospital Guidance Center provides on-site mental health counseling; Manhattanville College runs a summer school program; the school district and the Port Chester Council for the Arts provide other after-school and summer activities; and the Board of Cooperative Educational Services gives ESL and GED programs for parents and other adults. Job readiness and computer classes are offered by a local career counseling center (Services, Education, Resources of Westchester). And the Edison Family Service Network brings together staff from schools and community-based organizations (CBOs) to plan and coordinate workshops and community events.

Countee Cullen is a Beacon community school operated by the Rheedlen Centers in central Harlem, New York City (Canada, 1996). Its comprehensive program is open seven days and nights a week at PS 194. Beacon's community orientation is clear; it offers youth leadership opportunities, helped create a play street, and participates in neighborhood beautification projects, voter registration drives, and forums on community issues. The arts program fosters creative expression through writing, drama, photography, and video. Many partnerships make this all possible: The Child Welfare Administration supports a Family Development Program with services to prevent foster care placement; career awareness and job preparation come through the Department of Employment; and city and state departments of youth services and mental health support the efforts of this school-based program.

The Birmingham, Alabama, board of education has been supporting its Community Education Program since 1973, predating any of the other efforts mentioned so far. At that time, the mayor and city council put up two-thirds of the necessary funding and the board the other third (Sparks, 1996). Some 11 schools are designated as community school sites, each with a full-time coordinator and secretary. Links to human service agencies make counseling, health services, and employment help available at school sites. The board of education's policy manual calls for four sets of activities: adult education, family education, parent education, and dropout prevention with after-school classes. A summer camp and educational enrichment program are also offered.

In Birmingham, each community education site is mandated to have an advisory council that links to a citywide council, the Birmingham Community Education Advisory Council. Their charge is to identify needs, set goals, develop resources, and advise the Birmingham School System, which runs the program. About 450 people, including youth, are involved.

Link to Learning

No matter what the model, the goal of community schools is enhanced learning. What goes on in the classrooms is vitally important to the success of the program. You can surround students with a whole array of wonderful services, but test scores will not rise very much if the classroom teaching is not of high quality. Yet only a few of the community school models are actively involved in the classroom. CAS attempts to work closely with school authorities to link before- and after-school programs to classroom work. Efforts are made to help teachers deal with student problems and learn how to access the helping professionals who are in the school. At CAS middle schools, students are divided into four academies, and each has an assigned CAS social worker.

In university-assisted community schools, curricular changes often come first, when university professors work with schoolteachers to design more challenging courses. In some schools that are in the process of change, principals are under pressure to implement school reform models at the same time they are involved in developing community schools. Some of these places have incorporated the Comer School Development Program, using technical assistance available from the Yale Child Study Center. For example, both Quitman and McCoy schools are working on implementing Comer concepts such as intensive and inclusive planning, a mental health team, and parent involvement. Implementing the Comer school development model complements the process of adapting the CAS community school model. It appears possible for a school to transform classroom approaches and at the same time develop collaborative programs with outside agencies. An environment of change may further both educational enhancement and strong support mechanisms.

The New Jersey School-Based Youth Services Program (SBYSP), in all 29 of its sites, made a particular effort to work with schools to enhance students' access to learning (Warren, 1999). School-based staff from community agencies participated in various school committees, crisis management teams, prevention initiatives, and school safety programs. Events were planned, such as freshman orientation. The SBYSP staff conducted classes and workshops on psychosocial issues, counseled students on substance abuse and anger management, and advocated for particular groups of students, especially teen parents and special education students. In some cases, SBYSP staff assumed traditional school roles, such as sports coach or class advisor, freeing school staff to concentrate on teaching.

Observations

Molly Stark School has a singular story concerning how its model was built. It could best be described as "internally grown." The school was not initially part of any larger initiative, although at some point in its history it did have a relationship with Schools of the 21st Century, Edward Zigler's effort to create school-based early childhood experiences. But most of the services that Sue reports came about in a rather serendipitous fashion. A need was identified, and she and her staff set out to address it.

McCoy's experience was similar in the sense that a very committed principal, Jo Nemeth, pushed for the transformation. Jo's focus is on student achievement, but she does not believe that the school can be successful without significant parent and community involvement. One of her colleagues observed, "Her passion is health and human services delivery systems" (Blue Ribbon Schools Application, 2000–2001). McCoy is now one of Missouri's Caring Communities schools. With state grants through the Local Investment Commission (LINC), McCoy is able to offer health, mental health, and social services.

The bottom line here is that you can bring almost any service into a school if the need is really there, if you can find the resources to do it, and if you can find the space to house it. We have identified a number of different CBOs, such as CAS, Boys and Girls Clubs, and YMCA/YWCA. In addition to community agencies, businesses are eager to sponsor programs, especially if they are related to their products. Media people like the exposure they get by contributing time to community projects. Faith-based organizations can also participate in building community schools, often providing space for events and food, clothing, and other assistance for needy families.

The quality of the leadership, particularly the principal and the coordinator at the school site, may be more important than the mix of agencies. The most critical ingredients seem to be an active imagination, an ability to envision a new kind of institution that both educates the children and enriches their families, and a willingness to work hard.

MOLLY STARK'S FAMILY CENTER AND HEALTH SERVICES

This section summarizes the services we offer at the Molly Stark Family Center, a 3,600-square-foot building attached to the school, and describes the various health services we provide. The Family Center is the cornerstone of our full-service community school. Many of the services and programs we offer are found in some form in many schools throughout the country; others are more unusual.

The Need for Child Care

In fall 1998, our second year of offering after-school programs, the number of activities had increased, and we noticed that more and more parents were using these activities to fill their need for after-school child care. We knew safe and stimulating child care could provide our students with positive learning experiences while their parents were working. We also knew that children who receive early language stimulation in safe and healthy environments are far more likely to do well in school.

We began to discuss the factors that would determine whether we would be able to provide child care for school-age children. A community needs assessment survey sent to parents (see Appendix B) showed that 36 parents were interested in sending their children two or more days a week and another 17 would send their children on a more irregular basis. Parents needed both before- and after-school care, and 43 inquired about summer and vacation care. As a result of this information, our interest in providing child care increased.

Our biggest obstacles at this point were space, human resources, and funds to get both. We knew that the younger children are when they begin receiving care and education opportunities, the better off both they and their families are. However, the younger the children, the more expensive and complicated quality programs must be. And in an already overcrowded building, the space problem especially seemed insurmountable.

By this time, we had been contracting with Chuck Putney, a local grant writer who had written many successful grant applications for us. Equally important, he had become an advocate of Molly Stark. He believed in what we were doing and scouted out grants that he thought would fit our mission. In fall 1998, as he heard me talk about how lack of space was affecting the development of our programs, he suggested that we write a Community Development Block Grant to try to get money for an addition to our school. I'm glad I didn't know the challenges that lay ahead.

Building the Family Center

The Vermont Community Development Program, part of the Vermont Agency of Commerce, provides financial and technical assistance to identify and address local needs and priorities in the areas of housing, economic development, public facilities, and public services for low-income individuals. It uses federal money that is distributed by the states. The problems for Molly Stark in gaining this funding were many. First, we would need approval from the local school board. Second, this kind of grant must go to a town, so we would have to sell the idea to the Town of Bennington Select Board so they would apply for the grant on our behalf. Third, we would have to find an agency in town to partner with, and we would have to lease the new building to this partner, which in turn would make sure we used the facility for the purpose proposed. To get the go-ahead to lease the building, the school district had to hold a meeting at which interested community members could vote on this proposition. Because we already planned a partnership with Sunrise Family Resource Center, choosing a partner wasn't a problem. However, the thought that someone had to "watch" us to make sure we did what we said we would do was discouraging.

Bureaucracy is always a challenge. We made presentations to both boards (school and town) as well as the Vermont Agency of Commerce. But getting support from the town and school boards was the easy part. The greatest obstacle turned out to be that these particular funds had never been awarded for use in a school. The message from the Agency of Commerce was summed up by one of its employees, who told me that schools were considered a "black hole"—that is, once one school received money, other schools would ask.

Two weeks before the grant application was due, I received two different sets of questions. These questions were called "impediments to a funding decision," which was certainly an appropriate name for them, and addressed complicated issues of operating funds and project expenses, as well as plans for programming, personnel, and construction. Around the same time, I was told by someone who should know that this might not be the right time to apply. However, I ignored this and worked into the late hours of many nights answering the questions.

Discouraged and frustrated, I wasn't sure the project would ever really happen. But in February 1999, I attended a ceremony and was presented $291,300 by Governor Howard Dean to build a Family Center at our school.

The process had begun in October 1998, when the idea was presented to the board of education, and we moved into a partly completed building in September 1999. Although the building wasn't quite finished, it was important to offer child care at the beginning of the school year. Parents wouldn't want to have their children begin with one child care provider and then switch to the school when our center opened. So with no hot water and insufficient heat, we opened a small portion of the center in September. Each day for over a month, the lunch dishes were carted in a little red wagon to the opposite end of the school building to be washed.

We signed a 40-year lease with Sunrise Family Resource Center for $1 a year. The state told us that we must "meet benefit" within two years or the school board would have to pay back the grant money. Meeting benefit meant that we would have to have a certain number of low-income beneficiaries who received services because of our programs. The building was finished in October and we met benefit by March.

In fall 1999, we had a celebration of the center's completion. Government officials, guests from the Department of Education and Agency of Human Services, town officials, school officials, and 400 children and many of their parents attended the festive occasion. With available space, we were able to offer many new programs.

Child Care

In each of the first two years of the Family Center, approximately 25 children attended either or both before- and after-school care. We have learned a lot from this experience and have made changes along the way.

Things to Consider About Child Care

- Children need a variety of choices of activities, including small- and large-group as well as individual projects. After-school enrichment programs are natural extensions of our child care program. Children have the opportunity to choose enrichment, homework, or academic clubs and then can go back to the child care space at the conclusion of the program. Finding appropriate activities for the older kids was the big challenge. When the kids were included in the discussion of what to offer, it became easier.

- Children should have clear and fair rules to follow.

- An appropriate space should include a large, open area as well as classrooms for projects and calm activities. Other things to consider regarding space are building code regulations, accessibility to bathrooms and sinks, and storage space for toys, art materials, and equipment.

- Written policies and procedures concerning enrollment, fee collection, days and hours of operation, snacks provided, and parent participation are essential.

- The child care center should have a focused vision that all employees share. Although difficult to fit in, ongoing discussion about issues and ideas is important.

- The staff should be skilled and caring individuals with training in developmentally appropriate practices.

- Because many of the jobs in our Family Center are not traditionally found in a school, it was important to develop job descriptions before hiring staff. This helped determine how employees are paid. All new job descriptions had to be presented to the supervisory school board (because the grant money is funneled through them).

- Look at the staffing regulations for your state. This should include staff qualifications and ratios of adults to children. We now have a site coordinator, a child care lead provider, a preschool teacher, a kindergarten care teacher, and teaching assistants. Enrollment helps determine our staffing needs.

- After Molly Stark became a licensed child care facility, families could receive subsidies for child care. To learn what you must do to become licensed, contact your state's child care licensing office. Molly Stark parents pay for child care services on a sliding fee scale. Your state government may subsidize families at or below the federal poverty level. It is a good idea to determine the current rate in your community and the current state market rates, which can be obtained through your state's association of child care resource and referral agencies. It is important to seek outside funding sources to cover the shortfall for those who pay less than cost.

Our child care handbook is reproduced in Appendix C.

Kindergarten Care

Kindergarten care, which we call kindercare, is a way we found to build on and enrich our half-day kindergarten experience in a secure and nurturing environment. Children in the morning kindergarten can stay in the center for the afternoon, and children in the afternoon kindergarten can come early and stay until their session begins. Parents choose this option for a variety of reasons: Some feel their children are ready for a full day at school, some are at work and want their children in a quality-care situation, and some we recruit because we know they could use the additional experiences.

Preschool

We knew that when the Family Center opened, there would be space to provide a range of programs. We planned to begin with before- and after-school child care and slowly add on more programs, including a preschool. But then Judy Cohen, Family Center site coordinator, brought in a copy of the High/Scope Perry Preschool Study. The study, which followed children's progress from 3 to 27 years old, showed that over the years, the group that attended the preschool scored higher in intellectual performance, were in fewer special education programs, and had higher school achievement and general literacy in school. As adults, study participants who had attended the preschool had significantly higher monthly earnings, a higher percentage of home ownership, a higher level of school completion, a lower percentage of receiving social services, and fewer arrests (Schweinhart & Weikart, 1993). In May 1999, Judy announced that she would rather not wait a whole year to start a preschool. She wanted to begin in September, the same time that we planned to begin child care. So much for slow, steady implementation. Staff would need to be hired, and a class of 15 three- and four-year-olds would need to be in place, all by mid-August.

Throughout that summer, Judy frequently walked through the nearby housing project with her basket of toys, visiting parents and their children. One day, she talked to a mother who reported that her three-year-old daughter had never been enrolled in a preschool program. Judy helped her set up a developmental screening at the district's Early Education Program, and when the mom came in, she brought along her four-year-old daughter as well. The two children, who had many needs—severe language deficits in addition to emotional and social delays—enrolled in our preschool. We had planned to enroll an integrated mix of students that first year: five with special needs, five at risk, and five developing typically. But that first year, 13 of the 15 children were eligible for special education or Title I services, and 10 had no previous group experience. Most lacked adequate skills, both academically and socially. We quickly learned and continue to accept the fact that sometimes you just have to roll with it. Kids don't always fit themselves into your preconceived plan. However, in its second year, because we had more time to plan, our preschool had a much more integrated mix of children.

From the beginning, our goal was to develop a high-quality, developmentally appropriate program that could meet the needs of a wide range of children. The staff would work through an emergent curriculum that allows the children the opportunity to select activities and materials that interest them. In addition, we wanted to provide a safe and respectful environment for both children and their parents. For all these things to happen, it was crucial to hire staff members who had appropriate knowledge of the development and learning of young children. The nice part about starting a new program is that the people you hire are people that you have chosen.

Knowing how many staff members to hire for our preschool program was a challenge. We had often discussed how some programs for early care and education were not successful simply because they did not have enough staff. This is an even more significant factor when working with children of poverty, many of whom have had limited opportunities and have a variety of special needs. We decided that at minimum, we would follow the accreditation criteria and procedures generated by the National Association for the Education of Young Children. Their recommendations are for one staff for every 7 three-year-olds and one staff for every 8 four-year-olds. But these are the *minimum* recommended ratios. We find that the children's needs dictate the ratios. During the 2000–2001 school year, for 15 preschoolers, we had one teacher and two teaching assistants. Our ratios will continue to depend on the needs of the children in each year.

A major step we took was to become a licensed child care facility. We found Vermont's Licensing Division (which is part of the Agency of Human Services) both supportive and encouraging. A field specialist came to visit and told us what needed to be done, which turned out to be more labor intensive than difficult. We had to have written job descriptions, résumés of all staff on file, and criminal checks on all employees. In addition, we had to increase our child space (we decreased storage area), put a fence around the playground, and post emergency exit plans. These efforts were a small price to pay for the ability to receive child care subsidies for the children who qualify because of their level of poverty—subsidies that can generate between $4,000 and $5,000 a month to help run our programs.

In addition to our Family Center preschool, the district's Early Education Program is housed at Molly Stark. This program screens young children in the community and provides many services, including preschool, to those who are developmentally delayed. In addition, it enrolls a small percentage of typically developing children who pay tuition. Having the district's Early Education Program housed in our building has enhanced our program. One of their special educators consults regularly with our preschool staff, and we work closely with the director.

When our Family Center preschool opened, parents had one more option to choose from. Some parents view the Family Center preschool as part of Molly Stark School. Since involving their kids isn't categorical (that is, they don't need to be poor or have developmental delays to be eligible), it is sometimes less intimidating for them to send their kids to the place where they will later receive their elementary school education. This seems to be true for many of the services we offer and is one of the advantages of locating services at the school: Everyone goes to school, so there is no stigma.

Health Services

Access to adequate health care is difficult for many of the children and families at Molly Stark. Many parents seek help only at the emergency room and only during crises. Offering health services at our school was an effort not only to provide affordable, accessible health care but also to encourage parents to consistently seek these services for their children in hopes of developing healthy patterns.

Health Insurance for All Children

An important first step to helping all children be healthy is to make sure that they have adequate health insurance. Although health insurance is available to all children in poverty, many parents don't or can't fill out the necessary paperwork. At Molly Stark, this process is facilitated by the school nurse, beginning with a question on the initial school information forms filled out by parents. Since 1999, for students who do not have health insurance, school personnel have application forms available and assist parents in filling out the form when necessary.

Mental and Physical Health Services

Children and families who live in poverty often lack access to both physical and mental health services. In spring 1997, I went to a state meeting at which information was given out about health clinics in schools. The more I heard, the more sense it made to have these services more accessible to our families. In the 1998–1999 school year, we developed the PHASE (Providing Health and Supporting Education) Team, which includes a clinical psychologist and a pediatrician (the same two people who were in our focus group). Both professionals come to the school site a few hours a week to provide ongoing consultation and short-term direct service, discuss medical and psychological interventions and strategies with staff and parents, and make outside referrals when necessary. The pediatrician might see a student with chronic head lice or parents who want their child thoroughly assessed before deciding if a diagnosis of ADHD (attention deficit hyperactivity disorder) warrants medication. The psychologist might strategize with a teacher and parent about a child's aggressive behavior or work with a child whose school experience is affected by anxiety and depression. In addition, we have found it much easier to get a child seen by a specialist when a pediatrician or clinical psychologist sets up the appointment rather than a parent or school personnel.

In 1999, we added a family outreach worker to the PHASE Team. An employee of Sunrise Family Resource Center, she works 15 hours a week with Molly Stark parents and their families, assisting with information and referral or with daily living support. Some work is long term, like giving parents regular encouragement and direction in their lives. Other work is short term, like helping a family through temporary homelessness or illness. Most of the family outreach work is done in homes, and it looks different with each family because the purpose is to meet the individual needs of a family when they need help.

In spring 2000, a clinical social worker began working with us. She provides play therapy and consultation for young children and their parents. In addition, she spends time each week in the preschool classroom and then consults with the preschool staff to help create a classroom environment that will help the children develop socially and emotionally. In fall 2001, she began parenting support groups for young mothers.

All our health consultants are paid hourly from a variety of sources, including Medicaid money generated through special education case management as well as small private and state grants.

Referrals to the PHASE Team can be made by teachers, staff members, or parents. We discovered that having a screening process to decide which children and parents will be seen and how often is essential to avoid confusion and duplication of effort. Part of the process is a short Request for Consultation form (see Appendix D), which goes to a committee that includes a few key staff members and pertinent people who work with the child. We keep records on each student and ask each health provider to write a summary of the diagnosis and recommendations that can be added to the child's school health files.

A positive aspect of this model is the collaborative approach to working with a child and family. Again, too often a variety of professionals working with a child go in many directions without communicating with one another. The collaborative model looks at each child within the context of school, family, and community and allows school personnel, the family, and the providers to work together.

Well-Child Physicals and Inoculations

Well-child physicals and inoculations are offered to third- and sixth-grade children who don't have a primary care physician. Two physicians provide these services through contracted time. Inoculations are coordinated with the local Department of Health by our school nurse. After the program's first year, we decided to increase parent involvement by making it mandatory for parents to be present at the third-grade physicals. We felt the sixth-grade physicals were a bit different because children at that age might hesitate to talk about some tender subjects with their parents present. This decision illustrates the kinds of questions we discuss and decisions we continually make as our programs grow.

Dental Services

One day in May 1999, Dr. Michael Brady, a local dentist who had recently retired, came to our school. He had heard about the Family Center concept and thought he might like to do some dental work for children who had no access to a dentist. I often tease him that making that statement was his first mistake. The timing of that meeting was perfect. Although we had received the grant to build the center, the contractors had not yet begun. Within a week, I had met with the contractors to rethink the space. By making a few of the other rooms a bit smaller, it was possible to build a dental office with all the equipment needed to do preventive and restorative care.

Because dentistry wasn't in our initial plan, we didn't have the money to build the room or to buy the necessary dental equipment, but Dr. Brady had heard about a state dental access grant offered by the Vermont Department of Health. We applied for and received a $40,000 grant, which paid for the room and about half the large dental equipment, but we were still short about $20,000. Dr. Brady generously purchased the rest of the equipment. Five months later, at the opening celebration of our Family Center, Governor Howard Dean talked with Dr. Brady and pledged the additional $20,000 from Vermont Department of Health funds. Our local hospital gave another $1,700. Thus we were able to begin providing dental care to those Medicaid-eligible children across our entire school district who don't have a primary care dentist.

The first year's data were impressive. In the 1999–2000 school year, this new dental practice enrolled 362 children. By not having to pay rent and utilities, Dr. Brady's overhead was reduced from 60 percent to 30 percent. The practice produced $111,000 in fees entirely from Medicaid while spending only $38,000 on staff and materials, making it a viable practice. In addition, Dr. Brady spent only 75 percent of the time he used to spend at his private practice.

Dr. Brady explains his practice as follows:

Molly Stark children's dentistry is really a private practice in a public school. The school owns the dental equipment, furniture, and the room in the school building. The dentist does not pay rent or any utilities or maintenance charges. The Medicaid fees generated are the dentist's compensation, and he or she is responsible for employee salaries and all the consumable supplies needed to treat all the children in a comprehensive manner. Since the overhead is significantly reduced, it offsets the lower level of compensation from Medicaid fees and makes the Molly Stark practice a viable and sustainable small business, equal to a private practice in the area. For a dentist like me, a 53-year-old who sold his practice yet still wished to treat patients, this is a great opportunity to begin a worthwhile effort in a new setting. For a younger dentist, this would provide an opportunity to practice as he or she would in a private setting yet enjoy the more community-involved atmosphere the school and Family Center provide. Children who would never have full access to reliable dental care can see their own dentist in a setting that is comfortable for both the patient and the doctor. The social, economic, and staffing problems that inhibit comprehensive and sustainable dental care can be dealt with.

Dr. Brady captures the idea of a Family Center and partnerships within a school when he says, "A school-based practice has several advantages that permit us to meet the special circumstances that can be barriers to treatment for many eligible children. Often, private practices encounter problems with missed appointments and lack of parental follow-up for recall, maintenance, and preventive office visits. School personnel help with difficult contacts with parents and, at times, transportation. It is a team effort for these kids."

For children with extensive dental needs that cannot be easily or comfortably addressed in an office setting, Dr. Brady works with the local hospital that has made operating room time available for area dentists to treat children. In the first year, he saw 62 children at the Bright Smiles program; the following year, he treated more than 100. One five-year-old boy came in with an oral infection that had required hospitalization and antibiotics; 14 of his 20 teeth had to be extracted due to decay.

For me, the importance of this service to our community became very clear one day when I stopped at a local fast-food drive-through. The woman waiting on me had been my student when I taught fifth grade at Molly Stark years ago. Now all the visible teeth in her mouth were totally black and decayed. As I drove away, I was happy to think that years from now this would no longer be an issue for children who attend Molly Stark. Having good teeth would make them more socially acceptable and more employable in the future. Here is an example of a service clearly making a lasting difference.

Healthy Snack Cart

Sometimes seemingly small ideas that are relatively easy to implement can make important contributions. Our healthy snack cart, run by students and teachers in one of our classrooms a few days a week, promotes nutritious eating. By stocking and selling a variety of low-cost items such as bagels, cheese, fruit, pretzels, popcorn, and juices, we hope to establish healthy eating habits.

Other Early Support and Intervention Programs

With the goal of providing ongoing support to students and their families, we have created a variety of programs. Some are offered by our staff; others are in partnership with community organizations. All have the common purpose of providing building blocks for future success.

Playgroups

Some parents do not know how to play with their kids in ways that will help them learn and grow. This lack of knowledge is often misconstrued as a lack of caring and concern.

In our playgroups, an employee from Sunrise Family Resource Center who has knowledge of child development works closely with parents and their infants or toddlers. Offered once a week at our school, playgroups provide an opportunity for a small group of parents to connect with one another, discover new ways of interacting with their young children, gain access to information about parenting and community resources, and develop an early and positive familiarity with the school their children will later attend.

Kindercamp

Although entering kindergarten can be an exciting time, it can also create apprehension in children and their parents. One activity that has helped both groups develop a sense of comfort and confidence is a three-day orientation program held at the school at the end of the summer. Parents are invited to participate so they can become familiar with the staff, the building, and new activities in a nurturing environment before the first day of school. Children spend time in large and small groups listening to stories, playing games, enjoying art activities, and engaging in other experiences designed to give them an introduction to what kindergarten will be like. In addition, parents begin to develop positive relationships with the adults who will be working with their child and to learn how home activities can support the kindergarten program. Since it began in 1998, this has become a popular program, with over 75 percent of the children and parents participating at least part of the time. The smooth transition of kindergartners on the first day of school illustrates its success.

Lending Library

This addition to our school site provides educational toys and books that parents can borrow for their young children to use at home. In addition, parents can borrow videos that provide information about child development, discipline, and the many issues facing families (such as divorce, blended families, and alcohol abuse). When choosing materials to add to our lending library, we respect the needs, interests, and literacy abilities of the many families who might use it. However, so far our mentors have used the contents of the lending library much more than parents have. Issues we need to iron out include how materials are checked out and who in the Family Center is responsible for the process, what the hours of operation are, and how to let families know this service is available.

Parent and Family Opportunities

Some of these offerings are ongoing; some we have offered only once; some we offer as needed.

Graduate Equivalency Diploma

Parents can work toward their GED at the school. Classes are taught by an employee from our local adult basic education facility, the Tutorial Center. The Family Center provides scholarship funds and transportation on test-taking days. Recently, at the parents' request, the Tutorial Center has decided to offer a course at Molly Stark to help parents get driver's permits.

Community Leadership Training

This training is offered in conjunction with Sunrise Family Resource Center and the Bennington County Child Care Association. It is designed to help parents and other community members become more active citizens and advocates for themselves, their children, and their community.

UFOs (Unlimited Fathering Opportunities)

This 10-session program meets weekly for children and fathers (or other males significant in their lives). It was developed and sponsored by Bennington Head Start PLUS and provides a dinner and recreation for participants. In the 1999–2000 school year, we first provided this program for fathers and their children aged 3 to 6. It was so popular that the next year we offered a second session to fathers and their children aged 7 to 10.

Cooking for Life

This program was developed by the Vermont Campaign to End Childhood Hunger and the University of Vermont Extension Expanded Food and Nutrition Education Program. It is facilitated by our local Bennington Rutland Opportunity Council. The goal is to encourage parents to cook healthy, affordable meals for their families. The group meets once a week for six weeks to prepare healthy meals.

Family Literacy Programs

This program is sponsored by the Vermont Council on the Humanities. Called the Connections Program, it is taught by a Molly Stark reading teacher, and each series meets for three Saturday mornings. Parents discuss ways to read and talk about books with their children and leave with free books in hand.

The services described in this chapter are examples of the many ways Molly Stark reaches out to our school community. We have reached out to potential partners as well, and they have responded with innovative ways of partnering to offer what children and families need. Having a range of services provides a menu of options. Although each program or service addresses different needs, each shares the important qualities of being proactive in nature and designed to enhance the lives of children and their families. Schools don't usually work this way. Often, they operate in a crisis mode, as we did, trying to put short-term Band-aids on large-sized wounds. We hope that we have begun to build a comprehensive, preventive program that will change and grow to meet the needs of the children and their families in our community.

What Goes on During the Extended Day?

DIFFERENT APPROACHES TO AFTER-SCHOOL PROGRAMS

Extracurricular activities have long been available to students in sports and arts, particularly in middle- and high-income districts. In recent years, after-school programs have become a major focus in almost all communities. A survey in spring 2001 by the National Association of Elementary School Principals revealed the enormous growth in extending the hours that schools are open. Some 67 percent of public school principals reported that their schools or school districts offered after-school programs, and 27 percent of those offered before-school care as well. Another 15 percent were trying to develop such programs. Only 19 percent did not appear to be interested. The proportion of schools with extended hours was just 22 percent in 1988, rising to 28 percent by 1993. Most of the increase in programs has taken place since 1996.

Most educators and youth workers agree that after-school programs can help improve academic achievement, provide safe harbors, prevent high-risk behaviors, provide enriching experiences, and improve socialization. Beth Miller (2001) of the National Institute on Out-of-School Time points out that after-school programs in low-income communities can expose disadvantaged students to the same variety of developmentally supportive experiences and opportunities that middle-class students take for granted. As she puts it, "The schedule of one program reads like a parent's dream: Spanish lessons, electric guitar lessons, chess club, creative cooking lessons, gymnastics, Boy Scouts, choir, and softball, plus daily homework help and tutoring" (p. 8).

Three kinds of after-school programs have been identified in the literature (Fashola, 1998; Miller, 2001):

- *School-age child care* provides young children (typically preschool to Grade 3) with a safe haven from 3:00 to 6:00 p.m. Licensing and accreditation are required for day care program staff who provide mainly cultural and recreational enrichment. Some centers also provide homework help and reading programs.

- *After-school youth development programs* involve school-age students (aged 5 through 18) and emphasize academic as well as nonacademic activities. Many are offered by youth agencies (Boys and Girls Clubs, Y's, 4-H, faith-based groups, and public recreation centers) and are staffed mainly by youth workers. Some provide instruction in the arts, others in sports, and some include educational enrichment.

- *School-based academic extended-day programs* are seen as continuations of the school's effort to educate its students. Often, teachers are hired to stay after school to conduct small group classes, supervise homework clubs, and teach study skills. Other youth workers and volunteers may be involved in providing non-academic services, such as sports and arts. School achievement is the overall goal.

While the education and youth development fields operate in different domains, almost everyone agrees that keeping schools open for longer hours should have a beneficial effect on school achievement, crime prevention, and social behavior. And, of course, the increasing numbers of working parents are pushing up the demand everywhere, not just in disadvantaged communities. One of the big questions is, who should be in charge of these programs—the school systems themselves or community agencies with solid experience in youth development? A related question is, how much emphasis and time should be devoted to educational remediation and how much to recreation, fun, and youth development activities?

Influencing this debate is the availability of large amounts of federal and state money to fund new after-school programs. While funding will be discussed in greater detail in Chapter 10, several significant developments must be mentioned to explain why after-school programs are proliferating so rapidly.

A National Initiative: 21st Century Community Learning Centers

In 1997, the U.S. Department of Education (DOE) began to fund after-school programs through the 21st Century Community Learning Centers (CCLC) with $1 million. The program grew to almost $500 million by 2000, to $846 million by 2001, and to a full $1 billion in the 2002 budget. This growth is further evidence that after-school programs appear to be the "program of the moment"; both sides of the aisle in Congress see it as one solution to today's problems. Until 2002, the DOE administered CCLC as direct project grants to school districts. Beginning in 2002, new grants will go through state departments of education and be distributed through formula grants according to the size of each state's Title I population (eligibility for free or reduced-cost lunch). The state will then distribute the funds as project grants through open competitions between districts. However, community groups will also be able to apply for the funds in collaborations with schools.

It is hard to overestimate the tremendous influence of CCLC after-school programs. As of September 2000, the DOE reported that 900 school districts had been awarded three-year grants for 3,600 schools (there are about 85,000 public schools in the United States). Many thousands more competed for the grants and received good ratings, and as of May 2001, these numbers had grown to 6,600 schools in 1,600 communities. According to the DOE, the demand has been overwhelming. A survey in late 1999 showed that adults support the idea of after-school programs that provide children with a safe environment, structured tutoring, and homework help. The average grant in 2001 was nearly $600,000 and supported three or four school centers.

Beginning in 1998, the C. S. Mott Foundation entered a partnership with the DOE to support CCLC and other after-school initiatives. The DOE gives grants to communities, and the C. S. Mott Foundation provides support and has committed more than $100 million over several years. Mott has funded the following: (a) annual training sessions in every state and region to assist CCLC applicants in program planning; (b) training of more than 20,000 local people to train others to run effective programs; (c) evaluation of the centers and other after-school programs; and (d) studies of promising practices. In addition, Mott and the DOE together created the Afterschool Alliance, a coalition of public, private, and nonprofit organizations whose purpose is to raise awareness of the importance of after-school programs and to advocate for quality, affordable programs for all children. Other Alliance partners include JCPenney Afterschool Initiative, the Advertising Council, the Entertainment Industry Foundation, the Creative Artists Agency Foundation, the Open Society Institute/the After-School Corporation, and American Isuzu Motors, Inc.

The one area of controversy surrounding CCLC has been who in the community gets the grant. Despite efforts by the National Collaboration for Youth (representing community-based organizations, or CBOs), grants have gone only to school districts. Grantees, however, were required to have community partners with whom they can subcontract for after-school services. This issue was decided by Congress in 2001, when Republicans and Democrats agreed that CBOs should be allowed to receive the grants as well as school systems. The program requirements for CCLC grants are quite flexible (U.S. Department of Education, 2001). An array of comprehensive and supervised services must include expanded learning opportunities, such as enriched instruction, tutoring, or homework assistance. However, programs can select any four (or more) of the following activities:

- Literacy education
- Senior citizen programs
- Children's day care services
- Integrated education, health, social service, recreational, or cultural programs
- Summer and weekend school programs in conjunction with recreation programs
- Nutrition and health education
- Expanded library service hours to serve community needs
- Telecommunications and technology education for all ages
- Parenting skills education
- Support and training for child day care providers
- Employment counseling, training, and placement
- Services for individuals (of any age) who leave school before graduating
- Services for individuals with disabilities

According to Robert Stonehill of the DOE, the department is encouraging the use of the Safe and Drug Free Schools fund and Title I money for after-school programs. In addition, federal support for after-school programs is available from the Child Care Development Fund and Temporary Assistance for Needy Families (welfare) sources (see Chapter 10 for more on funding).

State Initiatives

In addition to the 21st Century Community Learning Centers program begun by the federal government to stimulate before- and after-school care, at least 26 states have implemented their own initiatives to extend learning opportunities (Miller, 2001). In a sense, these states are attempting to develop systems of school-age care, integrating before- and after-school time with classroom time (Halpern, Deich, & Cohen, 2000). In a study of six states, the Council of Chief State School Officers (2000) found that four states offered programs that could lead to full-service community schools; the other two, Texas and Illinois, narrowly focused on preventing students' academic failure.

California

California's After-School Learning and Safe Neighborhoods Partnership Program came about through creative lobbying of a receptive state legislature by key nonprofit agencies. In 2001, the legislature made $85 million available to schools and communities to develop partnerships that would provide academic and literacy support as well as safe, constructive alternatives to high-risk activities for students in Grades K–9. Programs must operate in school sites and/or parks adjacent to the school. Any local education agency can apply, as can a CBO approved by a local education agency. The program's doors must be open at least from 3:00 to 6:00 p.m., five days a week.

This is clearly an after-school program, not day care. Licensed providers are not required, and the child to staff ratio can be as high as 20:1. The program targets schools in which at least 50 percent of students are eligible for free or reduced-cost meals. To qualify for funding, a 50 percent local match is required, such as in-kind facility or staff costs. Criteria for selection focus on the quality and strength of the educational and enrichment components, staff training and development, the inclusion of nutritional snacks, and the capacity to respond to evaluation components.

Kentucky

Extended School Services in Kentucky were begun under the comprehensive Kentucky Education Reform Act of 1990. The 2000 Extended School Services budget allocated about $37 million for distribution to every school district to fund before- and after-school, evening, Saturday, intercession, or summer school programs in every school. The Extended School Services program is intended to prevent academic failure and is regarded as an extension of the regular classroom program. Although the funds can be used for noninstructional services, it is expected that those kinds of components will more appropriately be covered under the state's Family Resource and Youth Service Centers Programs, referred to in the previous chapter.

Strategies that have been helpful in implementing this program include requiring each district and each school to designate a coordinator. State staff from the department of education have spent considerable time in teacher training through conferences and publications. Among the issues that have arisen are transportation, interference with extracurricular activities, motivating students to attend, collaboration between Extended School Services and regular school staff, and individualizing instruction for students.

Massachusetts

Massachusetts initiated the After-School and Other Out of School Time Program in 1996. In 2000, about $5 million went to 78 communities to extend the school day and/or year for K–12 students. These funds could be used to coordinate and deliver services before and after school, during vacations, and on weekends.

To be eligible, communities must form a local council or partnership including the local mayor, school superintendent, representatives from schools and CBOs, students, and families. The council determines who will be the applicant agency for the council; this lead agency is responsible for establishing an infrastructure with the capacity for keeping the school open for extended hours. Another lead-agency function is to increase the integration of after-school programs with those occurring during the regular school hours.

Major concerns focus on funding and coordination. Since the program was begun, the demand for grants has been far greater than the appropriation. Flexibility in program design and the required council structure have led to turf battles over the best use of after-school hours; different groups have supported priorities for child care, violence prevention, community service learning, educational enrichment, tutoring, and other goals. In 2000, councils were required to negotiate these differences based on documented needs in each community.

In addition, Massachusetts started two after-school academic remediation initiatives in 1999: Academic Support Services Program ($18 million) and Individual Tutoring in Reading Program ($2 million). Academic Support targets districts in which large numbers of students have difficulty meeting statewide standards; Individual Tutoring focuses on failing fourth-grade students, giving them one-on-one instruction.

Minnesota

The Minnesota After-School Enrichment Program, started in 1966, is administered by the Department of Children, Families and Learning, the state education agency. It awards $10 million in grants to community collaboratives that include representatives of CBOs, schools, parents, and youth. Each group must develop a plan, based on an assessment of community needs, to provide after-school programming at least five days a week to youth aged 9 to 13. Certain neighborhoods in Minneapolis and St. Paul are targeted for this intervention. CBOs are eligible to be the lead agencies.

According to the report by the Council of Chief State School Officers (2000), when this initiative was originally conceptualized, state policymakers agreed on one primary issue: Communities are best served by collaboratives that include schools, local units of government, grassroots agencies, youth-serving organizations, parents, and youth. State officials reinforce this standard by holding quarterly coordinators' meetings and by making frequent site visits to the community.

Various issues have created barriers at the local level, such as transportation, problems in developing a stable collaborative of program providers, the need for more volunteers and volunteer training, and frequent staff turnover.

Some transportation problems have been overcome by enlisting volunteer drivers or seeking other sources of funds for buses.

The demand for after-school programs far exceeds the size of the initiative. The state looks for solid collaboration and inclusiveness in policy and funding decisions.

Local Initiatives

The After-School Corporation

In 1998, George Soros's Open Society Institute committed $25 million per year for five years to support after-school programming in New York City. The City of New York, the board of education, and state agencies have committed large amounts of matching funds, as have other foundations. A new nonprofit organization, The After-School Corporation (TASC), was charged with creating a network of high-quality programs, using community-based agencies in partnerships with schools. The first effort in New York City reached hundreds of schools, and more recently the initiative has worked in Baltimore and other communities.

The program spends about $1,000 per child per year for daily care from 3:00 to 6:00 p.m.; this covers the cost of a full-time, year-round after-school coordinator and a student to staff ratio of 10:1. Programming focuses on educational enrichment, problem-solving and team-building skills, and homework help, along with participation in sports, arts, and community service. For high school students, there are peer counseling, internships, violence prevention, mentoring younger children, college prep courses, and job training. TASC staff provide ongoing technical assistance and training.

Beacons

Beacons are prime examples of CBO-operated after-school programs. A visit to a middle school, IS 143, in New York City's Washington Heights revealed a very active Beacon program involving most of the student body (1,800) and thousands of neighborhood people. Students are exposed to creative experiences not available during school hours, such as an extensive mask-making project tied to the Latino culture of the community. The program director works closely with the school principal to make sure that they are on the same track.

Citywide Programs

San Francisco has adapted the New York Beacon model and built on it. The initiative started in 1994 when a group of local leaders reviewed community school models around the country. They selected Beacons as appropriate to their community and by 2001 had organized eight centers in schools, with plans for at least three more.

A citywide steering committee includes the Mayor's Office of Children, Youth and Their Families (the lead agency), the school district, and a local foundation (Haas Fund), with technical assistance from the Community Network for Youth Development. Funds come from the city (San Francisco Children's Fund) and 15 foundations, while the school district provides in-kind contributions of school facilities, maintenance, and personnel. Some 40 community agencies and eight public entities are partners in the initiative.

Each center is managed by a CBO. The Beacons' lead agency for the A. P. Giannini Middle School is Aspira Foster Family Services. A detailed report on each Beacon shows that this school-community partnership offers a large number of activities in the five requisite areas for children and youth: educational support (10, from math assistance to Russian language); leadership (9); health (8); career development (6); and arts and recreation (18, from kickboxing to a performance of the Nutcracker ballet). Some nine activities were listed for families and adults (mostly educational), as well as 15 community events.

A review of the San Francisco Beacons suggests how comprehensive community schools can become when they are backed up by a powerful combination of public (mayor's office) and private (foundations) resources. Access to on-site technical assistance is given credit for the growing impact of Beacons on transforming school environments, creating new neighborhood strengths, and bridging home, school, and community. Few programs have such strong guidance and support from an array of significant agencies in the city.

San Diego's 6 to 6 extended-day program is operated and funded by the city of San Diego in cooperation with the San Diego Unified School District in every elementary and middle school (196 schools). Initiated on the recommendation of a task force that was part of Mayor Susan Golding's Safe School Initiative, 6 to 6 receives funding (more than $15 million in 2001) from the city and other public and private sources. The 6 to 6 program provides a safe, supervised place for children to have fun and learn new skills; offerings include academic enrichment, arts, recreation, and sports. It is not a licensed child care program.

Many other cities have strong after-school programs, including the private nonprofit LA Best in Los Angeles and the 2 to 6 program in Boston.

Other Community Schools

Quitman Street Community School in Newark, New Jersey, in conjunction with its partner, Community Agencies Corporation of New Jersey, has made a major effort to develop extended-day services at the school site. In 2000, almost 300 children (out of about 500) were enrolled in the after-school program, and the average daily attendance was more than 90 percent. Almost two-thirds of the participants' parents volunteered at the school, totaling 1,380 hours for the year. The *Quitman Community School News* conveys the spirit of the school:

> Third and fourth graders in the after-school program took the stage to show what they have been working on all year during the time they spent together with Arts Horizon and Alvin Ailey . . . including West African Dances, Mansa Mussa and Manjani, and modern dance. Through visual art, dance, music, and story, third graders with Arts Horizon explored peace, friendship, joy, and beauty. They have practiced speaking and listening to each other by sharing ideas, feelings and leadership.

Quitman also offers a four-week summer camp to about 150 of its students. In 2000, first through fourth graders attended academic classes in the mornings, and kindergarten students received an enrichment program. In the afternoon, all students were scheduled for classes in cooking, computers, and art and could also take drama, music, Spanish, healthy living, creative writing, karate, and physical education. Free swimming classes were available at a nearby facility. Every Friday, the campers were taken on a Fabulous Field Trip—to the Bronx Zoo, Camden Aquarium, a farmers' market, and other places that they probably would never have visited without the program. The Quitman summer program attempts to integrate academic support with all the other activities.

Marshalltown, Iowa, is committed to full-service community schools. Its program, Caring Connection, has been widely cited as a model. It recently received a CCLC federal grant to support before- and after-school, weekend, and summer programming in two middle schools. Activities are organized around seven components: recreation, literacy intervention, tutoring and home support, applied academic units, substance abuse and violence prevention, outreach through family development, and adult education programming. Students participate in a variety of activities, such as homework assistance, sports, crafts, cooking, computers, and field trips. Family members can take advantage of such courses as GED preparation, English, Spanish, family finances, and computers for families.

Factors Promoting Effective Programs

The amount of material available to help people set up after-school programs is becoming overwhelming. The Thirteen Ed Online/Disney Learning Partnership online workshop (see Resources) on how to set up an after-school program contains a thorough list of the resources in this field. Many sources seem to agree that certain factors are conducive to implementation of a good after-school program (Fashola, 1998, pp. 51–56; U.S. Department of Education, 2000b):

Create a program with structure. Good programming starts with clear goals and well-developed procedures for attaining those goals. You need a solid organizational structure with hands-on, site-based management and regular oversight and accountability. Effective management and sustainability require annual operating budgets, multiple funding sources, accurate bookkeeping systems, and affordable fee structures. Attention must be paid to legal requirements for licensing, liability, and parental consent.

Give high priority to recruiting and training staff. A full-time coordinator is essential, as is access to high-quality technical assistance. Enough personnel should be recruited to ensure a low student to staff ratio. If regular teachers are used, they still need extensive professional development and supervision. If staff comes in from other agencies, they need training to work within the school community. Volunteers must be carefully supervised to make sure that they know how to work with children and are capable of implementing program components.

Evaluate the program. If goals are well defined, the expected short- and long-term outcomes should be clearly delineated. Evaluation should be built into the program from the beginning. It is possible to find and use prepackaged evaluation programs.

Have an active advisory board. The California after-school program found that the best programs were conceived, built, and implemented by the people closest to the children who benefited from them (Fletcher, n.d.). Program administrators recommend bringing together educators, parents, local government officials, and community organizations that care about making a difference for young people. Students should be actively involved in planning and implementing after-school programs, since they are the ones who "vote with their feet."

Researchers looking at the Extended Services Schools Initiative of the Wallace-Reader's Digest Foundation found that positive adult-youth relationships were the most important component of high-quality after-school programs (Walker, Grossman, & Raley, 2000). Staff worked hard to make time spent with youth both fun and meaningful, and many seemed to exude a natural fondness for their young charges. Offering caring attention and positive reinforcement to individual young people was characterized as an essential marker of quality, even in group activities.

Observations

The list of allowable activities under the CCLC legislation covers just about everything one could envision for a full-service community school. And several state programs, such as after-school initiatives in Massachusetts and Minnesota, require collaborative arrangements very similar to those that bring together the constituents for model community schools. These pioneer after-school programs are of great interest because they are often the entry point for a school's transformation. Certainly, extending the hours that the school door is open is an important first step in changing the whole environment.

Adriana de Kanter La Perla, liaison to the C. S. Mott foundation from the U.S. Department of Education, views the CCLC program requirement that school districts must have partners in the community as fostering needed collaboration in communities. She sees the coming together, the "commingling of philosophies," of three camps: youth development, child care, and expanded time for learning. She told me, "What has been exceptionally brilliant about this process of collaboration is that everyone has been willing to basically check his or her ideology at the door to come together and talk about common points" (personal communication, November 16, 2000).

I have observed in some community schools that not everyone has been quite so willing to relinquish authority. Principals still rule the roost. At one site I visited, I was told that the CBO staff were not allowed into the school until 1:00 p.m. and were not supposed to be visible before 3:00 p.m. when their activities began. This meant that the CBO case managers were not around during the school day to help deal with the highest-risk students or to spend time in class-rooms to directly observe trouble points and relate to the classroom teachers. This community school had an excellent after-school program but experienced substantial barriers to integrating the after-school activities with classroom work.

One of the most frequent challenges in the work of school-community part-nerships is finding ways to bring the work of the community partner into the classroom and the work of the classroom into the after-school program. The same situation exists in dealing with psychosocial issues; discipline and behav-ioral approaches may differ substantially between the school personnel and out-side mental health workers or prevention specialists.

At each level—local, state, and federal—certain issues appear to come up frequently in the administration of after-school programs at school sites. These include level of academic support, parent role, transportation, range of youth activities, use of classrooms by youth workers, safety and maintenance in and around the school, and sustainability. At every level, solutions include careful planning, use of technical assistance, effective collaboration skills (communica-tion, open decision making), access to training, and of course, adequate funding.

Why are after-school programs growing so rapidly? Obviously, the need for quality child care is enormous, and working parents are more forthright than ever in articulating the demand. Welfare reform programs around the nation have also stimulated the demand as they require welfare moms to obtain em-ployment or go to school. When funding is available, it is not very difficult for a school to stay open, either using its own staff to work with the students or con-tracting with a CBO to provide an after-school program.

It is interesting to ponder why after-school programs have increased so dra-matically over the past few years while school-based primary health centers have not. First, after-school programs are not controversial and are sought eagerly by upper-income and lower-income families alike. But this is not true of clinics; most advantaged students have access to private pediatricians and do not seem to need the same level of subsidized care that disadvantaged students do.

Given the impetus of federal, state, local, and foundation support, it is quite possible that keeping schools open for extended hours will soon be universal. The debate about how these 3:00 to 6:00 p.m. hours are best used and whether the focus should be on educational enrichment or youth development will undoubtedly continue. If faith-based organizations are allowed to compete for CCLC grants, the picture could change significantly. Without more research and greater consensus on goals, resolving the differences in approaches may rely more on political actions than on rational planning.

From the point of view of community school advocates, rapid development of after-school programs can only be a plus. The schoolhouse doors are open. What happens inside will differ in every school and every community, depend-ing on the needs and resources. As you will see, at Molly Stark School, after-school activities are a big deal. The offerings are imaginative and ever changing, depending on what Sue and her staff think will challenge the current crop of students and what unexpected resources appear in the community.

AFTER-SCHOOL PROGRAMS AT MOLLY STARK

After-School Enrichment Programs

The first extensive project we implemented was after-school programs. This seemed like a logical place to start. After-school programs would be good for all kids, not just those coming from poverty. It would be relatively inexpensive, and we could use classroom space not already occupied after school. Often, I am asked how we got the teachers to let us use their spaces. This was really never a controversy; we began by asking who wouldn't mind, and very few were worried about it.

We started with four enrichment programs to see if there was interest in the idea. I found four volunteers to offer programs in their areas of interest once a week for four weeks. They included a retired principal who helped a group of students learn facts for the National Geography Bee, a teacher who worked with students interested in weightlifting, a parent who taught outdoor games, and a local college student who shared her French language skills. Twenty-four kids signed up. That was in 1997.

Table 4.1 shows our after-school activities for the winter session that began in January 2001. It shows what can develop over a relatively short time.

Now about 200 children—more than half the student body—stay after school at least once a week. Our goal is to have a variety of choices encompassing a wide range of interests and skill areas. Some offerings are academic, some are not. We found that not all kids are ready to sit down and participate in an academic activity after school. Some just want to be active and have fun. The ratio of adults to children differs depending on the program, the management skills of the participating adults, and the specific group of children.

These programs are taught by teachers and other staff, parents, and community members. Although we frequently offer some old favorites (such as computers, Lego, and cooking), we also have new offerings each session; some examples are tai kwon do, quilting, Ping-Pong, rock-and-roll band, baby-sitting, gardening, auto mechanics, running club, sign language, meteorology, model building, and karate. The choices continue to multiply over time. I went to get a haircut, and a hair care club for fifth and sixth graders was soon started; I sat with a retired administrator at a high school basketball game, and she was soon quilting with a group of our students. No matter where I am in the community, I find myself recruiting people with hidden talents.

After-school programs fill many needs for children, families, and the community. They provide supervision by a caring adult, offer enriching experiences not readily available to all children, support positive peer interactions, and promote improved academic achievement. But an equally important result is that these after-school programs provide a hook for our students. One day I had to take a third grader home early because he had been verbally abusive to a teacher. At 3:00 p.m., when I was outside monitoring the buses, he showed up and said, "I know I was bad at school today, but can I go to tai kwon do if I promise to be

Table 4.1   Winter 2001 After-School Enrichment Programs

Monday	Tuesday	Wednesday	Thursday	Friday
Reading (K–6)	Reading (K–6)	Math club (1–3)	Computers (4–6)	Indoor soccer (2–4, boys only)
Baking cookies (K–3)	Clay beads (K–4)	Dance (K–4)	Arts and crafts (K–3)	
Computers (1–4)	Orient Express (K–4)	Pet care (K–4)	Cooking (1–4)	
Indoor soccer (2–4, girls only)	Computers (1–4)	Computers (1–4)	Musical: "Pandora's Box" (4–6)	
Card and board games (4–6)	Watercolor and drawing (3 6)	Chess club (4–6)	Calligraphy (4–6)	
Set design for musical (4–6)		Charcoal drawing (3–6)	Mural paint-ing (4–6)	
		Musical: "Pandora's Box" (4–6)		

good tomorrow?" We had found something that would make this child, who was disconnected from both school and life in general, want to be at school, and that was a good thing. Our hope is that if we can offer a good variety of after-school programs, each child will find something to shine in, something that encourages exploration in new areas of skill and interest. Although it is great for all kids, it is most important for those children who would otherwise never have the opportunity to participate in some of these activities.

As our after-school program expanded, it became clear that we needed coordinators to keep track of the activities and personnel. We now hire two parents, who are paid $10 an hour, to organize our after-school enrichment programs. We also began to pay the after-school facilitators a $90 stipend for each after-school offering because it was a way to help ensure sustainability. At times we use flexible scheduling; for example, a Title I reading teacher who organizes the after-school reading program could choose to begin work at 9:00 a.m. instead of 8:00 a.m. and leave at 4:00 p.m. instead of 3:00 p.m. These are contractual issues that we formalized in a document signed by the teachers' union and the board of education.

Things to Consider About After-School Enrichment Programs

- Our programs run in eight-week sessions, meeting once a week for an hour. This means students have different activities to choose from each day, and we're not reorganizing the schedule too often.

- Our after-school coordinators are responsible for hiring the facilitators, sending out and collecting the sign-up sheets, organizing the groups, selecting spaces for the various programs, making sure sufficient equipment and materials are available, and answering questions from parents and facilitators.

- Our program facilitators are teachers, staff members, parents, and community members. We realize that parents and community members may not have a background in teaching, so, when necessary, we pair them with a staff member to help run the program until they feel comfortable with management skills.

- We require facilitators to sign a written agreement to clarify roles and responsibilities.

- To avoid confusion, we also provide clear procedures for the facilitators to get reimbursed for materials and to reschedule a class if necessary. The clearer and cleaner the policies became, the more smoothly our programs ran.

- To create after-school programs that are sustainable, it became important to pay all the facilitators a small stipend. As we expanded, we applied for and received a yearly grant from the Turrell Fund in New Jersey. Fortunately, more and more grants are now available for after-school programs.

- We created a gathering place where children can go right after school to enjoy a snack and wait for the program facilitators to come get them. There are government subsidies available to help with the cost of snacks.

- Each afternoon at the conclusion of the program, an adult is available to make sure each child leaves safely with an adult. In some communities, providing transportation will be essential.

- You will need to consider whether you want to charge a small fee for after-school program enrollments. We charge just $4 per eight-week session for each after-school offering. Although we would never exclude a child because of a lack of money, we found that charging a small fee produces a greater commitment to the program. This small fee also allowed us to create a supplies fund. In addition, many local stores and organizations are willing to donate materials or money for materials.

- We have a short evaluation form that each facilitator, parent, and child can complete to help determine program effectiveness. The data help us make continuous improvements and also provide information for grant applications.

Appendix E contains samples of our facilitator sign-up sheet, our student registration form, and our facilitator evaluation form.

Homework Clubs

In 1998, a year after the enrichment program was under way, a third-grade teacher approached me with the idea of starting a homework club for fifth and sixth graders. The goal was not only to provide students the support they needed to get their homework done but to help them develop study habits and organizational skills that would promote academic responsibility. The teacher sent out a survey to staff, and with the help of the information this generated, our first homework club was established. Seven students signed up to participate.

Four years later, the club has expanded to include more than 20 students in Grades 3–6, and the teacher has the help of a paraprofessional who works in our school. The club meets three days a week, and students can attend as often as they choose. There is no charge for participation, and twice a year we treat students who consistently attend to a special dinner at a local restaurant.

Other homework clubs have since come into existence. In 1999, in looking at our detention data, we noticed that a small group of students consistently ended up in detention because their class work and homework were never completed. We decided to organize a mandatory homework club for these students who just don't have the support, interest, and self-discipline to get their work done. Like the original homework club, it is run by one of our teachers. There are fewer students in this group, so they can get the one-to-one attention they need. This is not presented as a detention or a punishment but as a constructive way of helping students catch up and develop good work habits.

Also, since the 1998–1999 school year, we have had an off-site homework club run by students from Bennington College in the housing project where many of our students live. A year later a second off-site program was added in a second housing project. These are both drop-in clubs that any student can attend. Even some middle school students who no longer attend our school have dropped in for support. At least once a year, as a special activity, the college students conduct a visit to Bennington College to show the kids what a college campus looks like and what they can strive for.

Homework clubs are not used as a punishment, and there is no charge to participate. We try to make them a positive experience, helping students develop good work habits, responsibility, and a chance to stay current in their work. Communication between the classroom teacher and the homework club facilitator is encouraged.

Academic Clubs: Reading and Math

Reading has been a clear focus in our school. We know that students who are successful readers are much more likely to find success in school and in life. During the 1998–1999 school year, a Title I reading teacher suggested that we offer an after-school reading opportunity. The concept was simple: Children would be invited to stay after school to enjoy a snack and read with an interested adult. These adults now include college students doing work-study and community members interested in volunteering their services, as well as staff members. As with the enrichment programs and homework clubs, it was important to remember that these activities need to be fun and motivating. Besides one-to-one reading with an adult, the students have practiced reading skills through games as well as computer programs.

After two years of successful implementation of reading clubs, we decided to begin a math problem-solving club. The first project was creating juice-box robots. Students had to group the boxes in tens and work together to assemble the parts of the robot. Each week brings a new challenge in problem solving. Like the homework clubs, the reading and math clubs require no fee.

Appendix F provides samples of written communication that can be used when implementing after-school enrichment, homework programs, and academic clubs.

Mentoring Programs

Even before 1996, when we began to look at what else we could offer students and their families to meet their needs, we had some strong programs in place. One of our first collaborations, starting in the early 1990s, was the PALS mentoring program.

We knew that a positive connection with a caring adult always has a significant impact on a child. Many adults who have experienced success in their lives speak about a trusting and trustworthy adult with whom they have had a positive relationship over a long period. This match can reduce a child's likelihood of using drugs and alcohol, engaging in physical violence and risk-taking behavior, and dropping out of school, and it can increase the likelihood of a better family relationship (Public/Private Ventures, 1995).

Every year, the PALS program pairs about 15 high school students with Molly Stark students in one-to-one relationships. The pairs meet each week outside school time for a few hours. The high school student (PAL) receives community service credit, and both enjoy a positive learning experience.

The challenge of a program like this is making sure that the PAL, the child, and the parent of the child maintain good communication. One problem we run into each year is a child's parent withholding time with the PAL as punishment for bad behavior at home. Often, our guidance counselor has to visit the parent to talk through the importance of this program being unconditional for the child.

One sixth grader recently showed me a letter from her PAL who had just gone to college. They had been in a PALS relationship for four years. The child was delighted to share her PAL's news, but what struck me most was her final comment as she walked away with her letter: "I like it that she really loves me." For me, this sums up the power of this program.

Our mentoring programs grew in 1999 when Judy Adams, who was assistant principal at the time, received a JUMP (Juvenile Mentoring Programs) grant for $95,000. With this grant from the U.S. Department of Justice, we began an on-site program. We were able to hire a program coordinator who, along with our guidance counselor, recruits, screens, and matches adults and children.

Employers allow their employees to come to the school for an hour per week to be with the children. Time can be spent on whatever the child and mentor enjoy doing together; they might eat lunch, play games, do art activities, catch up on homework, or just talk. In the initial training sessions for the mentors, we urge them to talk with the children about the importance of school and learning and their vision of future opportunities that might be available.

The program grew to 30 mentors in the first year, including people from local businesses as well as the police department. In the second year, mentoring programs were set up in other schools in our district; some mentors stayed with their students as they went on to middle school, and a few matches were made in another elementary school. The goals are that the program will expand throughout the district and that many of the kids will develop relationships that will encourage them to take a safe and productive road.

Things to Consider About Mentoring Programs

- You will need a person to oversee your mentoring program.

- It is important to develop a screening process to carefully select mentors and create good matches. This also helps spread the word so other mentors will come on board. Mentors are not necessarily trained educators or psychologists. Children who could be too difficult to handle because of severe emotional or behavioral problems are not candidates for this program.

- Strong communication among the school coordinator, the mentor, the child, and the child's parents is essential.

- Effective mentoring programs include training and support for the mentors in their efforts to build trust and develop positive relationships with children. Several hours of training before matches are made and regular supportive contact with the mentor by the school coordinator are important factors in our program's success.

- An agreement signed by mentors that clearly states their role and responsibilities helps formalize and strengthen their commitment to the program.

5

What Are the Staffing Considerations?

LEADERSHIP AND STAFFING

To state the obvious, a program is only as good as the people who operate it. My observations of community schools have led me to believe that these innovative programs attract very special people—people who are particularly concerned about child welfare, who are interested in equity issues, who enjoy the challenges of working with different groups. To make sure that others can follow in the footsteps of these special people, it is important to understand what drives them.

Leadership

What makes community schools different from other schools is the sharing of responsibility between the school and one or more nonschool organizations. Ideally, the responsibility for running the school and for managing the work of the outside organizations is also shared. Leading these two strands of activity are the principal and the full-time coordinator.

The Principal

We have seen how Sue Maguire came into her school and offered strong leadership during the transformation process, and I've mentioned other examples of dynamic principals. I do not believe that an effective community school can be implemented without the support of the principal.

The principal has to buy into the whole idea and be willing to open the schoolhouse doors to a multitude of other youth workers. The principal must be able to make the school staff comfortable with the additional staff and with the new programs developed as part of the community school transformation. He or she must collaborate willingly and consistently with the coordinator.

At the Quitman Street Community School in Newark, New Jersey, Principal Louis Mattina established an open-door policy for both the teachers and the community school staff. Committees were formed across domains; communication was encouraged through frequent events, such as parties, and a newsletter. The sense of ownership and pride in the community school was evident throughout the school.

The Coordinator

One shared attribute of almost all the different approaches to community schools is the presence of a full-time coordinator. Someone has to be in the school building along with the principal to share the responsibility of keeping the doors open for extended hours. Someone has to make sure that all the various activities are in place as scheduled and that all the staff are performing according to set standards. In a school that is jointly operated by the school itself and a community-based organization (CBO), the coordinator usually is employed by the CBO. For example, at most of the Children's Aid Society (CAS) and Beacon adaptations, the coordinator is hired by a CBO such as a local Y or a Boys and Girls Club. However, a few school systems, such as Birmingham, Alabama's, include funding in their school budgets for community school coordinators. Often, the coordinator's employer is determined by the source of funding and by whether a grant goes to the school system or to an outside agency.

A study of the Wallace-Reader's Digest Extended Services Schools Initiative found that running after-school programs required the presence of a full-time rather than a part-time coordinator (Walker, Grossman, & Raley, 2000). Typically, a program that started with a part-time leader soon sought additional resources to fill the position for longer hours and to add another half-time person for administrative chores. A Beacon school coordinator who had been hired by a local CBO said, "My schedule? From 8:00 a.m. to 9:00 p.m. It's supposed to be a 40-hour week, with me leaving 2 hours before the program closes. But it's hard to leave. My morning is taken up with meetings or office work. I go to a lot of community things, like CBO monthly meetings or meetings with the hospital staff." And then, of course, she had to be on duty running the program from after-school to closing time.

One principal's view of the position of coordinator was, "If we really wanted to integrate day and after school into a real extended-service school, we needed a coordinator who knew the teachers. So we revised the job description to hire someone full time who was a certified teacher to get the input of the day teachers." Apparently, coordinators who had previous experience working in the schools were able to establish firmer relationships with the school staff.

The question of whether the coordinator of the community school should work for the district or the partner agency frequently arises at conferences. I have heard Eileen Santiago from Thomas Edison Elementary School in Port Chester, New York, claim that she preferred to hire a known person from within the school, while Catalina Montes from Thomas Gardner Extended Services School in Boston maintains that her program sought an "outsider" because school people were not accustomed to working the long hours required of a community school coordinator.

It's always interesting to ask people what they did before they got involved in community schools. One coordinator of a citywide effort told me that before her current challenging job, she had worked in her family's business. But she also was a parent activist and had organized a parent organization. So although she did not come out of either the educational or the social service sector, she was prepared to deal with the realities of running a complex office that had to relate to both school and city politics.

Other School Staff

The transformation from a traditional school to a community school involves existing school staff as well as staff from other agencies. Many schools employ guidance counselors and school nurses, who until the advent of the community school initiative have had the major responsibility for providing support services. Some schools put these people together into a pupil personnel team and include the school psychologist if one is employed by the school system (usually for special education testing). But the reality in many schools with high numbers of disadvantaged students is that the existing services supported by the school system are totally inadequate. That is why the additional services are needed.

Community schools have to find ways to integrate existing school personnel into the plan. In schools with primary health care clinics staffed by hospitals or health centers, the school nurse becomes the triage person. Students see the school nurse first, and then she directs them toward the services they need, such as physical exams, dental care, or mental health counseling. In programs like Communities-in-Schools, guidance counselors serve as major referral agents to the case managers who come into the school. They are in a position to assess which students are neediest and require large amounts of individual attention.

In some communities, concerns have been expressed that a community agency's provision of services in a school will obviate the need for a school-employed nurse , social worker, counselor, or psychologist. Quite the opposite is true. All hands are needed, but with the new personnel, it is possible to divide the responsibility. The school-supported staff should be free to concentrate on issues that will enhance quality educational experience, such as attendance, course selection, testing, and classroom behavior.

While the role of teachers in the transition to community schooling is not so obvious, they, like the principal, can make or break the program. Teachers need to be included in the design of the school from the beginning. They need to understand how bringing in all the outsiders can reduce the barriers to learning and help them do their jobs better and that the more classroom teaching is reinforced in after-school programs, the higher the potential learning curve for the students.

Up to this point, the growth in numbers of community schools appears to be piecemeal, one school at a time and only a few in any given district. However, in 2001, several cities—Boston; Hartford, Connecticut; San Francisco; Buffalo; Portland, Oregon; Tukwila, Washington; and Plainfield, New Jersey (where I grew up)—began to move toward systemwide programs. School systems interested in furthering the concept of community schools have to create leadership in the central office. An associate superintendent, for example, could be put in charge of districtwide planning and coordination.

Community Agency Staff

The workers who come into a school have to be aware that they are, at least initially, the outsiders. Training and upgrading of community-based agency staff are very important. Making the Most of Out-of-School Time (MOST) is an initiative started in 1994 by the National Institute on Out-of-School Time (NIOST) with support from the Wallace–Reader's Digest Foundation (NIOST, 2001; see also Resources). In Boston, Chicago, and Seattle, through the MOST initiative, CBOs were designated to organize after-school efforts that involved various stakeholders in those communities. Seattle's School's Out Consortium, led by the YWCA, provided 1,500 hours of on-site training and technical assistance each year to licensed, government-subsidized school-age care program staffs (Harvey & Shortt, 2001). In addition, the consortium offered professional development workshops for youth-serving providers and caregivers and discussion groups for parents.

Staffing Problems

Among the barriers to implementation of full-service community schools (discussed in Chapter 9) are a number of staffing issues, including salary differentials, turnover, and training.

Salaries

School-community partnerships sometimes get bogged down over the salary differentials between the teachers and the CBO youth workers, with teachers usually at higher levels. In some parts of the country, almost all teachers belong to unions, but few youth agencies anywhere are organized into unions. In one large-scale citywide community school program, teachers were paid about $30 per hour for after-school work compared with $16 per hour for youth workers from community-based organizations. Although they probably do not offer identical approaches to enrichment, they do work in adjoining classrooms with similar groups of students. Sylvester and Reich (2000), in their report on after-school programs, show that staff salaries for out-of-school time programs average less than $10 per hour and turnover is about 40 percent a year.

Turnover

This is a story told too often: We were just about up and running when the principal left and a new person came in; we had to start all over to convince the new principal of the importance of community school concepts.

Turnover is endemic in all human services. However, in the case of a community school, changes in leadership can be quite traumatic. The same applies to community-based agencies. The founding leader of the school-community partnership leaves and is replaced by someone who does not believe in outstationing personnel or who has no experience working with schools. Such situations mean that the original plan and design has to be strong enough to withstand the pressures of changing leadership.

Training

Neither the educational establishment nor the youth services field has a training program that encompasses the kind of cross-disciplinary thinking required to run community schools. Few teachers' colleges, other than those with university-assisted school connections, include course work that focuses on community schools. Newly trained principals know very little about these kinds of school-community partnerships. And most social work schools and psychology departments, which produce many of the leaders of the community-based organizations that will partner with schools, do not feature school transformation models in their curriculum.

That is just the beginning of the training issue. Most training in this new field takes place inservice (within the employing organization). Much can be accomplished through making technical assistance and training widely available to current and future practitioners.

Technical Assistance

Intermediary Organizations

Intermediary organizations are national programs that have the capacity to help local school and community groups adapt the organization's models. The programs mentioned in Chapter 2, for instance, all have staff that can help local communities. The Beacons in New York were originally set up in 1991 by the Department of Youth and Community Development with technical assistance provided by the Fund for the City of New York. This fund has focused heavily on youth development issues, running frequent workshops and training programs for the coordinators and staff of the New York City Beacons and organizing site visits to model Beacons.

CAS's National Technical Assistance Center for Community Schools, also in New York, sends staff all over the country to help set up CAS adaptations. The Salome Ureña Middle Academies (IS 218) in New York City is a training site that has been visited by hundreds of interested people from the United States and many other countries. The center's mission is to increase the ability of schools and community organizations to work together in long-term partnerships that benefit children and families. These are some of the topics covered in their training:

- Partnership building
- Needs and resource assessment
- Criteria for determining capacity and readiness
- Program and curriculum development
- Integrating school-day and after-school programs
- Parent and community engagement
- Getting from planning to implementation
- Sustainability—long-term strategic planning

These topics are typical of those covered in other training programs.

CAS encourages site visits not only to their New York City models but to national adaptation sites in San Francisco; Boston; Salt Lake City; Long Beach, California; Washington, D.C.; and Newark, New Jersey. They encourage parents and leaders of schools and community agencies to get involved in training programs as a group.

The United Way's Bridges to Success and the Communities-in-Schools program also have technical assistance staff that travel from their offices in the Washington, D.C., area and offer similar substantive training.

A study of extended services adaptations in 80 schools throughout the United States found that such intermediaries played important roles in implementing the models at local sites (Walker et al., 2000). Acting almost as management consultants, they helped school and community partners clarify decision-making roles and promote positive relationships between the parties.

The researchers observed, "Although they [the intermediaries] clarified grant requirements when necessary, their extensive experience in school-community collaborations allowed them to make suggestions for mediating tensions that arose in allocating resources and responsibilities among partners" (p. 73). Both their expertise in negotiating political conflicts between schools and community agencies and their status as neutral outsiders helped them work out solutions to the problems.

Making visits to existing community school sites has become an important part of the technical assistance challenge. Potential program developers are encouraged to observe an array of programs to clarify models and understand how they work. During the planning period, when school and community representatives first come together, a site visit out of town is a useful way for participants to get to know each other.

Grantees of the New Jersey School-Based Youth Services Program receive continuous technical assistance from the New Jersey Department of Human Resources. A highly qualified support team provides ongoing access to information, training, and other resources. Project directors attend monthly meetings where they can interact with each other and be exposed to programming and coordination assistance.

Quality Advisors

The MOST initiative, run by NIOST in Boston, Chicago, and Seattle, encouraged its providers to develop a quality program and at the same time create an infrastructure capable of supporting and maintaining a system. These programs have been carefully tracked and evaluated over time. The biggest problem encountered has been staffing shortages.

One strategy that seemed to have a positive impact on staff retention was the use of what they called quality advisors. These advisors were intensively trained by NIOST and placed for prescribed amounts of time to work directly at the program level with the project site directors. Not only were they helpful with mentoring, training, and finding resources, they could also function as more personal "guidance counselors" for the staff.

The National School-Age Care Alliance has created an accreditation system for after-school programs. The standards are directed toward ensuring that programs provide educational enrichment, encourage personal growth and development; involve families; respect cultural diversity; and encourage linkages to the community.

Safe Futures Experience

In 1996, the U.S. Department of Justice launched a delinquency prevention program called Safe Futures, which encompassed many of the same components as full-service community schools. The selected grantees (six local governmental groups) were to put together community collaboratives that would offer a continuum of care built into a multidisciplinary system for prevention, intervention, treatment, or correction services. Components included after-school programs; mentoring; family support services; mental health services; programs to prevent drug abuse, violence, and teen pregnancy; and community-wide approaches to helping schools get rid of gangs.

A study of the implementation of Safe Futures (U.S. Department of Justice, 2000) provides relevant lessons. Researchers found that the selected communities needed access to ongoing training and technical assistance, both to implement complex components and to adapt models to the local context. Providers were able to tap into technical assistance resources for a particular component (for example, the National Mentoring Center) for help in specific fields. Not surprisingly, small agencies with fewer staff and lower budgets needed more technical assistance, especially with accountability, record keeping, reporting, program evaluation, and other common requirements for demonstration programs. Some sites needed specific assistance with issues requiring cultural sensitivity.

The Role of Universities in Training and Staffing

Universities have many roles in the future development of community schools in terms of both models and personnel. Some of the most innovative work in schools has been promulgated by university faculty. But that is only the beginning of their responsibility. Since all teacher, social work, mental health, primary health, and psychology training is conducted under university auspices, universities have a major role in the design of graduate education and its ability to cross disciplinary lines. The professional staff of both the school systems and the partner agencies are influenced by their experiences in college and graduate school. For the community school concept to be widely accepted, universities must make sure that their students in all domains understand what it means to enter collaborative relationships.

The University of Pennsylvania has been the leader in developing university-assisted community schools. Two historians, Ira Harkavy and Lee Benson, set the stage in the university more than a decade ago with their interest in historical precedents and their focus on John Dewey's community school orientation. They believe that both students and faculty need to be exposed to building responsive neighborhood schools. In their community, they have worked to establish the West Philadelphia Improvement Corps (WEPIC) at the Center for Community Partnerships.

WEPIC was launched in 1985 with an honors history seminar called "Urban Universities—Community Relations: Penn-West Philadelphia, Past, Present, and Future." By 2001, WEPIC was actively engaged with 13 schools in the area of West Philadelphia surrounding the university and had developed more than 100 university courses that link Penn students to community service work. Through this medium, Penn professors and students (both graduate and undergraduate) have developed collaborative relationships with school personnel to upgrade the quality of education and to introduce other program components, such as parent involvement, health services, and after-school activities, into the emerging community schools. The approach is described as community oriented, real world, and problem solving.

WEPIC has played a major role in instructing other universities in how to develop university-assisted schools. It holds an annual conference and offers on-site consultation. Yale University has also been the site of important contributions to this field, through the work of James Comer's School Development Program and Edward Zigler's Schools of the 21st Century. Both of these models are packaged for replication purposes and have technical assistance people who can help schools with implementation.

Two Centers for Mental Health in Schools are university-based: one at UCLA's Department of Psychology under the leadership of Howard Adelman and Linda Taylor and the other led by Mark Weist at the University of Maryland. Both offer extensive support in terms of published manuals and documents, annual meetings, and consultant services.

Observations

A new field cannot be created without the necessary workforce. A well-functioning, comprehensive community school requires excellence in both the educational components and the support services. This implies good leadership and well-trained staff in the school system and in the agencies that partner with the school to provide the services.

One aspect of this work that never ends is training. Because the collaborative concepts are new, school and community agency personnel have to work hard to incorporate them into their thinking and their actions. And even when everyone seems pretty comfortable with the emerging community school, the turnover issue is ever present, and each new person who comes on the scene has to be integrated into the school's particular environment. Continuous inservice training must be available to make sure that everyone is aware of the procedures and programs that cross domains.

Principals and coordinators are key figures in this conceptualization. Not only must each perform well in his or her own domain, but they have to relate well to one another. The responsibility for ensuring this quality rests at many levels. The local school is, of course, the scene of the action. Over it stands the local school board and superintendent and the community agencies and their boards. If the program is coming from the state, another level of hierarchy and leadership must be dealt with. And in the long run, if legislation continues to be promulgated in Congress, oversight from the federal level could be forthcoming (as it already is for thousands of after-school programs). As a first step at any level, it will be useful for the emerging field to define the coordinator's role in the community school and outline what qualifications and certification are necessary for that position.

MOLLY STARK'S STAFF
AND HOW IT DEVELOPED

As a school principal, my most important task is to hire high-quality staff. In fall 2000, we had almost 100 staff members. Besides the administration and site coordinator, this included 19 classroom teachers, 20 specialists (special education, reading, art, music, and physical education teachers; a librarian; and a nurse), 36 support personnel, 12 staff in the districtwide Early Education Program housed at our school, and 7 Family Center staff. Whether teaching in a classroom, assisting students in a homework club, providing stimulating child care, offering guidance in a medical consultation, running the Family Center, or connecting with parents, the competence and commitment of the staff are critical.

It is difficult to provide a job description for a principal of a community school. Each day is different and its own challenge. I am the one who is ultimately responsible for the students' academic outcomes. I must answer to the school board, the district administration, the staff, the parents, and the students. This is true for all principals. Add on after-school programs, a preschool, child care, mentoring, an array of health services, professional development for the staff, grant writing, all the necessary paperwork, parent programs, and the problems and issues to be coped with daily, and it makes for a busy job.

At Molly Stark, having the services and programs school driven, as opposed to having an outside organization in charge of the community school services, makes me accountable for the overall coordination of everything that happens in our school. How do the instructional programs fit into the comprehensive social and health programs we offer? Who are the community people we work with? What are their roles, and how do their roles affect the staff, students, and parents at Molly Stark? What are their schedules? What is the role of the Molly Stark staff? How do we maintain open and productive communication about families and kids? How do we make sure that other community service providers understand our goals and our vision? Who gets paid what, and how do we find the money to make it all sustainable? There are a lot of questions, but I don't look at the support services we provide as a source of problems; instead, I think of them as a menu I can turn to when we are trying to help a child and his or her family.

Hiring Teachers

The teachers and other staff members are the core of what happens for the students at Molly Stark, which is why hiring excellent staff is such a crucial task. When I need to hire a teacher, I look for someone who can provide both high-quality instruction and a comfortable, caring atmosphere for children and their parents. The ability to create a positive relationship seems to be one of the most important sources of our students' willingness to work hard toward academic achievement.

Beyond that, our teachers can choose how much to take part in the nontraditional programs we offer. Some were part of the planning in the original focus group, others watched quietly from the sidelines. Some have chosen to be facilitators in after-school programs; others are mentors. Still others have come to me throughout the process with ideas that have been successfully implemented. The climate here is one of innovation and positive risk. Staff members know that if they come up with an idea that is good for children and/or families, we will make our best effort to find a way to carry it out.

Hiring a Site Coordinator

Early in our process, a workshop instructor at a community school conference gave me a piece of advice: Hire a site coordinator to oversee the Family Center programs. At the time, I thought that although this would be a good idea, it
was absurd to think we would ever have enough money to do it. Since this certainly wasn't a typical position found in a public school, it wouldn't be funded by
local money. I figured that I would just have to add these responsibilities to my
own schedule. Of course, back then I had no idea how our plan would evolve and
grow. Now I realize how naive I was to think that we could possibly run a center
without a site coordinator.

Since Judy Cohen became our site coordinator in 1998, her responsibilities
have grown and changed. On paper, Judy oversees the Family Center components, such as child care, preschool, family outreach, and literacy programs. She
schedules staff, works with parents, prepares and reports data, and makes sure
that fees and subsidies are collected. We knew these duties would be necessary.
The part that is missing in her job description, however, is the unpredictable
daily responsibilities that must be addressed if a program is going to be truly
responsive to the needs of kids and families. On any given day, Judy may change
a diaper, baby-sit a toddler whose parent has an appointment at the Family Center, transport a parent and child to an appointment in the community, help a
parent understand and fill out paperwork for an agency, or talk with a parent
who is coping with a crisis. The point is that it would be very difficult to write a
real job description for many of the positions in a community school.

In 2001, the Family Center had seven employees: a full-time site coordinator, a preschool teacher who works six hours a day, a half-time kindercare (child
care for kindergartners) teacher, a lead child care provider who works from
10:00 a.m. until 5:30 p.m., and three teaching assistants, two of whom are full
time. Many of the staff in our Family Center were "recruited." They were well
respected and had reputations for doing excellent work with children and families. One of the strong advantages of beginning a new program is having the
opportunity to choose all your staff.

In the first three years of the Family Center's existence, the positions changed
each year. Needs change, district programs change, Family Center programs
evolve. For example, since the 2001–2002 school year, our school district is supporting full-day kindergarten for all the elementary schools. We therefore no
longer need a kindercare teacher, so our staffing has changed. Some years we
have children who need extra assistance, and we hire accordingly. We continue
to take pride in having a high ratio of adults to children so we can meet the needs
of all the children.

Part-Time Staff From the Community

Many people from our community provide services at our school. Most work
hourly; for others, we pay a portion of their salary to the community agency
where they are employed. Some already serve our school's families, and they
provide services as part of their organization's regular service delivery, but they

Table 5.1   Community-Based Staff

Position	Organization
Clinical psychologist	Bennington Psychotherapy Association (private practice)
Pediatrician	Green Mountain Pediatrics (private practice)
Family outreach worker	Sunrise Family Resource Center (state parent-child center)
Clinical social worker	Self-employed (private practice)
Parent education teacher	Tutorial Center (local adult basic education center)
After-school program coordinators	Parents from our school
After-school program facilitators	Staff members and community members
Local physicians (inoculations/physicals)	Bennington Family Practice (private practice)

do so at the school site instead of the organization's site. One example is the Tutorial Center, the local adult basic education facility that helps many Bennington citizens work toward their GED. Two afternoons a week, a Tutorial Center teacher provides these services at Molly Stark, conducting free courses for adults from the Molly Stark school zone and any other interested community adults. This is a service provided in our community, and we do not need to pay this teacher.

Table 5.1 lists community members who work at Molly Stark. Notice that this list does not include the dentist, because his practice is an independent business located in our school.

These consultants are paid hourly except the family outreach worker; we pay a percentage of her salary to Sunrise Family Resource Center, where she works.

We need to be able to depend on these people to be professional and competent. I learned early on that no matter what agency or organization they come from, it's the individual that counts. When we are looking to fill a position or to engage a consultant, we look for someone who works well with all types of people and who can collaborate and work as part of a team. Having our programs coordinated by the school means that we can choose who works with us—a crucial part of ensuring high-quality staff.

Challenges of Staffing

Job descriptions for our Family Center employees were written by the site coordinator (see Appendix G). This was a difficult task since these positions weren't typically part of a school and we had to present the descriptions to the board of education for approval. We had discussed trying to fit the positions into established jobs, but we decided against this. Although it took much more time and energy to create and define new positions, we felt it was important to recognize the unusual nature of these jobs and to make the pay consistent with the positions. Our irregular hours and days—school vacations, school closings, and the Family Center hours of 7:00 a.m. to 5:30 p.m.—all add to the problem of staffing.

A challenge that is subtle but nevertheless present is integrating the Family Center staff so they are seen as part of the Molly Stark staff—that is, making sure the Family Center employees who work with kids during child care are included in parent meetings, special education meetings, and other pertinent conferences. More than once I have had to remind people on the Molly Stark staff that the Family Center staff have much information to share. I feel sure such unintentional oversights occur only because it takes time for the school staff to adjust to a new structure. But I also know that if we are to truly work as a team, the Family Center staff must be an integral part of the information channel when decisions are being made about children they have worked with over a long period.

We are always looking toward next year. What staffing do we need to change? What resources should we be thinking about now that might help us to make the program work? The process is dynamic and ever changing, and it should be. This is the only way that what our staff does will be responsive to the actual needs of families.

The Bigger Challenge

For the last few years, I have taught a graduate course in school administration, titled School and Community, at Massachusetts College of Liberal Arts. In addition to presenting the typical educational leadership issues and concepts, I am determined to challenge the students, who will be future administrators, to think differently. I want them to explore the purpose of education in the 21st century and how it will meet the needs of children and their families, as well as to identify their role in developing and leading schools that can carry out this mandate. It is crucial that education courses offer a vision of the connection between education and health and social services if we are to see an increase in the number of schools that really do meet the needs of children.

6

How Are Effective Partnerships Developed?

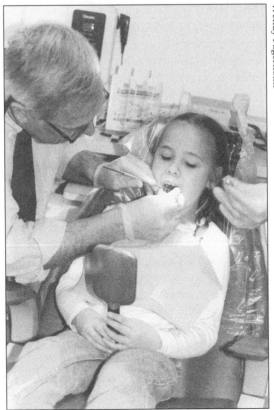

Wendy Fagerholm

GOVERNANCE STRUCTURES
AND LEAD AGENCIES

Our discussion of governance is framed in idealistic terms:

> Collaborative governance refers to a closely linked set of oversight, man-
> agement, and site-level activities in which a broad cross-section of
> shareholders share authority and accountability for agreed-upon goals.
> . . . The essential purpose of collaboration is to achieve results that no
> single institution or segment of the community could achieve acting
> alone. (Coalition for Community Schools, 2001, p. 2)

Developing partnerships and shaping the array of formal and informal relationships that will govern the project is the most challenging aspect of creating a
community school. Partnerships can occur on many levels, fostered by everything from formal contracts to personal contact or custom. Molly Stark School is
among the less complicated examples of school-community partnerships. The
principal is the controlling figure; she is the "lead agency," and all the financial
arrangements go across her desk. So do most of the decisions about what services are provided and when and where they are provided. The Bennington
school district has oversight responsibility and appears to be supportive.

Other models are much more complex, with Children's Aid Society (CAS)
schools probably at the opposite end of the continuum. In the most fully implemented CAS school, the turf is really shared, with the principal running the academic part of the school and the CAS coordinator clearly in charge of all the
other components, including the funding. Decision making is done together.

Tim Garvin, executive director of the Allston-Brighton YMCA, the lead
agency in a partnership with Thomas Gardner Extended Services School, has
become a strong advocate for collaboration. With help from Boston College, this
partnership has created an adaptation of the CAS model. Garvin told a conference group,

> This is hard work. I think the only reason we have been successful is
> because we are a true partnership. A partnership is not just on paper. It
> is not a vision statement or a mission statement. And it is not a hierarchy
> or bureaucracy or government stuff. All of that is important. But it is a
> partnership when you share bad experiences . . . and you come to realize
> that partnerships aren't institution to institution, but person to person.
> (Building Strong Full-Service and Community Schools, 2000, p. 5)

Gardner's principal, Catalina Montes, confirmed the strength of this partnership, saying that when she called Tim for help moving furniture, "he pulled
people out of the Y swimming pool to come to the school and volunteer."

This chapter describes various approaches to governance and examines
some actual practices in various parts of the United States. Who makes decisions
on what level? Who has fiscal responsibility? Who directs the staff at the school-
site level? Some examples I cite appear to be specific to their particular geo-

graphic locations. Clearly, every state and community operates under its own set of policies, regulations, and agencies. But the concepts of governance can cross boundaries, and it may be useful for those in one area to learn from another.

Governance Structures

In their study of school-community initiatives, Tia Melaville and Martin Blank (1998) describe a two-tier level of governance: primary oversight, where policy and finances are dealt with, and day-to-day management in the school building, where programs are implemented and activities coordinated. The oversight typically takes place at a higher level than the service site—in a school system, county offices, or a nonprofit like the United Way. Decision making at the site level involves school and agency staff, and possibly parents and students.

Communities-in-Schools (CIS) offers an example of the two levels of governance. At the higher level, usually a city or county, a nonprofit board is organized with business people and community agencies. They raise funds and contract with community-based organizations (CBOs) to relocate services such as case management, tutoring, and school-to-work programs into the schools. At the school site, the CIS coordinator, employed by the nonprofit board, implements the program in the school and relates to school personnel. Melaville and Blank determined that 47 percent of the oversight groups for school-community partnerships were community collaboratives like CIS; 27 percent were local school boards like the Community Education Program in Birmingham, Alabama; 17 percent were not-for-profits or private agencies like CAS or United Way; 7 percent were noneducational public agencies like health departments; and a few did not fit these categories. But when it came to who was in charge at the school-site level, more than half the direction was provided by school districts, usually building on existing site-based management schemes. Nonprofits managed more than a third of the school sites, and a few schools were run by interagency or community collaborative groups.

The U.S. Department of Education spells out its take on governance of comprehensive school-linked strategies in *Putting the Pieces Together* (1996). In support of the two-tier notion, this report describes a large oversight group (with 30 to 50 members) at the top that meets periodically and a small management group (with 10 to 15 members) that does the day-to-day work at the school level. The oversight group is expected to break up into subgroups or committees to encourage participation.

Richard Negron, CAS's director of technical assistance, has had considerable experience working with community groups and schools in developing governance arrangements. The CAS model attempts to integrate the support services with the educational interventions. Negron's approach focuses on what he calls the cabinet—a site-based governing body that includes the school principal, assistant principals, the coordinator of the community school program (employed by a CBO), key community school CBO-employed staff, other school faculty and personnel, and PTA representatives. This management body meets weekly to conduct the joint operations of the community school, make decisions, and solve problems. Negron points out that many schools now have site-based management teams that focus on the school's academic agenda. In his view, it is essential that community school coordinators are members of the site-based management teams as well as the cabinet (telephone conversation, June 15, 2001). In this model, oversight is provided jointly by the school authority and the CBOs that are the lead agencies in the schools.

In New York City, the superintendent of School District 6 and the CAS director of community schools work closely together to track developments in the CAS community schools in that district. Anthony Amato, the School District 6 superintendent who oversaw the implementation of the CAS community schools, left in 1999 to become the head of the Hartford, Connecticut, public school system. He immediately instituted reforms that picked up on many community school concepts. His replacement in Washington Heights, Jorge Izquierdo, was delighted to find the CAS program operating so well. "I was really impressed. I wished I had had all those services at my school when I was a principal. You can talk about raising test scores . . . but until you do something concrete to meet children's most basic needs, you can't begin to deal with instructional issues" (Pardini, 2001). Clearly, in this instance, the collaboration between the school system and the community agency has continued across major staff changes.

In *Building a Full-Service School,* a manual based on experiences of the Florida Full-Service Schools Program, Calfee, Wittwer, and Meredith (1998) describe two kinds of governance structure. Site-based governance is a three-tiered pyramid. On the bottom, holding up the whole structure, is a site-based planning committee that makes decisions on a day-to-day basis. This group includes parents, teachers, counselors, community health and human service workers, other school services staff, at least one teacher, and the site coordinator. Over this group sits a policy committee made up of managers, who are generally the supervisors of the planning committee people (principal, agency head, health department director). They meet monthly to establish policies and procedures needed for site-specific program implementation and operation, such as resource allocations. On top of the whole structure sits an "elite" steering committee to resolve problems, advocate for program funding, and maintain a political basis for community support. It meets bimonthly and includes VIPs such as the superintendent of schools, mayor, judges, sheriff, other government figures, and business leaders.

Community-based governance, according to the Florida group, builds on existing interagency councils and is applicable to communities where more than one school is involved. Here the steering committee members act as both advisors and decision makers for the program. They direct a local oversight council, which in turn brings together representatives from full-service schools, family care coordination teams, and existing interagency councils.

Lead Agencies

The oversight group is typically organized by a specific organization. As we have seen, many different types of agencies may assume the lead-agency responsibility, from the school itself (the principal) to public agencies and youth-serving organizations. If a community lacks a "natural" lead agency, one with the capacity to perform the necessary policy and administrative functions, it is possible to bring a group of interested people together and form a new nonprofit organization. That is the approach favored by Communities-in-Schools. Program developers from the national organization work with local people to set up such councils. Some of the new councils are built on a framework of existing networks or consortiums of agencies. An existing community planning agency may also get involved.

For Linkages to Learning, a school-linked program in Montgomery County, Maryland, the lead agency is the County Health and Human Services Department's Division of Children, Youth and Family Service. The agency's functions are to coordinate the community needs assessment, contact partners, organize meetings, develop memos of understanding among partner agencies, facilitate training, provide coordination, and staff the program.

Joint-Use Agreements

For his doctoral dissertation, Ken Testa (2000) made a unique study of how school districts and community agencies collaborate in planning and developing facilities that can be shared. Testa documents the importance of creating school environments that accommodate the 21st century notion of multiple-use buildings. Yet in all of the emerging literature about school-community partnerships (some of which I have written), there is little recognition of this area of study.

Testa's dissertation contains interesting examples of school systems in California that have made "deals" with an array of organizations to develop joint ventures. In the city of Paramount, playing fields for the school are located in an adjacent public part. In Elk Grove, a public library is being constructed within a school building. In other places, swimming pools, athletic fields, shopping malls, technological learning centers, and other programs are being combined with school buildings. After studying these various joint-use arrangements, Testa concluded that crafting these agreements is a "highly complex matter, one full of subjectivity, circumstance and intangibles" (Testa, 2000, p. 298).

Interviews and focus groups with joint-use practitioners produced important insights into how these agreements are arranged. (The findings were similar to my own observations of school-community collaboration.) Some of the important attributes for partners include a cooperative attitude, willingness to build trust, understanding of others' points of view, the belief that joint use produces benefits, and willingness to give up control. Testa found a strong sense of entrepreneurialism, the need to "get out of the box," and a "never say die" mentality.

Testa (2000) reports that the strongest barrier to progress appeared to be turf issues, or territorialism. "A mentality of 'we do things this way here' was referenced by respondents in describing unwillingness to change, fear of losing power, or need to maintain special interests" (p. 300). Multiple layers of bureaucracy also stood in the way of progress. As one school leader said, "It's been so time-consuming. When you can't get consensus, then the process of collaboration becomes cumbersome and stressful. At that point you just want to say, someone make a decision and tell us what to do." The importance of preplanning was emphasized: "If you don't plan, joint use becomes an afterthought and almost impossible to implement" (p. 301).

An example of joint use is the Wilder Foundation's Achievement Plus initiative in St. Paul, Minnesota, which encompassed the remodeling of two schools and the construction of a new one, all fitted out to accommodate the requirements of full-service community schools. At the Dayton Bluffs School, for example, a new city-run recreation center that added space for a theatre, dance studio, community kitchen, warming room for winter sports, and gymnasium was actually attached to the school. Extensive renovations of the two existing schools included space designated for the recreation programs provided by the city of St. Paul. At both existing schools, additional space was carved out for medical services, child care, community and counseling rooms and family resource centers. All these facilities are available to the school during the school day and open to the public afternoons and evenings.

The new site was an abandoned high school built in 1909. The newly refurbished school, John A. Johnson Achievement Plus Elementary School, includes a media center, early childhood classes and facilities, a community and family room, medical services, and offices for community agencies. The building was designed by the St. Paul school system as a demonstration site for Achievement Plus programs and includes designated spaces for teacher training. The YMCA of Greater St. Paul, chosen as the recreation partner for the community school, built a new facility attached to the school.

Advisory Committees

In the Jacksonville, Florida, Full-Service Schools Program, each full-service school is governed by a neighborhood oversight committee consisting of parents, teachers, students, principals, other school officials, and local citizens. The committees identify the health and service issues they believe need to be addressed in their respective schools. Each committee monitors its full-service school throughout the year, ensuring that appropriate services are located on site.

Almost all community school models include some kind of advisory committee. However, many of these groups are on paper only. At site visits, when one asks when the committee last met, the response is often "not recently." It may be that site coordinators do not always have the community organization skills needed to recruit and work with grassroots people. Working with an advisory group is time-consuming, and you have to pay attention to its advice when you call the group together. Some foundation and public grant programs require documentation that advisory groups have met and specify their composition, which often must include youth representation.

Contracts and Memos of Agreement

I believe it is important for schools and community partners to enter into formal relationships with each other, using written statements such as contracts or memoranda of agreement to specify roles and responsibilities. Leadership has to be firmly in place and a system for decision making agreed on. As the Center for Mental Health in Schools (n.d.) states, integration of school-community interventions "requires weaving school and community resources together in ways that can only be achieved through connections that are formalized and institutionalized, with major responsibilities shared" (p. i).

In their guidelines for school community centers, community school pioneers Joseph Ringers and Larry Decker (1995) suggest that policy statements should include the intent of the governing body, what is to be accomplished, legal authority or constraints, and relevant prior actions or projects. Laws and regulations should be referenced and agreements about procedures should be documented. This means giving thought to organizational charts, operational matters such as management, administration, staffing, and programming, and financial subjects such as budget preparation and approval procedures, sources of funds, authority to spend, and authority to revise allocations.

Examples of Lead Agencies and Governance Approaches

School Operated: Molly Stark

In this school, the principal works directly with the community school staff through an informal "cabinet" that includes the assistant principal, the site coordinator of the Family Center, the school guidance counselor, and other core staff members. They meet very frequently on an ad hoc basis.

City Operated: Buffalo, New York

The Buffalo, New York, Mayor's Community Schools Project (MCSP) is a unique effort within city government to foster community schools. Mayor Anthony Masiello has brought together many different resources to create initiatives in 15 schools in his city. Amy Prentiss of the city's Division of Citizen Services acts as community-school liaison.

In 1994, Mayor Masiello launched the MCSP, making community schools one of the main education objectives of his administration. The groundwork had already been laid when two schools received funding from the New York State Education Department's Community School Program in the early 1990s. These schools receive grants of $175,000 to $200,000 a year to hire a community education leader or community school coordinator, pay teachers and aides for after-school programming, and contract with outside agencies.

The mayor first used Community Development Block Grants, selecting three schools in partnership with the Superintendent of Buffalo Public Schools. Additional funding has been sought from an array of public and private sources. Twelve schools are now funded by the city program and three by the state.

City grants of $5,000 to $25,000 are also made to community-based organizations to support after-school services. Schools contribute the cost of keeping buildings open. In addition, the MCSP administers a portion of Buffalo's local law enforcement block grant, which is used in schools for multicultural drum and dance classes and a swimming program.

Currently, Buffalo's MCSP has working relationships with more than 100 organizations, including youth agencies, businesses, TV stations, health and social support groups, churches, and Americorps volunteers. No two schools have the same menu. Several have school-based health clinics, others have family resource centers, child care, employment training, adult literacy, anti-violence projects, and just about any program you can think of (including the dog training mentioned in Chapter 3).

Commission Operated: Kansas City, Missouri

The Local Investment Commission (LINC) in Kansas City and Jackson County, Missouri, is a unique citizen-driven community collaborative set up in 1992 to help improve the lives of families and children by working on issues such as school-linked services, health care, employment, housing, welfare reform, and community economic development. Governed by a 36-member commission, it has 35 full- and part-time staff members, a professional cabinet made up of public agency staff and representatives of private service providers, and more than 700 volunteers. The commission is representative of the city, with strong leadership coming from the corporate and business worlds as well as from neighborhood groups.

LINC is also the community partnership that administers the Missouri Caring Communities grants through Comprehensive Neighborhood Services in 28 neighborhoods. Through this channel, LINC funds 60 schools in five school districts with 15,000 students. (The McCoy school mentioned in previous chapters is one of those schools.)

Schools are the hubs for services. A council made up of residents and parents is created in each neighborhood to guide the development and implementation of the neighborhood's plan. LINC reviews each plan, funds some or all of the planned activities, and provides technical assistance and training.

Council Operated: Central Falls, Rhode Island

When the United Way of America, with support from the Wallace-Reader's Digest Extended Services Schools Initiative, was seeking locations to adapt its Bridges to Success community school model, the United Way of Southeastern New England in Providence was quick to respond. In 1997, Allan Stein, United Way vice president for public policy, set up a collaboration with the Central Falls School District and other community agencies called Schools and Communities Organizing to Promote Excellence (SCOPE).

SCOPE is now in transition, broadening its goals and establishing additional programs. In 2001, the Central Falls School District was awarded $1.2 million through the federal 21st Century Community Learning Centers program. This has extended SCOPE's goals, which are

- Improve academic performance
- Enhance social and emotional skills and competence
- Increase employability
- Encourage parent involvement

Programs that are being integrated here include (a) the original adaptation of the Bridges to Success model in three Central Falls schools, featuring a collaboration with the Rhode Island Youth Guidance Center; (b) a statewide early childhood integration effort called Child Opportunity Zones (COZ); (c) Even Start; (d) Head Start; (e) parent engagement and family support activities; (f) school-to-work programs; and (g) career exploration and development.

This project has a structure that holds it all together—SCOPE's districtwide steering council. All the stakeholders sit on this board, including the superintendent of schools, other school district personnel (such as the coordinator of federal grants and the supervisor of buildings and grounds), representatives from United Way and provider groups, parents, students, teachers' union representatives, Rhode Island Department of Education members, and representatives from each school through their School Improvement Teams. All these people (as many as 18 to 20) meet every month.

What makes SCOPE's council unique is that it appears to have power. It controls the distribution and administration of about $2 million from state and federal grants. A full-time executive director runs the council, with a program coordinator at each school. Three committees now function: allocations, evaluation, and public engagement (public relations). It is in the allocations committee that the real work of this initiative takes place. Decisions about what activities to support have to be tied to SCOPE's four goals. The council applies its standards to each proposal to make sure that it is not duplicative and is relevant. In 2001, some 25 programs were spread among the three schools. The framework is described as flexible, with the capacity to move financial support around to meet various needs.

Mario Papitto, Central Falls's coordinator for federal grants and one of the prime movers of this initiative, believes that the strength of the council is the desire of all concerned to do things differently, not just to load a bunch of programs into a schoolhouse. This theme was reiterated by the superintendent of schools and one of the local building principals. They were eager to establish partnerships with youth agencies and to reorient their teaching staffs to integrate classroom work with after-school activities. Staff training takes place at each site with all the constituent agencies participating. Papitto also believes that even without the dollars, the council would still exist as a means of communication between the school system and the CBOs, which share a common concern with the welfare of the children in this community. At a meeting in Providence (February 26, 2001), Papitto said, "SCOPE is not a place where you come to get money. . . . You come here to coordinate services for kids."

The United Way, having tested this strong council model over four years, is ready to go statewide. In a new community school initiative, United Way will work with three or four middle schools in disadvantaged areas in Rhode Island to try to adapt the model. In addition to the SCOPE adaptations, they will set up a Learning Network to involve other schools in what Stein calls "community building" work and to provide technical assistance around the state. United Way will also work closely with the state in shaping policy for the Children's Cabinet, a unique Rhode Island attempt to integrate children's services at the state level. Finally, United Way will bring experts to Rhode Island as they develop within the field of community schools. About $1 million has been put together from state government and foundations to further this activity in the United Way.

School-Community Collaboration: Indianapolis, Indiana

Since 1994, United Way's Bridges to Success (BTS) program in Indianapolis has brought together schools, community agencies, businesses, colleges and universities, cultural institutions, parents, community members, and youth. The goal is to help schools provide for children's basic needs—health, mental health, vision, dental, nutrition—and to support after-school programs and whatever else is needed to reduce barriers to learning. Building on partnerships with more than 300 local organizations, BTS now operates some services in 43 schools, each with a different configuration. This whole program is governed by the BTS council, a collaborative body of high-level institutional partners and service providers, nonprofit organizations, business leaders, principals, parents, and students.

The United Way and Indianapolis Public Schools (IPS) provide day-to-day management; IPS pays for five school coordinators, each of whom oversees the work in a cluster of eight schools. In each school, a site team representative of the school and the constituent agencies oversees the program, meeting once a month. Someone from the team, either school staff (the principal) or community lead-agency worker, is designated as the school contact person for the coordinator.

BTS was funded in 2001 through United Way ($350,000), which supports BTS central staff (the director and administrative assistant), and IPS ($250,000), which pays for the coordinators. A substantial Robert Wood Johnson Foundation grant initiated the development of school-based clinics. The 19 current clinics are supported by five hospitals and the local health foundation; a dental mobile clinic goes from school to school. Other leveraged resources from community agencies for services have added up to almost $3.8 million since BTS's inception.

BTS also maintains an information clearinghouse for local use and for adaptation sites around the country. In 2001 a database was designed that can capture demographics of participants and details on partnerships and outcomes for each school. Debbie Zites, BTS director, told me, "It's amazing what happens when you put a bunch of people in a room and give them an opportunity to create new kinds of programs" (personal interview, October 15, 2001).

Community Based, Agency Operated:
New York City Beacons

Community-based agencies have considerable flexibility in operating Beacons in New York City. They receive grants from the New York City Department of Youth and Community Development to provide services at school sites. Each site is required to have an advisory committee, including the school principal, local police precinct representative, parents, students, community members, and the Beacon director, who chairs the committee.

The operations of the advisory committees vary significantly from strong to weak, and the amount of power they wield at the school level is largely self-determined, though the city requires the submission of minutes from their meetings. The strongest committees drive the activities of the program; for example, they might insist on programs celebrating cultural heritage or involve local merchants in conducting fund drives.

Oversight is provided by the CBO, which employs the director and the staff and receives the grant of $400,000 a year. Another $50,000 goes from the city to the school to pay for space and maintenance. But the Department of Youth and Community Development also provides oversight, employing a staff of 15 to monitor the $43 million program and provide accountability. In addition, another agency, the Youth Development Institute of the New York Fund for Children (a foundation), provides technical assistance and training to the Beacons, with support from other foundations.

Collaborative: Schools Uniting Neighborhoods

This initiative, started jointly by the mayor of Portland, Oregon, and the administrator of Multnomah County, puts together public and private resources in a collaborative relationship called Schools Uniting Neighborhoods (SUN). Oversight is provided by what is called the sponsor group. In addition to the city and county offices, other partners include seven local school districts, two cities, Legacy Health Systems, Casey Family Programs, Casey Foundation, Caring Communities of Multnomah County, and the Bank of America. The sponsor group makes the decisions about which schools should receive grants, based on the schools' responses to requests for proposals. This oversight group meets two or three times annually. Once a quarter, everyone connected with the SUN initiative comes together (school principals, lead agency representatives, site managers, parents, and so on) for training and each site shares key accomplishments with the others.

The Multnomah County Department of Community and Family Services is the managing partner or lead agency and employs the director of the initiative, Kathy Turner. She works with a management advisory team that meets monthly with local site managers and facilitates technical assistance to the sites as they request help. Each school that receives a grant has selected a nonprofit agency (usually a family service or youth service agency) to act as partner in the effort. The school and its community partner hire a SUN site manager to bring together networks of services and volunteers to offer programs.

The governance model calls for a site-based advisory committee, typically involving the principal, the site manager (coordinator), parents, community leaders, a faith community member, and a lead agency representative. However, not all of the SUN schools have fully functioning advisory committees. The most developed sites also have an operating team that meets weekly to consider specific issues relating to children and families in crisis. In these schools, a partners team convened by the principal and site manager meets three or four times a year to look at program mix, operations, safety, and other issues for that specific site.

Business Operated: Simon Youth Foundation

Simon Property Group, the nation's largest mall owner, has created the Simon Youth Foundation, whose first initiative is a partnership with CIS to develop Education Resource Centers in Simon malls. Students with special learning needs can attend classes and receive their high school diplomas in the nontraditional setting of an open learning center. Career training opportunities in sales and management are located right in the mall. The first centers were established in Wichita, Kansas, and Pittsburgh, with others in El Paso, Texas; Palm Beach, Florida; and Indianapolis soon to follow.

CIS manages the day-to-day operations, recruiting teachers, mentors, counselors, and other educational personnel and working with school superintendents to identify students who would benefit. The Education Resource Centers are used for other community-based programs as well, such as adult education and cultural events.

State Models

Many states have created mechanisms at the state level to promote collaboration of services related to children.

California

California's work provides a very comprehensive example (Pioneer Initiatives, 2000), but it's not easy to wend one's way through the daunting bureaucracy and then figure out who does what. In the state's Department of Education, one branch—Child, Youth, and Family Services—through its Learning Support and Partnerships Division, supports Healthy Start (school-linked services), After-School Partnerships, School Health Connections, Family and Community Partnerships, and the Healthy Kids Program. The other branch—Educational Equity, Access, and Support, which includes the Education Support Division—encompasses Student Support Services and Programs, Safe Schools and Violence Prevention, Adult Education, and Educational Options. If you have read this far, you may have observed that at least the titles of the programs represent just about every aspect of full-service community schools.

All this state effort is backed up by the work of the California Center for Community-School Partnerships at the University of California, Davis, School of Education. The center, with support from the state and foundations, provides technical assistance for the Healthy Start initiative and other programs and conducts research on community school practices.

In a guidance document, the state has laid out some of the dimensions of school-community partnerships. They point out that while it is one thing for a school to advocate partnerships, it is another thing to create conditions that allow for effective participation. A key element in fostering effective partnerships is to establish opportunities and procedures specifically to welcome and engage partners in the educational program. It's also essential to provide stakeholder development programs for school staff, families, and community members so that they have the skills to promote and participate meaningfully in collabora-

tive partnerships. The partnership is formed when school and community partners involved in a collaborative, ongoing, and equal working relationship
assume joint responsibility for meeting the needs of the "whole child" and
improving student results. They receive and provide training on education and
learning support issues and clearly understand their roles and responsibilities in
the education sphere.

Oregon

As I write, new legislation is being introduced in state houses around the
country. Oregon provides an interesting if confusing example that involves collaboration at the state and local level but no new funds to set up programs. This
initiative grew out of the Multnomah County SUN project previously described.

In 2001, the Oregon legislature approved an act submitted by the Coalition
for Community Learning Centers. It directs the Departments of Education and
of Human Resources, the State Commission on Children and Families, and the
Oregon Criminal Justice Commission to support the development and implementation of community learning centers. The Department of Human
Resources is responsible for administering the grants and the Department of
Education for evaluating effectiveness. However, the State Commission on
Children and Families in conjunction with local commissions on children and
families or other organizations provides training and technical assistance in
developing these programs.

Community learning centers are defined as school-based or school-linked programs providing informal meeting places and coordination for community
activities, adult education, child care, information and referral, and other
services. Included in this definition are community schools, family resource centers, full-service schools, lighted schools, and 21st Century Community Learning Centers.

It is recommended but not required that (a) school districts provide opportunities for parents to participate in decision making at the school site; (b) employers help parents get time off to allow them to do that; (c) school districts enter
partnerships with business and labor to provide workplace-based professional
development; and (d) school districts form partnerships with recreation groups,
faith-based organizations, social service and health care agencies, businesses,
and child care providers to support the creation of community learning centers.

Schools can either provide the services directly or coordinate with programs
provided through the local commissions on children and families. The following
principles are to be observed: (a) Services should be located as close to the child
and family as possible; (b) attention is to be paid to diversity and cultural differences; (c) continuity of care is a goal; (d) urgent needs are to be addressed; (e)
and services should be coordinated and collaborative to reflect the understanding that no single system can serve all the needs of the child and family. Further,
community learning centers should have an advisory committee to offer guidance on program development and conduct a needs assessment to plan the
effort. The act lists 13 different services and activities (ranging from after-school
enrichment to counseling) that can be coordinated.

The act specifies how the state agencies can evaluate and monitor the program and directs the Legislative Fiscal Office to consult with several agencies to identify resources within existing budgets that may be available for local community learning centers.

Missouri

The Missouri Caring Communities initiative started in 1989 with a cross-systems reform effort among four state agencies—the Departments of Elementary and Secondary Education, Mental Health, Health, and Social Services—in conjunction with the Danforth Foundation. Later the Departments of Labor, Economic Development, and Corrections were added to the collaboration. Leadership is provided by the Family and Community Trust, which was established by the governor to bring together the directors of the constituent agencies and nine private-sector members responsible for advancing management reform and implementing policies to improve the well-being of Missouri's families and children through the Caring Communities program. By 2001, 21 community partnerships had been organized at the local level, along with three collaboratives bringing services to more than 100 local school sites. Communities, businesses, and government continue to help with the planning and delivery of services.

The state sees its role as providing financial and technical assistance, removing bureaucratic barriers, encouraging innovative ideas, and promoting broad participation at the local level. Caring Communities is built around six core goals that are measured annually to evaluate the progress of the initiative:

- Parents working
- Children and families healthy
- Children safe in their families and families safe in their communities
- Children prepared to enter school
- Children and youth succeeding in school
- Youth ready to enter productive adulthood

Although the goals are the same across the communities, each program is unique to meet a variety of needs and resources.

Observations

I find the subject of governance the most difficult to write about. I know what the research says about the importance of formal contracts and carefully planned structural relationships. I am convinced that it is important to have an oversight council that brings together the constituent agencies at the top level, a site-based management team to conduct the work at the school level, and a representative advisory committee to relate to the families and the community. The examples from Kansas City, Indianapolis, and other places show that it is possible to construct these arrangements and make them work. However, I must admit that Sue makes a compelling case, especially in a small school, for one person (probably the principal) just "doing it." She doesn't want to create a new bureaucracy, and maybe she doesn't need to in the setting of a small semirural elementary school.

But, and it's a big but, not every principal wants to work as hard as Sue does. More important, many schools need massive amounts of outside help to overcome barriers to learning, as well as additional managers to facilitate complex programs. Some community agencies have the strength to come into a school and take over responsibility for the support services side of the equation, while others do not. If our goal is to see these models adopted in thousands of communities, we have to be more specific about how to do it. Some community schools will be school led, and others will be CBO led, depending on the resources available in their communities. I believe that in the most desirable form of governance structure, the work of the school system and the community partners becomes so fully integrated that designation of a lead agency ceases to be an issue.

Reflecting on the Canadian experience with full-service schools, the Ontario Secondary School Teachers' Federation resource book states,

> The success of shared governance depends on the strength of the network of relationships formed and the degree to which teachers, support staff, students, parents and community have a voice in school governance. Relationships must be able to withstand the give and take of working through a multiplicity of problems with a group of individuals who have a diversity of beliefs and opinions. Whatever form of shared governance is worked out in the collaborative school, one concept remains constant—the team approach. (Rusk, Shaw, & Joong, 1994, p. 150)

The experience of the Safe Futures initiative, a juvenile delinquency prevention program that called for comprehensive services, provides some insights into the process of collaboration (U.S. Department of Justice, 2000). The study found great variation in the degree of actual systems reform. Just getting the actors from different institutions together was regarded as a good first step. Viable collaborations were perceived as requiring considerable time, effort, and trust. People in authority had to exert their leadership to secure resources and support. Partners had to learn each other's language and the values and norms of the respective fields. And after all the work that goes into building relationships, partnership programs can be discontinued for reasons unrelated to the collaboration. Turnover is endemic, not only among staff but among leaders as well.

Pat Edwards (1996), associate director of the National Center for Community Education in Flint, Michigan, has been involved with community schools for many years. In a review of a number of community school programs, she observed one commonality of most of the evolving models:

> All take place in public schools, yet they are using a nonschool entity (i.e., city government, university, foundation, agency) as the lead agency for the community school. Almost all of the community schools being showcased by national media are using an outside agency in a major capacity. One wonders if most of these efforts have come about in

response to the seeming impenetrability of our bureaucratic school systems. School systems, perhaps more than any other institutions, need to "come up to speed" on the superhighway or they may find themselves playing catch-up from the back of the pack. (p. 33)

MOLLY STARK'S PARTNERS

There is no way that Molly Stark School, on its own, could provide all the services we offer. Our main focus is, and should be, on quality education. All the rest is what we give students to help them be more available to learn.

Many of our community organizations and providers have always served children and families. And of course, schools have always served children and families. Unfortunately, both groups have often served in isolation, giving services piece by piece with no comprehensive, long-term plan.

Some years ago, we saw the need for interventions that can help children and families over a long period of time and are directed toward changing the causes of problems, not just the symptoms. An effective program meets the immediate needs of children and families and, after helping the family through the crisis, works to prevent the problems from resurfacing. In an effective intervention, all parties communicate for the good of the children. To provide such interventions at Molly Stark, we had to begin to define our role as a school differently and look at the relationships between the school and the community in a new way.

Several Types of Partnerships

There are levels of partnerships at Molly Stark. Sunrise Family Resource Center, our earliest collaborator, is an example of a community organization we would consider a full partner. Sunrise is a nonprofit organization in Bennington that provides an array of services to help strengthen children and families, including advocacy for families in crisis, teen parent education and support, and early care and education (child care) for infants and toddlers.

Our partnership with Sunrise has taken many forms. Sunrise is the agency named as our partner in the building of the Family Center (we had to have a local organization as a partner to make sure we carried out community development services in the center). We've shared grant money and resources. At different times, staff members from Sunrise have taught a community leadership course for parents and community members at our school, and since 1999, we have contracted an employee from Sunrise to serve as our family outreach worker, working with Molly Stark families 15 hours per week. We pay the salary for those hours to Sunrise and split the cost of her benefits.

The Tutorial Center, the adult education center in our community, is a somewhat different kind of partner. It has provided GED classes at our school since the Family Center opened. Any interested community member is welcome to take these classes. We do not have to pay for these services because they are open to the public and the Tutorial Center is just using our Family Center as another site.

Another example of this type of partner is Head Start, the organization that has provided the Unlimited Fathering Opportunities, a program for dads and their kids, several times at our school. Again, they are using our site for no fee, and Molly Stark families have easy access.

The pediatrician and psychologist who work with us are also partners. We pay them an hourly fee, and they have provided consultation and direct services to children and their families since 1997. The dentist is considered a major partner, with a practice in the Family Center. We pay him nothing, but he provides an invaluable service to children, and he and his assistant have become significant additions to our school. It isn't unusual to find kids chatting with him in his office. As providers work with us successfully over time, we begin to see them as partners that are helping us help our students.

In addition, many community members act as mentors or teach after-school programs. Although for some it is only short-term, they are all partners in that we share the goal of providing something beneficial to strengthen the lives of children and their families.

Developing Partnerships

Developing strong and effective partnerships was one of the most difficult challenges we faced, because cooperating as genuine partners is hard work. It takes a great deal of effort to share decision making and to let go of turf issues. It helps if all the people involved can see that they will gain something positive from the partnership. In our case, the agencies and providers supply expertise, materials, and sometimes part of their pot of money. On the other side, the school provides easy access to children and their families, facilities, critical information, and sometimes a part of its pot of money. Each party benefits from what the other has to offer. The importance of the link is so basic; communities have a difficult time attracting people and being healthy without good schools, and, of course, it is difficult to have a successful school without good health care, safe children, and access to effective community programs.

Since Molly Stark is clearly the lead agency in our version of the full-service community school model, we have had the opportunity to choose our partners from those who are interested in working in collaboration with our school. When we invite a person to work in our building with the kids and their families, we are less concerned with the agency and more interested in the person. It has become clear to us that agencies don't make the difference; competent, effective people do—people who are willing to do "whatever it takes." Most of the people (or members of their agencies) who were at that original meeting in spring 1996 eventually came on board in some capacity, some more quickly than others. Early in the process, I decided that it truly didn't matter when people joined us as long as what they ended up doing was good for the kids and their parents.

Here are some questions we asked before choosing our partners and service providers:

- Which agencies and providers have Molly Stark children and their families as common clients?

- Is there duplication of services among several providers serving the same clients?
- Who has worked well with our school in the past? Who has a history of making a difference in the lives of children and families?
- Who has shown the ability to work as part of a team and is willing to give up some turf to do so?
- Which agencies and providers will offer the most direct service? (Many agencies are very bureaucratic and require much paperwork and meetings, which doesn't really advance the goal of helping children and families.)

Different agencies use different language, guidelines, and policies. Although these differences are important to consider and discuss, we didn't take too much time worrying about them. Instead, we looked at our common mission and purpose and proceeded with this in mind. We looked for key providers that were willing to look past the way services historically had been delivered and had a passion for helping kids and families.

In addition, we had to determine who at Molly Stark would be responsible for setting up the service providers' schedule. For instance, our site coordinator sets up all the parent and family programs that take place at the Family Center, I set up the schedule for the pediatrician and psychologist, and the dentist and his assistant set up their own schedules and do their own billing. Except for the dentist, I am responsible for making sure everyone is paid from the correct fund.

Things to Consider About Partnerships

- Be sure to have clear letters of agreement between your school and the partner agencies. The agreement should include

  - The time period of the agreement
  - Clearly defined expectations of services
  - The exact amount of money to be exchanged
  - Supervision and hiring policies (it is extremely important that both parties have input in this area—again, the person, not the organization, will make the difference)
  - Provisions for related expenses, such as mileage, office space, equipment, supplies, and telephone
  - A procedure for personnel problems that might arise
  - A staff development plan, if any

- Having enough space for services is always an issue. Before we built the Family Center, we used whatever space we could whenever it was available. The pediatrician and psychologist were sometimes in my office to meet with children and parents. We found ourselves using rooms or parts of rooms that were empty part of the time. We made alternative schedules to use the same spaces.

- Sharing responsibilities is a good way to collaborate when working with families. For example, you might offer a literacy night for parents and children at your school. The school offers the snacks and child care; the agency facilitating the program provides the materials and facilitator.

• Financial reimbursement of outside staff should be discussed and determined by both parties. Outside providers who work with children and families at your school are often paid hourly. Another option when a person from an agency or organization works a certain number of hours per week at your school is to pay a percentage of the person's salary directly to the agency. Who pays benefits and related costs must be determined. One other possibility is to have a person run a business within the school; the school provides space but the service provider receives fees (Medicaid or hourly) and is responsible for the costs of running the business, such as salary and materials. The dental practice at Molly Stark is a good example of this arrangement.

• Because some of the service providers will be at the school only a short time each week, someone at the school must always be available and responsive to the needs of children and parents. Troubles don't arise only when the service provider is available. The ideal situation is to have an array of trusted people (administrator, site coordinator, teacher, guidance counselor) so someone is always available when needed.

• Provide a form for parental permission to share information that encompasses all service agencies—educational, social, health, and the like. It is important that all of the people working with a child and family can share their perspectives.

Like everything else that happens at Molly Stark, nothing about our partnerships is etched in stone. The partnerships and services change as the needs of children and families change. We continue to learn what works and what doesn't work along the way.

7

How Are Parents Brought on Board?

PROGRAMS TO INVOLVE PARENTS

Everyone pays lip service to the importance of parental involvement in school reform programs, but the evidence of accomplishing this goal is quite thin. I have been told repeatedly, "We had a parent program, but nobody came." I think this dissonance between vision and reality reflects poor communication between the staff in many schools and the families in the local community.

Full-service community schools are designed around parent-friendly concepts. This chapter reviews several examples of responsive parent programs, looks at some special components, and supports the centrality of parental involvement in school-community partnerships.

Exemplary Parent Programs

Feinberg-Fisher Elementary School

Katharine Briar-Lawson, dean of social work at State University of New York in Albany, helped initiate a comprehensive parenting program in the Feinberg-Fisher Elementary School in South Miami Beach in 1993 (*Building Strong Full-Service and Community Schools*, 1996). She described the beginning stages:

> A lice crisis was about to close down our school. . . . Nothing worked. Finally, they [school authorities] went to the parents with the most lice who said in effect, "The problem is not bottles of shampoo. The problem is having 18 mattresses in one-room apartments with no electricity and water. You are asking us to use shampoo when we don't have a place to use it. Give us battery-operated vacuum cleaners, coins so we can take the linens to the laundry, and scissors to cut our children's hair. And by the way, there is no place for the kids to do homework. Maybe we need to open up a homework club." (p. 10)

These same parents were invited into the school to create a unique program called RAIN (Referral and Information Network). It provides free assistance to parents and promotes awareness of social services, government agencies, and the school's programs for the students. Parents serve on school management and improvement teams, help in classrooms and in the family resource center, and participate in Saturday and after-school programs with their children. Over the years, the parents have pressed for one-stop social services, a health and mental health center, a child care center, and two Head Start classrooms, all located on site. A full-time parent coordinator/social worker does outreach to parents in the community to promote their increased involvement (and to make sure they have coins for self-service laundries). The RAIN parents have become a potent force in the school community; for example, when the neighborhood was threatened with "gentrification," the parents appealed to the mayor and council to protect low-income housing.

Quitman Street Community School

The Community Agencies Corporation of New Jersey (CACNJ) is the lead agency for the Quitman Street Community School in Newark, an adaptation site of the Children's Aid Society community school model supported by the Prudential Foundation. Under the leadership of Deputy Executive Director Dorothy Knauer, former coordinator Denise Shipman, and current coordinator Josette Mundine, all employed by CACNJ, the school places a heavy emphasis on parent involvement. An attractive family resource center staffed by a full-time parent program coordinator provides focus to this effort. Every parent whose child participates in the after-school program is invited to sign a contract that a family member will volunteer in the school for at least 6 hours during the year. As a result, more than 2,500 hours of time were donated in 2000 by the parents during school hours or before or after (the school is open till 9:00 p.m.). And it was projected that by the end of the 2001–2002 school year, more than 7,000 hours would be contributed.

A rich menu of parent activities is offered. Well-attended adult education classes include GED, karate, aerobics, computer and office skills, dance, and art. At least six parent workshops are held monthly on topics such as breast cancer awareness. More than 60 families participated in a weekend family retreat held at a mountain resort. Many special events are offered to parents, including a Back-to-School Breakfast, Black History Luncheon, and Turkey Dinner Giveaway.

In 2001, CACNJ employed 12 parents as part-time group leaders, youth counselors, and aides in the after-school program. At the end of the school year, 5 of these group leaders were hired by the school principal to serve as full-time paid teachers' aides, qualifying them for benefits from the school system. This seems to me to demonstrate the power of such programs.

The Quitman school staff have received training from Bank Street's New Beginnings program and the Comer School Development Program, helping to create a school environment that encourages parents to participate as volunteers and paid staff. Denise Shipman described Quitman's approach: "Our parents learn that our extended day is not just a baby-sitting service or a homework club; everything we do in the community school is directed toward our mission, to enrich the children's lives" (telephone conversation, September 20, 2001).

Florida Full-Service Schools Program

Calfee and colleagues (1998), in their manual on building a full-service school, present a composite picture of how one community school can deal with family problems. They describe a multiproblem family, referred by a teacher to a case team because one of the two children was acting out. The team—consisting of the teacher, a counselor, and an administrator from the school and a psychologist, nurse, caseworker, and juvenile justice worker from the partner organizations—set up a meeting with the parents. A family care coordination plan was drawn up to document the family's strengths, concerns, and goals. In this case, the plan led to counseling and a specialized after-school program for the son and health services for the daughter. The mother enrolled in evening GED classes and dance lessons held at the school and started volunteering in the school's computer lab. Both parents began attending family counseling sessions with a mental health professional and learned how to use their eligibility for food stamps. They checked out educational materials and attended parenting workshops.

Four years after becoming involved in the full-service school, the family is in much better shape. The mother is employed, the children are doing better in school, and the father has a better job. As they move off welfare and Medicaid eligibility, they are able to enroll in Florida's school-based health insurance, Healthy Kids, for $5 per month per child.

Wake County Education Partnership

The Wake County Education Partnership in North Carolina has launched a major initiative to promote school readiness, literacy, and parent/family involvement. For each of these three categories, action steps were laid out by citizen committees at a countywide summit. The parent program provides a list of activities that are relevant to community schools:

- Provide opportunities through parent groups, work sites, and community agencies for parents to expand their knowledge and skills.
- Help parents gain access to resources about parenting and child development, and teach them to set high expectations for their children and to provide a good learning environment at home.
- Make a family advocate available to each family to plan coordinated family services and create a catalogue for parents of all public and private services.
- Encourage employers to review and revise family-focused policies and programs, such as making time available for parents to attend school events.
- Work through parent groups and community agencies to include more parents, and appoint parent liaisons in each school to help enhance student achievement.

In addition, three groups—Communities-in-Schools, the school system, and the PTA—are seeking 2,000 volunteer parents and community people to establish one-on-one relationships with low-achieving students in Grades 3–8.

Special Components of Parent-Involvement Programs

Family-School Compacts and Contracts

A *compact* is an agreement between families and schools that identifies how a student, parents, and school staff will work together to ensure the student's success in school. This tool for promoting close working relationships between families and schools was developed in California. A *contract* is an agreement between a family and a community school to ensure that the family contributes volunteer time to school-based activities. The Quitman Street Community School has instituted this approach.

Home Visits

A foolproof way to contact parents is to visit them at home. Although this sounds pretty simple-minded, it is amazing how few programs "get it." Of course, staff have to be available to go out into the community and see people. But some programs have successfully trained community members and parents to do outreach, either as volunteers or for very low wages. At a community school in Mt. Vernon, New York, parent outreach workers surveyed the community to determine what the greatest needs were. Much to everyone's amazement, the answer that came back from the visits to the homes was "food." Although the neighborhood did not appear on the surface to be disadvantaged, those parents who had been contacted only through this outreach were in dire poverty. Food packages are now obtained through county food programs and distributed regularly. When these parents finally came to the school, they were able to access clothes banks and a toy-lending library.

The National Coalition for Parent Involvement in Education (NCPIE) offers further advice: Hire and train a liaison to directly contact parents and coordinate family activities. The liaison should be bilingual as needed and sensitive to the needs of family and community, including the non–English-speaking community. The home liaison teacher from the Del Norte Elementary School in El Paso, Texas, teaches parents about nutrition and meal planning, banking, and budgeting.

In some places, the school principal and/or the teachers make home visits. When Hanshaw Middle School in Modesto, California, was implementing its Healthy Start program, the principal visited 500 homes in the area, speaking to them (often in Spanish) about what they wanted the school to do for their children. The parents told him how alienated they felt from the school system, which had resulted in many of their children (and the parents themselves) dropping out.

The principal took the teachers on a bus tour to help them understand their students' lives outside the classroom. The design and character of the school program that emerged provided a challenging and relevant curriculum that supported the students' cultural background and encompassed a life-skills approach.

National Network of Partnership Schools

Dr. Joyce Epstein, director of the National Network of Partnership Schools, is the country's leading guru on parental involvement The organization identifies promising practices and brings together technical assistance and evaluation to help schools implement the framework of parent involvement that Epstein created. One version of her six types of involvement includes sample practices that are found in many full-service community school programs around the country:

1. Parenting—Help all families establish home environments to support children as students:
   - Parent education and other courses or training for parents, such as GED, college credit, family literacy

- Family support programs to assist families with health, nutrition, and other services
- Home visits at transition points to preschool, elementary, middle, and high school

2. Communicating—Design effective forms of school-to-home and home-to-school communications about school programs and children's progress:
   - Conferences with every parent at least once a year
   - Language translators to assist families as needed
   - Regular schedule of useful notices, memos, phone calls, newsletters, and other communications

3. Volunteering—Recruit and organize parent help and support:
   - School and classroom volunteer program to help teachers, administrators, students, and other parents
   - Parent room or family center for volunteer work, meetings, resources for families
   - Annual postcard survey to identify all available talents, times, and locations of volunteers

4. Learning at home—Provide information and ideas to families about how to help students at home with homework and other curriculum-related activities, decisions, and planning:
   - Information for families on skills required for students in all subjects at each grade
   - Information on homework policies and how to monitor and discuss schoolwork at home
   - Family participation in setting student goals each year and in planning for college or work

5. Decision making—Include parents in school decisions, developing parent leaders and representatives:
   - Active PTA/PTO or other parent organizations, advisory councils, or committees for parent leadership and participation
   - Independent advocacy groups to lobby and work for school reform and improvements
   - Networks to link all families with parent representatives

6. Collaborating with community—Identify and integrate resources and services in the community to strengthen school programs, family practices, and student learning and development:
   - Information for students and families on community health, cultural, recreational, social support, and other programs or services
   - Information on community activities that link to learning skills and talents, including summer programs for students
   - Service to the community by students, families, and schools, such as recycling, art, music, drama, and other activities for seniors or others (*Epstein's Six Types of Parent Involvement*, n.d.)

Research on the first 202 schools to join the National Network of Partnership Schools identified the ingredients of successful partnership schools (National Network of Partnership Schools, 2000). These schools had supportive teams that put together school, family, and community representatives. They were likely to have a plan for each of the six types of parental involvement and to evaluate the effectiveness of the plan at the end of each year. The teams were supported with funding, time, leadership, and guidance. The most effective programs were tied into the school's improvement goals, reached all families, were permanent, and were able to access schoolwide Title I funds to develop their programs.

Where Does the PTA Fit In?

During the 1990s, the national PTA experienced a significant decline in membership and support. Some of this was attributed to the impact of increasing numbers of working women and single parents, but questions were also raised about the relevance of a middle class–oriented organization to inner-city and minority families. Thomas Toch (2001), writing in the *New York Times*, suggested that such a model relegated parents "to the periphery of school life." The PTA has been responsive to such criticism and now supports a more contemporary approach that helps schools share with parents such items as homework assignments, involves parents as tutors and mentors, and invites parents to take a direct role in managing schools. In this "move beyond bake sales," the national PTA supports Epstein's six standards for parent involvement in schools. In Chicago, for example, the PTA is supportive of school councils composed of six parents, two teachers, the principal, and two community representatives; these powerful councils can hire principals and change budgets.

Observations

Parents will come if they are invited to participate in activities that are relevant, useful, and nonthreatening. I have seen parents crowd into family resource centers at the Children's Aid Society adaptation sites, eager to obtain information they need to improve their family welfare. This may include immigration law, housing assistance, and employment advice, as well as guidance on how to relate to their children. I have seen parents in great numbers participating in a school Christmas fair that sold gifts made by parent-child teams. Parents come in droves to community dinners and musical events. They love to watch their children perform.

I have emphasized repeatedly the importance of having a full-time coordinator in a community school. In a school like Feinberg-Fisher Elementary, parent activities can easily occupy the time of one full-time worker; Quitman Street Community School found the same time requirement. Schools cannot by themselves perform all the requisite activities to make parents feel comfortable in the school setting. The presence of staff from an indigenous community-based organization is often critical to building trust with people in the community who feel alienated and not represented in the school hierarchy. The rationale for partnerships is very strong in this area.

A number of activities have been outlined here that can be undertaken in community schools to bring parents into the process of educating their children. It is hard to rank these types of programs or say whether communicating with parents is more important than providing educational enrichment. One study of eight schools that effectively involved parents of limited English proficiency students found that they shared certain characteristics (McLeod, n.d.). These successful schools went out of their way to demonstrate respect for the parents, especially in terms of cultural and language differences. They were educational resources for the parents as well as the children and enlisted the parents as partners in their children's education. A concerted effort was made to involve the parents, particularly in the governance of the school. And finally, of importance to advocates of full-service community schools, these parent-friendly schools provided an array of social, health, and mental health services to the students and their families.

WORKING WITH FAMILIES AT MOLLY STARK

"You cannot provide services that touch the most intimate levels of a child's life without the understanding and recognition that many parents have a lot to say, whether they are poor, educated, opinionated, scared, or needy." In spring 2000, these words were spoken at a conference of the Collaborative for Integrated School Services by panelist Rosa Agosto, director of family and children's services of the Education Alliance in New York City. They are powerful, and I often think about them.

Parents *are* the most important and influential teachers for their children. I have worked with hundreds of parents throughout my career and have found that they sincerely love their children and want what is best for them. However, this doesn't necessarily mean that all parents have the skills and emotional wherewithal to know or do what is best for their kids.

We knew from the beginning that establishing and maintaining positive and productive relationships with parents so they could better support their children, although sometimes challenging, was an essential factor for improving outcomes for our students. Time and time again, researchers have concluded that family involvement is one of the most accurate predictors of student success. The children of parents who are involved stay in school longer, earn better grades, and produce higher test scores. We don't need to read more studies to know this. It makes perfect sense.

As in most schools, our relationship with parents has been inconsistent and often dependent on the interpersonal skills of our staff. Some staff members are naturally good with people and can work well with all parents; these staff can look beyond their own set of norms and beliefs and make each relationship a positive one. Although not necessarily consciously, others sometimes identify and stereotype parents according to the family situation, education, or income and may define them as intrusive, apathetic, pushy, or hostile. These attitudes, in turn, reinforce the parents' perception that the school is not a friendly place, which of course causes a serious block to maintaining a trusting and collaborative relationship.

On the other side, many parents have had negative experiences with schools and other public agencies; they may avoid contact or approach us in a defensive way, talking inappropriately. Some are engaged in day-to-day struggles over housing, food, lack of a job, or other family crisis. Sometimes what seems to be a lack of interest in their child's education is something much larger. On top of their daily challenges, they often have to face a confusing bureaucracy to help their children. Whatever the reason, we realized that the traditional ways to reach some parents hadn't worked. We had to find a way to communicate with all parents from widely varying backgrounds.

A valuable in-service around the issue of creating positive relationships with parents took place in September 1998, when I invited a teacher and parent from Norfolk, Virginia, to spend a day with us at Molly Stark. I had heard Rachelle Hayes-Ruff speak at a conference and was touched by her evolution toward working in a positive way with her children's school. She told us honestly that she and her sons were a "package deal" and described her transition to becoming an integral part of a school that welcomed and supported parents. She said, "Parents were always welcomed in the building, even parents that, on the outside, looked like troublemakers. There was always a soft, kind word to encourage them to think positively and change their negativeness into positive, good energy that would help light their child's way." It was a powerful statement, and she had the staff listening intently.

During her talk, she asked a very important question: How many staff members had visited the housing project where many of our families lived? I was shocked to see only five hands go up. It was the day before school was to begin. I told the teachers that anyone interested was to meet out front at noon and we would walk across the street to the housing project and talk with children and parents about how much we looked forward to beginning the year with them. More than 30 staff members showed up for the visit. Children and parents came outside to talk and seemed excited that we took the time to connect. The next day we had our annual family picnic to kick off the new school year, and there was a real feeling of interaction and solidarity.

That fall we took on a staff goal. It was parent-teacher conference time, and we decided we would try to get 100 percent participation; that is, every child would be represented by at least one parent at the conference. It became a real team effort. After the first attempts by the classroom teachers, they handed in lists of parents who did not or could not attend, and then a staff member (whoever had the best relationship with that particular parent) would make contact through a phone call or a home visit. As a result, parents represented all but three of our students at that round of conferences. This is a goal you have to keep on top of and show the same commitment to at each of the two conference periods each year. It doesn't always happen because it takes so much time and effort.

Another thing we learned that year is that we often make unfair assumptions about parents. One mother had four children at our school, all of whom were well-behaved, good students. But for some reason, she would sign up for conferences and never actually come. When the classroom teachers handed in her name as a no-show, we decided the guidance counselor should connect with her because they had had positive phone conversations throughout that school year. When the guidance counselor went to the house, the mom shared something that we hadn't known: She had a true phobia when around people, and each time she had tried to come up to the school, she hadn't been able to follow through. She asked the guidance counselor to take her to the school and stay with her as she met with the teachers. The conferences were a success, and her kids were thrilled with her visit to the school. Whenever I begin to judge a parent in my mind, I think back to this misjudgment we made.

Things to Consider When Working With Families

- Listen. Don't assume you know what the parent wants or needs.
- Try to have empathy. All families face challenges at times.
- Look for the strengths of the family members.
- Look at the child within his or her family, not in isolation.
- Give clear, understandable information.
- Give parents specific things they can do to help their children (like reading to the kids, asking about their schoolwork each day, and talking with them).
- Establish positive contact with parents early in the year.
- Take care in presenting bad news to parents: Don't wait; focus on the issue; avoid being judgmental; counterbalance it by mentioning the student's strengths.
- Make an effort to understand the family's background. Some parents have very different expectations and customs concerning their children, parent involvement, communication with the school, and so on. What sounds like a good piece of advice from us may be unrealistic in the context of what is happening in the lives of some families.
- Ask for continual verbal and/or written feedback.
- Encourage parents to ask good questions about their children. Understand that you may have to teach some parents these skills.

We began to make real headway when we stopped assuming we knew what our parents felt, wanted, or hoped for their children. Only when we began to sincerely listen did we really hear. We found that the best place to start when working with families is with issues of interest or concern to them. For some of our parents, it was the desire for their children to be challenged to reach their potential. For others, it included such issues as needing help to find housing or talking through a family crisis.

Today we have parents involved in our school in many ways. Some facilitate after-school programs and others are actively involved in their children's classrooms. Many participate in the wide variety of programs and activities we offer during the day and in the evening. We have found that parental involvement is a comprehensive, year-round effort that has as much to do with our everyday responsiveness and courtesy as it does with anything else. It is about stopping to talk with parents when we see them in the hallway or in front of the school, it's about returning their phone calls promptly, and it's about listening to what they need and want instead of assuming we know all the answers. It requires ongoing energy and effort, but in the long run, it is a crucial piece of a school community.

In spring 2001, a parent came to our site coordinator to ask for help. She had papers to fill out for an agency, and she couldn't read well enough to complete them. When I heard this story, I recognized the amount of trust a parent needs to be able to ask for this kind of help, and I knew we had come a long way.

8

Do Community Schools Work? Assessment and Evaluation

EVALUATION OF COMMUNITY SCHOOLS THROUGHOUT THE COUNTRY

Across the nation, initiatives for youth, families, and neighborhoods are under increasing pressure to demonstrate that they make a difference. The community schools movement is not exempt from such scrutiny. At this stage, we know that community school initiatives are beginning to produce positive results, and increasing numbers of principals and teachers are testifying to their value in helping to improve student learning and to strengthen families and communities.

As we have said, *community school* is an inclusive term, encompassing a growing number of school-community initiatives that feature both common themes and differing approaches. The names of the initiatives suggest some of their varying attributes: Caring Communities, Beacons, Bridges to Success, university-assisted schools, Healthy Start, Communities in Schools, Schools of the 21st Century, and many others. Some are broad in scope, promoting widespread replication or adaptation, while others are single entities. Programs are being promulgated at the national level (for example, the Children's Aid Society and Schools of the 21st Century), state level (for example, the New Jersey School-Based Youth Services Program), and local level (for example, the Polk Brothers Foundation Full-Service School Initiative in Chicago), and in individual schools (for example, Molly Stark). Community schools also vary in their goals. Some specifically aim to improve academic achievement, and others focus primarily on health and behavioral outcomes or enhanced family functioning.

This chapter builds on *Evaluation of Community Schools: Findings to Date* (Dryfoos, 2000), a monograph I wrote for the Coalition for Community Schools with a lot of help from Laura Samberg and Martin Blank. Here I summarize a range of results from a variety of research and present examples of local, state, and national community school evaluations.

How Do We Know Whether Community Schools Are Effective?

Policymakers and practitioners want to know what kinds of positive changes community schools can make. Before addressing this question, we must first ask, "Given our vision, what indicators of success should we be looking for?"

Because we believe that community school concepts belong in the domain of education reform, improved learning and achievement must be a long-term objective of this growing movement. In addition to test scores, indicators of learning and achievement include rates of attendance, promotion, graduation, suspension, and expulsion. It is important to note that many community school models are designed to affect not only education outcomes but also other outcomes that, in turn, are known to affect education outcomes. Such intermediate outcomes include improved social behavior and healthy youth development, better family functioning and increased parental involvement, enhanced school and community climate, and access to support services.

The data summarized here indicate that community school initiatives are moving in the right direction across many different indicators of success, giving us cause for optimism. The story is not complete, however. First, it should be noted that the programs cover a broad continuum, from fully realized community schools that have been in existence for a decade or longer to schools that are just beginning to open their doors and offer expanded opportunities such as after-school activities. Second, the quality of assessment reports varies enormously, from evaluations that relied on very small nonrepresentative samples to those based on carefully designed management information systems and control groups. At best, evaluation is difficult, expensive, and long term. Only a few programs can produce what would pass for "scientific" results. Many others can offer "preliminary findings," early returns on long-term projects.

Across the country, researchers are struggling to do a better job of documenting the effects of these programs. The constraints are many when one tries to track events in an experimental program offered in a setting (public school) that does not lend itself to experimental conditions. With these complexities in mind, Lisbeth Schorr and Daniel Yankelovich (2000) have argued for moving ahead with social programs and not getting bogged down in methodological warfare:

> Evaluating complex social programs is not like testing a new drug. The interventions needed to rescue inner-city schools, strengthen families, and rebuild neighborhoods are not stable chemicals manufactured and administered in standardized doses. Promising social programs are sprawling efforts with multiple components requiring constant mid-course corrections, the active involvement of committed human beings, and flexible adaptation to local circumstances. (p. 7)

What is most important is the growing evidence that community schools have begun to demonstrate positive effects on students, families, and communities. The preliminary data summarized here suggest that many of these models have the capacity to produce multiple impacts that include and go beyond the expectations of traditional education reform.

Sources of Information

The monograph I wrote in 2000 was a first attempt to compile documentation on the impact of community schools. Many evaluations are currently under way, and within the next several years, we should have access to much more information. My experience so far has been that the literature on community schools is mostly "hidden." Compiling the information involves extracting annual reports and unpublished documents from researchers and program administrators throughout the country. Web sites are a great benefit because one can download reports that are difficult to obtain in hard copy and have not been (and probably never will be) published (see Resources). A search on the Internet for "community schools" or "full-service schools" yields thousands of citations.

Measures of Effectiveness

In my research in mid-2000, I was able to obtain information on 49 school-community programs that have produced evaluation reports or data on results since about 1998 (although a few were conducted in the mid-1990s). No two initiatives are alike, nor are the research protocols. Of the 49 programs, 6 are after-school initiatives such as LA's BEST. Some reports, such as that on the large-scale California Healthy Start initiative, aggregate findings for hundreds of schools. Other programs, such as Communities-in-Schools (CIS), have submitted reports at state, community, and local site levels (counted as one report). Other evaluation efforts focus exclusively on one school, such as the study of the Broad Acres Elementary Linkages to Learning School in Montgomery County, Maryland. Thus the count of reports is rough and is intended to serve as an estimate of the large quantity of information that is becoming available.

All the reports present findings on one or more outcomes, such as improved academic achievement, change in student behavior, or increased parental involvement. In 46 of the reports, some positive changes were noted; 3 report no positive changes—that is, students in the schools with the programs either did no better than those in comparison schools or did not improve in performance or behavior over time. Highlights of the compilation on outcomes are presented in the sections that follow.

Learning and Achievement Outcomes

Achievement. Thirty-six of the 49 programs reported academic gains. These gains generally included improvements in reading and math test scores, looked at over a two- or three-year period. Many of the programs reporting academic gains were in elementary schools. In at least eight cases, the outcomes were not schoolwide. Rather, they were limited to students who received special services, such as case management, intensive mental health services, or extended-day sessions.

However, there were some instances of schoolwide improvements on academic measures:

- Charles Drew Elementary School, a participating school in the University of Pennsylvania's West Philadelphia Improvement Corps program, showed more improvement (an increase of 420 points) on the state's standardized reading and math tests than any other school in the state in 1999.
- At PS 5, a Children's Aid Society community school in New York City, the percentage of children reading at grade level rose from 28 percent in Grade 4 to 42 percent by the time they completed Grade 6.

Attendance. Nineteen programs reported improvements in school attendance. Several reported lower dropout rates, one specifically among pregnant and parenting teens. Several mentioned higher teacher attendance rates, suggesting higher levels of satisfaction. Here are examples of positive results in this area:

- A national evaluation of CIS found that about 70 percent of students with high absenteeism before participation in CIS improved their attendance.

- At Lane Middle School, one of the Schools Uniting Neighborhoods sites in Portland, Oregon, attendance increased from 85 percent to 91 percent over two years.

Suspensions. Eleven programs reported a reduction in suspensions. This may reflect changes in suspension policies rather than changes in behaviors leading to suspensions. As schools transform into more child-centered institutions, they are likely to change practices regarding suspensions and expulsions as part of the change in school climate.

- At the Woodrow Wilson Middle School (an Iowa School-Based Youth Services Program adaptation), the rate of suspensions in 1995 was one-sixth the rate five years earlier.
- At Lane Middle School in Portland, Oregon, suspensions declined from 50 to 15 in two years.

Behavioral Outcomes

High-Risk Behaviors. Eleven programs reported general improvement in behavior and/or reductions in rates of substance abuse, teen pregnancy, and disruptive behavior in the classroom. These are examples:

- An evaluation based on 138 grantees in California's Healthy Start initiative found that students receiving Healthy Start services decreased their drug use.
- The Blenheim School (one of Missouri's Caring Communities sites) reported a 40 percent decrease in disruptive behavioral incidents following the implementation of a system for referrals for clinical therapy.

Family Well-Being

Parent Involvement. At least 12 of the programs reported increases in parent involvement. For example, at the Bryant School, a Missouri Caring Communities site with an intensive family intervention program, volunteer hours increased from 43 in 1996 to 2,008 in 1998.

Family Functioning. In many programs with a strong family focus, improved family functioning was reported.

- Parents who received Schools of the 21st Century services were able to improve their child development practices, were less stressed, spent less money on child care, and missed fewer days of work.

- An evaluation of 138 grantees of California's Healthy Start initiative found that families reported improvement in filling basic needs such as housing, food and clothing, transportation, finances, and employment.

Community Life

Access to Services. Better access to health care, access to dental care, lower hospitalization rates, and higher immunization rates were reported at least once. After-school programs cited access to child care as a significant outcome.

- As a result of putting full-time school nurses in school sites in the Success Program in Des Moines's public schools, 97 percent of the children were immunized. Dental screenings produced a 34 percent increase in improved oral hygiene and a 36 percent decrease in referrals for cavities.

- At Broad Acres Elementary School in Montgomery County, Maryland, a Linkages to Learning site, access to health care was greatly increased, reducing the percentage of families who reported no health care access for their children from 53 percent to 10 percent, and of those with no insurance coverage from 38 percent to 10 percent.

Neighborhood. Six programs reported lower violence rates and safer streets in their communities. A unique finding was the reduction in student mobility reported by the Polk Brothers Foundation Full-Service School Initiative, as described in the next section.

It should be noted that most of the programs affected more than one outcome, reflecting both the design and the comprehensiveness of the research and the program. For example, the Marshalltown, Iowa, Caring Connection program appeared to have an impact on both academic achievement and youth development. The Children's Aid Society affected school performance as well as parent involvement and community safety. Elizabeth Learning Center in Cudahy, California, also improved school performance, lowered the dropout rate, and brought parents into the school.

Examples (compiled by Laura Samberg, formerly at Coalition for Community Schools)

*Polk Brothers Foundation Full-Service
School Initiative: A Local Program*

The goal of the Polk Brothers Foundation Full-Service School Initiative is to improve the physical and psychological well-being of children in three Chicago schools, thereby making a positive impact on their school-related behavior and academic achievement. Support services are brought into the school that meet the needs and desires of families and strengthen the relationships between parents and school personnel. Each partnership is required to set up a governance body and hire a full-time coordinator to oversee the operations.

The three schools and their partners are Brentano Elementary/Logan Square Neighborhood Association, Marquette Elementary/Metropolitan Family Services, and Riis Elementary/Youth Guidance. The schools are open after school and in the evening. Each has a different set of programs, including parent involvement, recreation, school remediation, and tutoring.

Emerging evidence from an evaluation of the Full-Service School Initiative conducted by the Chapin Hall Center for Children at the University of Chicago is promising:

- While mobility patterns varied, average mobility declined from 1996 to 1999 at all three schools to levels at or below the citywide average. More children are in school for longer periods, creating more chances to learn and participate in programs.

- Reading scores improved at rates exceeding the citywide average at all three schools. Improvement in reading has been among the toughest challenges facing Chicago public schools.

- By the first half of 1999, all three schools were actively acquiring resources from more than 25 outside organizations each. More organizations are using the school to reach children and families who need their services, one of the primary objectives of full-service schools.

- Parents surveyed reported an increase in the number of adults in after-school programs who could be trusted to help their children with serious problems. When parents see the school as a friend of the family and a safe haven, they are more likely to support the school in maintaining high expectations for learning and appropriate behavior, and the climate of the school improves.

- Teachers surveyed reported an increase in the number of adults in after-school programs who know children in the school well as individuals. As teachers are convinced that after-school staff are concerned and competent, they are more likely themselves to find new ways to get involved in the lives of their students.

Two of the three partnerships are continuing without direct financial support from the foundation. Both schools are using private, state, and federal funding to cover the coordinator's salary, security costs, and some programming. The third school will be supported mostly by the school system. This program is expanding to other schools in Chicago with support from the Dimon Foundation and Bank One.

The New Jersey School-Based Youth Services Program: A State Program

The New Jersey School-Based Youth Services Program (SBYSP), developed by the New Jersey Department of Human Resources in 1987, was the first major state program that gave grants to community agencies to link education and human services, health, and employment systems. The "one-stop" program has been initiated by schools and community agency partners in 29 school districts (at least one in each county). Each site offers a range of services, including crisis intervention, counseling, health services, drug and alcohol abuse counseling, employment services, summer job development, and recreation. Some offer day care, teen parenting education, vocational services, family planning, transportation, and hot lines.

The Academy for Educational Development conducted a three-year longitudinal evaluation of the SBYSP that compared survey responses and school data for two groups: students who took advantage of SBYSP services and activities and those who did not. The evaluation was statistically controlled for important background variables, such as family stress, access to support from family and other adults, and participation in positive youth activities. Findings showed that in the six schools studied, SBYSP was clearly reaching the most vulnerable students and had been able to make important differences in their lives.

Overall, analyses of students' responses to the baseline and follow-up surveys, controlling for baseline levels of behavior, family stress, family and other adult support, and participation in youth activities, showed positive change in 39 of the 45 outcomes studied in the evaluation and statistically significant positive change in 14 of the 45 outcomes. Factors that showed positive changes at statistically significant levels included (a) educational aspirations; (b) academic credits earned; (c) access to reproductive health information, peer support, and family support; (d) use of contraceptives to prevent pregnancy; and (e) use of condoms to prevent STDs. Significant reductions were shown in factors such as (a) trouble sleeping; (b) feelings of unhappiness, sadness, or depression; (c) worrying "too much"; (d) feelings of anger and destructiveness; (e) suicidal thoughts; (f) smoking; (g) deliberately damaging property; and (h) hitting others with intent to hurt. These are all important indicators of program effect.

Schools of the 21st Century: A National Model

Schools of the 21st Century (21C) is a model for school-based child care and family support services that transforms the traditional school into a year-round, multiservice center that is open from early morning to early evening. The ultimate goal of 21C is to help provide affordable, accessible, high-quality services for all families, regardless of income level, in order to ensure the optimal development of children. Although 21C schools vary according to local needs and resources, the model includes six core components: parent outreach and education; preschool-age programs; before- and after-school and vacation programs for school-age children; health education and services; networks and training for child care providers; and information and referral services. Since its inception in 1988, more than 600 schools in 17 states have implemented 21C programs.

Research indicates that the combination of services provided in the 21C model has strong benefits for children, parents, and schools:

• Children in 21C schools demonstrate improved academic outcomes. Children who participate in 21C beginning at age three start kindergarten more ready to learn, as evidenced by their scores on kindergarten screening tests.

- Additionally, children who participate in 21C for at least three years score higher on mathematics and reading achievement tests than children in a comparison non-21C school.

- 21C parents reported that they experience significantly less stress, as measured by a parental stress index, they spend less money on child care, and they miss fewer days of work.

- The addition of early childhood classes to the school has had a positive impact on teaching practices, with teachers in the primary grades incorporating the best aspects of early childhood classrooms, such as providing more individual attention within the context of appropriate developmental levels.

- The expanded services provided by 21C schools have improved their standing within the larger community, as evidenced by more positive public relations, the passage of significant bond issues, and a substantial reduction in school vandalism.

Observations

Anthony Masiello, mayor of Buffalo, New York, is enthusiastic about his Mayor's Community Schools Project:

> Community schools impact on our neighborhoods in many ways. Students are offered a safe haven, with academic enrichment and cultural and recreational activities, during extended-day and [extended-]year programs. Parents, who often had few positive early educational experiences, feel welcome at a community school. These parents are able to take advantage of adult education opportunities at a community school, with the added benefit of providing the example to their children that education is important. Community school programs "even the playing field" on which children and adults may achieve their fullest potential. (handout, February 2001)

We can be quite optimistic about the potential impact of full-service community schools. But because many interventions are taking place in these schools at the same time (for example, many are adapting school reform models while at the same time undergoing transformation to community school status), it is not always possible to attribute success to one aspect of the changes that are occurring. Much of the programming in community schools focuses on after-school initiatives targeted at a subset of the students. Often, special-education children are not included in these programs, and disruptive, high-risk kids are not encouraged to enroll. Yet the success of the program is often evaluated in terms of improvements in the whole school: For example, did the test scores rise for the school? If the participants are primarily low-risk students whose performance is already high, I would not expect any significant overall change.

A great deal has been written in recent years about the importance of starting out programs with strong "theories of change." This means that the planners must have a clear idea of what activities are expected to have what short-term and long-term impacts. The program should be focused on those activities. And the evaluation should measure what pieces have been implemented and what effects those pieces have. All this sounds easier in theory than it is in practice.

The authors of *Practical Evaluation for Collaborative Services* (Veale, Morley, & Erickson, 2002), based on their long experience with designing and implementing systems for Iowa's SBYSP, point out, "Assessment and evaluation should be considered essential and feasible. Plenty of aids are available to accomplish the task. . . . The satisfaction of being sure of service implementation and outcomes is gratifying and provides a feeling of stability and security. The reward of funding and public support ensures a future for everyone" (p. 138).

Community school advocates and evaluators may take solace in the fact that few school reform models have been able to produce solid evidence of success. A review in 2000 of 24 "whole-school," "comprehensive," or "schoolwide" approaches was not too encouraging (American Association of School Administrators, 2000). The study used a five-point scale ranging from strong evidence of positive effects (5) to no research at all (0). Only three school reform models were rated strong, five were promising, six marginal, one weak, and eight had no research at all (one model was left off the chart).

It is time for community schools to be recognized as an important component of the education reform movement. Most of these programs aim not only to improve school performance but to change the lives of children and their families and reduce social barriers to learning. These initiatives recognize that the forces for upgrading the quality of education must be joined with the provision of strong supports.

THE IMPACT OF MOLLY STARK'S PROGRAM

Assessing the outcomes of the opportunities we provide at Molly Stark is a difficult task. Simply saying that the support and opportunities we offer are good for children and families is not enough. We know that the public, the parents, the school district, and the state are interested in knowing if the programs and services that we couple with good instruction are indeed improving academic achievement. This is not an unreasonable question, given that our stated goal is to have our students be successful in school.

We know how health and social issues can negatively affect the outcomes of good instruction. But having to demonstrate that improvement in health and social problems actually leads to improvement in academic success is a real challenge.

The difficult part comes in knowing what is important to assess and how it can be done accurately. Early in this process, we decided to collect data in three outcome areas: reduction of physical and verbal aggression among our students (which had been a focal point for a long time), increase in parent interest and involvement, and, of course, academic success of the students.

Early Findings

To see "how we were doing so far," we commissioned a report from an independent evaluator through Harvard University, which was completed in 1999. The evaluator looked at such issues as parent support, student behavior, and academic success as measured by state standards tests in math and language arts. The findings for the three years from 1996 to 1999 were as follows:

- Parents who traditionally were not actively involved in their child's education were more involved than they had been three years earlier and were more likely to come to the school to participate in some way. For example, over three years, the percentage of parents attending parent-teacher conferences rose from 87 percent to 98 percent.

- Discipline referrals had decreased significantly over three years from an average of over 100 per month to 35 per month.

- In the Developmental Reading Assessment, a running record given to second graders each spring since the 1997–1998 school year, between 65 percent and 75 percent of our students had met or exceeded the state standard each year.

Progress of Fourth Graders, 1997–2001

Tables 8.1 through 8.4 show our school's achievement compared with the school district and the state over the last five years, from 1997 to 2001. It is important to note that we are compared on an equal basis with the other elementary schools in the Bennington district, even those that have very low poverty rates and very few students with special needs. For example, one school has 5 percent special education children in contrast to our 20 percent, and only 7 percent of its students receive free or reduced-cost lunches as opposed to Molly Stark's 54 percent (2000–2001 statistics).

Vermont state standards tests are scored in five categories: achieved with honor, achieved, almost achieved, below standard, and little evidence (which is the lowest category). As the tables show, our fourth graders improved in every subject and now are near, at, or above state standards. For example, from 1997 to 2001, in basic understanding in reading, the proportion of students achieving the state standard went from 41 percent to 84 percent. This 43-point gain is significantly greater than the district's gain of 19 points or the state's 20 points. In spring 2001, we scored in the same range as or even higher than the other elementary schools in the district and state, and in every test except math problem solving, the percentage of students who showed "little evidence" was reduced to zero.

(text continues on page 142)

Table 8.1 Percentage of Fourth Graders Achieving State Standards in Reading/English Language Arts

	1997	1998	1999	2000	2001		1997	1998	1999	2000	2001
Basic Understanding						*Analysis/Interpretation*					
Molly Stark	41	63	73	62	84	Molly Stark	22	39	47	36	74
District	57	73	83	73	76	District	42	52	65	50	69
State	59	79	86	83	79	State	59	57	68	64	67
Writing Effectiveness						*Writing Conventions*					
Molly Stark	39	21	30	32	58	Molly Stark	34	27	32	32	45
District	60	25	52	48	51	District	45	53	47	42	55
State	49	35	64	58	53	State	50	51	52	49	57

Table 8.2 Percentage of Fourth Graders Achieving Below State Standards or "Little Evidence" in Reading/English Language Arts

	Below Standard					Little Evidence				
	1997	1998	1999	2000	2001	1997	1998	1999	2000	2001
Reading										
Basic understanding	17	13	8	18	8	0	0	0	0	0
Analyze/interpret	32	15	7	0	5	5	0	0	0	0
Writing										
Effectiveness	15	35	22	8	11	2	2	2	0	0
Conventions	24	45	22	24	0	2	0	0	0	0

Table 8.3   Percentage of Fourth Graders Achieving State Standards in Mathematics

	1997	1998	1999	2000	2001
Concepts					
Molly Stark	3	11	22	14	42
District	12	29	31	25	40
State	No data	32	38	38	42
Skills					
Molly Stark	24	41	45	56	68
District	44	59	57	58	69
State	No data	62	67	68	69
Problem Solving					
Molly Stark	7	22	24	24	30
District	11	27	24	35	34
State	No data	27	35	30	31

The increase in test results didn't come from one particular factor. In my opinion, there are many reasons for the improvement, from offering relevant professional development opportunities to reducing the fourth-grade class size to having teachers convey the message to students that academic success is important.

And although the results are positive, as principal of Molly Stark, I know some important things that no test results can reveal. Academic success, parent involvement, and student aggression are ongoing issues—they are not going to suddenly get better so we can stop working so hard on them. Almost all the parents came to the parent-teacher conferences because the staff put in a determined effort through phone calls and home visits to make sure the ones considered not likely to come would show up. For many parents, these same supports and reminders will be required for every scheduled conference.

Physical and verbal aggression decreased significantly, but now we are revisiting our discipline policy because we can see a slow but sure increase in the number of students who are disrespectful and exhibit poor social skills. We have reconvened a focus group to once again look at this issue.

Our test scores have been rising since we began the full-service community school process. However, some of the results are dependent on the particular group of students being tested that year: how many students have special needs, how many simply can't sit and take such a long test, and how many came to school hungry, tired, or angry that morning.

Accountability for results is a national issue in education. We felt the pressures of high-stakes testing before we developed the community school, and we

Table 8.4 Percentage of Fourth Graders Achieving Below State Standards or Showing "Little Evidence" in Mathematics

	Below Standard					Little Evidence				
	1997	1998	1999	2000	2001	1997	1998	1999	2000	2001
Concepts	71	51	37	40	25	18	0	2	2	0
Skills	24	21	25	16	10	3	0	0	0	0
Problem solving	79	57	42	48	45	8	6	14	6	8

continue to feel it now. The state, district, and community members who look to these tests to define successful and unsuccessful students don't acknowledge that our percentages have increased so dramatically; we continue to be compared with other schools that have much more advantaged populations. We have collected data showing individual progress, but achievement of standards may not be attained by the crucial second and fourth grades, when the state standards tests are given. Too often, the gaps in experience and skills with which kindergarten students enter school will remain with them even as they learn and progress.

My point is that if you are working with a high-risk population of children, the test score hysteria is counterproductive. You must always continue to look at what you have to do at the present time to make it all work, and making it all work can mean different things for each child and family.

Assessing the Community School Model

Another area that we are continuously assessing is our collaborative partnerships. Effective collaboration should be judged by the positive impact it has on students and families, not by whether we follow the right procedures to deliver some services. For example, playgroups were started in the community room of one of our subsidized housing tracts. Repeatedly, their sponsors said how good it was that this opportunity was available. However, we discovered that not one of our low-income parents (the target population) was attending with their children. When we questioned some of our parents, they said they felt intimidated by the "other parents." Here was an example of a situation that appeared to be helpful but was not actually meeting its goal.

Another good example of ineffective collaboration was when we decided to hire a social worker through our community's mental health facility. She was required to spend several hours per week in staff and supervision meetings at her site rather than delivering services at our school. In addition, her first task was always to make the parents fill out multiple information sheets that included several personal questions. Although both of these practices were mandated by policy, neither was good for the children or their families. After assessing the situation, we decided not to use this service delivery model with this organization. Instead, we hired a clinical social worker and paid her hourly to work with our students. The bureaucratic obstacles went away, and we served children and families more effectively.

It is difficult to single out what factors actually caused the positive changes at Molly Stark. My theory is that the comprehensiveness of what we are doing is crucial, and what matters most is different for each individual. The biggest challenge is measuring prevention, measuring what our students would be doing in the absence of our programs.

We decided it was time to look at the long-term effects of our community school, so we hired a researcher from the University of Vermont to set up an evaluation design to begin in the 2001–2002 school year; it includes both quantitative and qualitative research methods and a broad-based assessment of outcomes. We began collecting data in our preschool with the expectation of following these children and families over time. We are giving the Ireton Child Development Inventory (Ireton, 1992) to teachers and parents to assess the children's progress in core areas of development known to be related to later school performance, including measures of emotional and behavioral progress. In addition, teachers are given the Achenbach Caregiver-Teacher Report Form (Achenbach System of Empirically Based Assessment, 1997), a measure of emotional and behavioral problems. Parents are asked to complete the Abidin Parenting Stress Index (Abidin, 1995), a parent report measure that assesses six child outcomes and seven parent outcomes. This index provides a base for assessing several important dimensions of the child's social and emotional growth, as well as the parents' sense of their effectiveness as parents and their relationship with their child. These quantitative measures are complemented by ongoing teachers' reports and anecdotal assessments, a summary of the child's physical and mental health history, and a parent interview designed to assess such things as the parents' feelings toward their child's program at Molly Stark.

Obtained at several points during the school year, these measures assess the degree of change associated with program participation over time. In addition, we use individual case studies to integrate qualitative and quantitative information. The kindergarten teachers are also asked to complete the Kindergarten Teacher Questionnaire (Burns & Gorman, 1999), a measure of school readiness and selected health outcomes designed for use in Vermont schools, and the Achenbach Behavior Checklist (Achenbach System of Empirically Based Assessment, 1991), a measure of emotional and behavioral issues.

As we proceed with these evaluations and think about the future of our school, we are moving into unknown territory and putting ourselves on the line in hopes of demonstrating that, when we provide the right opportunities and supports to children, their potential can be maximized.

9

What Are the Barriers to Creating Full-Service Community Schools?

Wendy Fagerholm

146

OVERCOMING BARRIERS
TO IMPLEMENTATION

This community school stuff is hard work. Sue Maguire and her core staff never stop, and neither do most of the people mentioned in this book who work in school-community programs. These efforts are, above all, time-consuming. Unquestionably, it takes more time to work in partnerships than just to do it all yourself. But time is not the only barrier to successfully implementing a full-service community school. I will mention other barriers here and try to figure out how to overcome them.

I'm indebted to my friends at Public/Private Ventures, a significant social policy research organization, for sharing their findings from a study of the implementation of the Wallace-Reader's Digest Extended Services Schools (ESS) Initiative in 10 cities (Grossman, Walker, & Raley, 2001). They have documented a number of barriers encountered by the selected schools: "The programming challenges faced during implementation have three major commonalities: they were formidable, they were typically unanticipated during the planning stages, and they occurred with consistency across programs, regardless of model type" (p. 11). Challenges highlighted by Public/Private Ventures included sharing of space, transportation, and provision of adequate staffing.

Another view of barriers to effective programming stems from the Thirteen Ed Online/Disney Learning Partnership online workshop titled After School Programs—From Vision to Reality (see Resources). The workshop mentions the same obstacles but also expresses concern about lack of attention to "child dynamics," failure to develop interventions appropriate to different age and gender groups, and failure to take into consideration different behavioral patterns and diverse cultures. This suggests the need for consistent high-quality training and supervision throughout all of the involved systems.

Thomas McMahon and colleagues (2000) at the Yale School of Medicine have conducted the most comprehensive review to date of integrated service delivery systems and identified "conceptual, fiscal, legal-ethical, and practical issues that can hinder local efforts to develop full-service schools" (p. 65). In addition to the problems already identified, they cite the lack of carefully documented information about how models should be replicated and the necessity for long-term hands-on technical assistance that will result in integrated school and human service systems.

In this book, I have mentioned a number of interesting models of full-service community schools and after-school programs established by school-community partnerships. The challenge is to take these models and replicate or adapt them in sufficient numbers to create massive social change. Failure to successfully adapt is a significant barrier.

Lack of Space

According to the U.S. Department of Education (2000), the life span of school buildings is about 40 years, after which they deteriorate rapidly. The average American school building is 42 years old. And few were built to encompass space for family and child services. It has been estimated that at least $250 billion would be needed to renovate old buildings and build new ones. The current expenditure is a tiny fraction of that amount, and in 2001, neither President Bush nor Congress appeared willing to face that fact.

Most schools were designed as purely instructional facilities with limited community access. Auditoriums, sports facilities, food service, libraries, media centers, computer labs, and other specialized areas of the school are not readily available to the community. Families have to rely on other locations for those services or go without.

New Buildings

A few places around the country have created new schools as the center of the community. I mentioned the Wilder Foundation's Achievement Plus schools and other examples in Chapter 6. Discovery Middle School in Vancouver, Washington, was cited by the U.S. Department of Education (2000) as "Innovative Design #1." This school campus was completed in 1995 after extensive input from parents, students, educators, architects, business partners, and other community members. It features "academic villages," each consisting of 10 high-tech classrooms designed to house a team of students and teachers organized as a school within a school. A large open area called the Tool Box stimulates integrated instruction, with zones for research with reference materials, wet and dry lab activities, art projects, technology applications, and fabrication. A special room near the entrance is set aside for community organizations, school partners, and social services to use, reaffirming the school's central place within the larger Vancouver community.

Educational facilities should be designed to strengthen the relationship between schools and communities and to serve a variety of needs in partnership with public, civic, and private organizations. As we have observed at Molly Stark, the building of the Family Center sent a powerful message to parents that they were welcome and encouraged to be involved in their children's learning.

Finding Space in an Existing School

Few full-service community schools will be built from the ground up. They will result from careful planning and redesign of existing facilities that may require considerable modification over time. I once visited a school in New York City where the Columbia University School of Public Health wanted to place a clinic. The principal was not encouraging, stating that the run-down building was much too overcrowded to find room for a medical suite. He begrudgingly allowed that one room at the end of the first floor might be converted to such a facility. The Columbia people, with financing from a state program and foundations, moved in and opened the clinic in the cramped space.

Five years later the picture had changed completely. Because of its supportive personnel (nurse practitioner, aide, health educator, and part-time physician), the clinic was so successful that the principal had thoroughly embraced the enterprise. He referred to it as *his* primary health center. By this time the suite extended to seven rooms, including a dental office, two examining rooms, a room for small counseling groups, two social workers' offices, and a pleasant waiting room. With help from the Columbia group to bring in educational consultants, the principal had completely reorganized the school, including the physical plant, and the whole climate had changed.

Undoubtedly, many schools are so run-down and overcrowded that they have difficulty finding space for new services. But it is amazing how a little ingenuity can go a long way, and a little-used closet can be extended to become an examining room or a social work office. At the full-service schools in Florida and other parts of the country, many mobile units have been parked on school property to be transformed into clinics, child care centers, family resource centers, and other aspects of community schools.

Turf

Whose space is it, anyway? The teachers in the school, many of whom have occupied the same classrooms for many years, think it is theirs. The new people who come in with the extended-day program and the outside grants assume that, at least during after-school hours, the space belongs to them. The underlying ethos of a well-functioning community school is that the space is there to be used for whatever purposes best serve the needs of the children. But resolving questions of turf, like those around all the other issues, takes time. One community school director felt that after three years, her greatest accomplishment was the acceptance by the teachers that their classrooms would be used for the after-school program. Some of the goodwill resulted from the teachers seeing the gains that children made because of the after-school enrichment. As the implementation of community school concepts began to change the environment in the school, the teachers felt more ownership and involvement and took pride in the school's improvement.

The school principal and the community school coordinator have to stay on top of the turf issue right from the beginning of the school change process. Use of classrooms, equipment, art supplies, library, computers, gyms, the auditorium, and other school property should be negotiated during the planning period.

Maintenance

Extending school hours clearly puts a lot of pressure on the custodians and janitors in school buildings. Practitioners report intensive negotiations, often with custodial unions, to work out schedules that cover early morning to late evening. In the Central Falls, Rhode Island, SCOPE (Schools and Communities Organizing to Promote Excellence) program, this tension has been greatly reduced by inviting the school system's supervisor of buildings and grounds to sit on the governing council for the initiative. He has become a major stakeholder in the success of the program and takes it upon himself to make sure that the buildings are available for the scheduled activities, whether in the gyms, playgrounds, auditoriums, or classrooms.

Transportation

The bus schedule is almost always cited as a problem for administering full-service community schools in both urban communities and rural areas. If the bus picks up the students at 2:30 p.m., how can they stay in school for extended hours? If the community lacks public transportation, how are disadvantaged parents without cars supposed to get to the school for all the programs offered to them?

Public/Private Ventures found that in four of the research cities, students who wanted to attend ESS's after-school programs but normally relied on school busing required alternative means of transportation (Grossman et al., 2001). Three of the cities had late buses available at the middle or high school level, but these were set up primarily for activities such as extracurricular sports. Using those buses would require that the ESS program end before the late bus left.

All the ESS programs encountered problems accessing transportation for off-site activities like field trips and hiking. Also, staff, volunteers, and parents who lived a moderate distance from the school were limited in the degree to which they could participate in programs unless they had their own means of transportation.

According to the Public/Private Ventures study, the main reason transportation was cited as a major problem was cost. The expense of additional busing was never included in the planning stages and only emerged as an issue after the programs got under way. One program estimated the costs of after-school busing to be $50,000 for the school year and $100 a day during the summer (the latter figure seems low). A principal proposed that the ESS program be made a mandatory part of the school day so the school district would have to pay for busing. Clearly, the solutions are costly. In some cases, school districts are willing to pick up the tab; in others, community agencies share the cost with the program.

The consequences of inadequate transportation were portrayed as "substantial." As one school coordinator put it, "Lots of kids say they can't participate because no one can pick them up." Another said, "We have to limit the program to 150 students a day because of transportation. We only have so many buses" (Grossman et al., 2001, p. 9). The feeling was that the children who were most likely to miss the program because of transportation problems were those who needed it most.

I often think about the school buses I see lined up around the athletic fields of a nearby suburban public school at all kinds of odd hours—as late as 6:00 p.m. on weekends and even in the summer. For sports events, the players, band, and cheerleaders are transported to and from neighboring communities. If bus schedules can adapt to sports schedules, they should be able to adapt to extended school hours. Transportation is one of the issues that must be dealt with during the planning process. It may be necessary to renegotiate contracts with bus drivers.

At the Quitman Street Community School in Newark, New Jersey, the lead agency partner provided one solution to the transportation problem. The Community Agencies Corporation of New Jersey made its van available for various purposes, including taking children and parents to medical and social services appointments and transporting groups of students and teachers on field trips.

Inequity

A unique study conducted in California to review after-school programs from the point of view of equity and access also concluded that the neediest children are not the ones found in after-school programs (Olsen & Sharf, 2000). These findings seem to reflect some of the experiences in community schools as well. In the country's most diverse state, youth advocates are concerned about ensuring that emerging programs respect the diversity of, and equalize access to services among, disadvantaged populations. A preliminary review of selected programs showed wide variation, reflecting different levels of resources in communities. Middle-class suburban kids have access to an array of enrichment activities not available to children from low-income areas. Facilities and space tend to be inadequate for after-school programs on school sites, particularly those on inner-city and overcrowded school campuses.

The California researchers also concluded that, "The arena of after-school programs is growing faster than its ability to create an infrastructure of training [and] dissemination of program models and materials, which are required to ensure more equitable access to quality programs" (Olsen & Sharf, 2000, p. 1). They suggest that the cultural, ethnic, and linguistic backgrounds of the staff affect their ability to communicate with parents and support youth development; training in cross-cultural services is lacking; and program content and design often speak more effectively to one group than another.

Confidentiality

When you try to integrate two very different cultures, such as school and social support, you encounter difficulties in sharing information. Constancia Warren (1999), the evaluator of the New Jersey School-Based Youth Services Program (SBYSP), observed that the program's health and mental health professionals appeared to be governed by medical confidentiality considerations and were careful to protect students' privacy. The school staff were less concerned about individual privacy than about their broad responsibility for ensuring the well-being of students, both individually and collectively, and therefore felt much freer to discuss sensitive information openly. In the SBYSP programs, time must be spent working out arrangements to share some information without revealing anything the student wants kept confidential. As Warren points out, the key is communication. One project director explained how she deals with boundary and confidentiality issues with her school: "Negotiation, negotiation, negotiation!"

Discipline

An area related to confidentiality is discipline. Often, school personnel and community agency personnel have different views about how to deal with "acting out" children. Many schools have adopted zero-tolerance policies that have quite rigid behavioral standards. School systems suspend and expel students for various infractions of the rules. People who come from youth service agencies may be more lenient and loath to pursue those avenues. Instead, they might identify the highest-risk students and surround them with supportive mechanisms, such as case management.

Policies about discipline need to be worked out during the planning process so that by the time the community school starts functioning, school and community agency staff have reached a consensus on how students should be treated. One approach is to designate a joint mental health team that meets frequently and discusses each case as it emerges.

The Need for Integration

In a fully realized community school, the partnership yields an integrated model: Whatever is brought into the school by outside agencies fits into the educational system. For example, after-school enrichment is tied to classroom work. What happens in the school health clinic is reinforced by health and mental health promotion in the classroom. The prevention message about sex, drugs, and alcohol is the same whether it is delivered by the teacher or the health educator who works for the health service provider. (The same health educator can also work directly in the classroom to relieve the teacher of the health education role.) In their study of California schools, Olsen and Sharf (2000) observed, "Integrating youth development and academic development agendas is difficult. . . . The goals for after-school programs are unclear and tensions exist between multiple and sometimes competing agendas. Due to time pressures and the intricacies of communicating across somewhat different orientations, collaboration between school-day and after-school programs can be extremely limited" (p. 1).

The Center for Mental Health in Schools (1999), expressing the ideas of Howard Adelman and Linda Taylor, has presented a significant caveat to advocates of school-community partnerships:

> It is essential not to overemphasize the topics of coordinating services and co-locating services on school sites. Such thinking downplays the need to also restructure the various education support programs and services that schools own and operate. [It would be a mistake to think that] community resources can effectively meet the needs of schools in addressing barriers to learning. (p. ii)

Integration is much more likely to happen if the full-service community school is perceived as a school reform program through which the entire school is transformed into a different kind of institution. It is difficult to imagine that educational outcomes in community schools can be improved if nothing changes in the classroom. The school staff and the support services staff have to work closely together, particularly in the planning stages, to make sure that a "seamless" product emerges.

Sufficient Funding

Most of the community school initiatives described in this book—Molly Stark, for example—depend on multiple sources of funding. In such cases, a huge responsibility falls on the principal to juggle all those resources and make sure that all the programs are covered year after year. Although some states have created integrated funding mechanisms and there is some movement toward creating community schools legislation nationally, it is unlikely that programs can move away from categorical funding in the near future.

In other models, like the Children's Aid Society, the funding burden falls on the community-based organization. McMahon et al. (2000) point out that having a nonschool agency as the lead can create a situation in which the school system feels that it has little financial stake in the long-term survival of the program. They conclude, "Despite being more difficult to create, . . . a wholly new organization established specifically to receive funding and administer the project may be an alternative to the concept of a single agency that ensures responsibility to secure and manage funding" (p. 76). This suggests a nonprofit agency in which schools and community agencies are equal partners.

Replication Difficulties

Many different models of community schools and after-school partnerships are presented in this book. Obviously, I hope this will encourage school and community people to come together and implement these concepts. However, some of the difficulties in doing this must be acknowledged. Jean Anyon (1997), in an important book on inner-city schools, cites the mid-1990s experience of two schools in Newark, New Jersey, in trying to adapt the Comer School Development Program. The main problem was that not enough resources were made available to the schools by the Newark School District to replicate this model. Not enough mental health personnel were added to aid more than a few students, and the mental health team met irregularly, was not trained adequately, and did not assist in school planning. Parents who were supposed to be paid to participate were not, and there were no funds for arts, athletics, or social skills programs or to buy materials for the discovery room. While this sounds like a funding problem, it also was attributable to a lack of committed leadership, staff development, and technical assistance.

I do not believe that effective replication of any of these complex programs can take place without considerable help from technical assistance agencies. Happily, many such resources exist, such as the intermediary organizations identified in Chapter 5 for adaptation of Children's Aid Society community schools, Beacons, United Way's Bridges to Success, university-assisted schools, Communities in Schools, Schools of the 21st Century, and the Comer School Development Program (see Resources). And, of course, funders, both public and private, have to allow school-community partnerships to purchase this valuable technical assistance time, which might require the presence of a full-time facilitator for a year or more just to work through the planning process and early implementation.

Naysayers

Not everyone loves the idea of full-service community schools the way I do. Some people are skeptical about the impact of these initiatives, wondering what difference it really makes in educational outcomes to have access to services. Others just don't believe the school building should be cluttered with a lot of programs that don't belong there.

Some of these differences came out during a "fishbowl conversation" at a national meeting of the Collaborative for Integrated School Services (*Building Strong Full-Service and Community Schools*, 2000). I expressed dismay that community schools seemed to be so invisible in education reform discussions. Lisbeth Schorr, an expert on community building, questioned whether "putting everything together in one mass is the best way to get things done." She continued:

> It may well be that . . . people whose responsibility is primarily for academic learning . . . shouldn't be worrying about community-building and health services, even though they recognize that if the health services are not there, and the community-building isn't happening, they can't achieve their ends. . . . Just because we all have connected outcomes to reach doesn't mean that we shouldn't have quite separate responsibilities. People who are charged with kids' academic learning should be able to focus their time, their attention, their energies very strategically on that, while some other people in the community are charged with support services, community-building, making community connections. . . . There is a high risk of crippling the ability of the schools to do academic stuff if they also have to take responsibility for everything else—for a child welfare system that isn't working, for communities that are unsafe, that are violent. . . . Maybe we are saying that we have to create a new institution . . . but maybe it is not the school. The only reason I persist in this is that I fear that by charging schools with these responsibilities, we are making it harder for them to do the job of educating all kids to high levels. (p. 15)

This view—that the provision of full services burdens rather than relieves schools—has been echoed elsewhere, and community school advocates have responded. Ira Harkavy, vice president of the University of Pennsylvania and chairman of the Coalition for Community Schools, responded to Schorr:

> Real community school development means creating systematic and systemic changes across a variety of agencies—including community development centers, youth service agencies, service providers, governmental agencies, and higher education. . . . What is required is that

schools function as organizing entities, not the sole provider of everything! They should be the center—but not the only center. (*Building
Strong Full-Service and Community Schools*, 2000, p. 15)

Lack of Visibility

It is likely that many people still misunderstand the basic community school
concepts that Sue and I have tried to convey here. They continue to believe that
bringing services into extended-day schools increases the burdensome tasks for
educators rather than relieving them of the total responsibility for attending to
the needs of children and their families. Some advocates have suggested that the
emerging field lacks adequate public relations and media exposure.

This issue was addressed in 2001 through a three-year media campaign
undertaken by the Children's Aid Society in conjunction with the Coalition for
Community Schools and the Advertising Council. Public service advertisements
about community schools generated 10,000 calls to the CAS hotline from parents, educators, funders, and policymakers who wanted more information
about transforming their local schools into community schools.

The Coalition for Community Schools encourages its 170 partners to hold
sessions on community schools at their national meetings; it also conducts an
annual national forum for everyone. Most of the education and youth development organizations have responded to this call. Community schools have been
encouraged to develop their own public relations campaigns, particularly by
inviting community leaders and political representatives to tour the buildings
and observe the programs.

The coalition's Web site has many visitors, as do the sites of the intermediary
organizations (see Resources). An Internet search for references to full-service
or community schools can produce many interesting citations. Increasingly,
schools and school systems are posting their own Web sites where one can learn
about the vast array of programs offered in school buildings.

I had the honor of escorting Congressman Steny Hoyer of Maryland on a
visit to Salome Urena Middle Academies (IS 218), a Children's Aid Society
school in New York City, and watching how warmly he related to the students,
teachers, and parents. He went back to Washington and wrote his significant
legislation, the Full-Service Community Schools Act of 2001 (still awaiting
introduction to the House as of early 2002; see Chapter 10).

Observations

Overcoming this array of barriers is certainly a challenge. Space shortage,
turf conflicts, transportation limits, funding complexities, attention to cultural
diversity, and staff turnover are all issues that must be dealt with in the planning
and implementation of full-service community schools. I'm always amazed to
see how committed practitioners in the schools and the community agencies
manage to overcome these barriers. They just keep plugging away.

In this book, most of our attention has been directed to the services side of
the full-service community school equation. Let us not forget that just dumping

a lot of services into schools may have very little impact on student achievement. The improvements in access to support systems must surely be accompanied by improvements in access to quality education.

My own vision is that thousands of schools that serve disadvantaged children and youth will be interested in these school-community partnership concepts when they learn about them and that many community agencies will want to participate in these collaborative arrangements. I hope we enter a community school building boom that will create physical plants designed to encompass all the necessary features of a full-service community school. But I do not see how the potential stakeholders can implement complex plans or overcome troublesome barriers without substantial help from well-organized and accessible technical assistance agencies. It would be unwise to assume that people can do all this work on their own without sustained guidance. It would also be foolish to assume that this work can be successful without significant financial support that relieves local people from having to piece together short-term grants from fragmented categorical sources.

MOLLY STARK MEETS THE CHALLENGES

In my training to become certified as a school principal, I was given an article by Michael Fullan (1993) in which he said that "problems are our friends" (p. 40). But as challenges continuously surface, they certainly don't feel like friends! I know the thought here is that you can't grow and learn without working through problems, but I must say that we could have done without so many "friends" throughout this experience.

Fortunately, some of the more common challenges that schools face were not problems for us. We have a building that provides much of the needed space. Many of our students live within walking distance, so transportation for our programs is not a major issue. The school district provides a cleaning service in the evening, so custodians are at the school until 11:00 p.m. each day.

However, we didn't lack our own set of challenges. And this wasn't much of a surprise—there are always issues that must be ironed out. But many of the problems we have dealt with were not expected because this was all new territory. Finding a place for the pediatrician to examine students, looking at how to fund child care staff, finding the time to set up a clinical psychologist's schedule and then making sure we have support systems to help the parents show up for appointments—I never thought I would be doing these things as a school principal.

In addition, the lack of community schools in our area left us with no one to consult with or learn from. Running a community school in a state with no other community schools makes us feel a bit isolated. With no real technical assistance, we have had to learn by trial and error.

Many of the challenges we face are about people. An ongoing goal is making sure that we are all looking ahead with a focus on solutions. It is easy just to say, "It can't be done," and be closed to all the possibilities, but this kind of blocking attitude interferes with positive change. The greatest asset we've had throughout this process is a group of people who say, "There are no excuses, how can we make this work?" It has become part of our school's culture to do whatever it takes to do what is right for kids. And this outlook, which started with a core group, has become increasingly pervasive among our staff. For that to happen, we had to build a community that has common goals and an atmosphere that allows for innovation and change. This required a great deal of conversation and a clear focus on our vision.

Turf

Turf issues emerged as soon as we started working with local service providers. When we first set up partnerships with outside health providers, I sent a letter explaining our plan and reassuring clinicians in our community that we were simply trying to provide a service that students and parents would not otherwise get; we were not trying to steal patients. In spite of this letter, I received a few phone calls from providers worried that we would be taking patients from their practices. The only thing that really calmed this fear was time—time to see that our purpose was to serve those students and families who had limited access.

Funding

Although finding enough money to fund programs has always been a challenge, it has become clear that if you can show a need as well as sound practice, there are many funding sources to tap. The stress comes in knowing that if you don't continuously find a certain amount of money, the quality of the programs will suffer. Searching for money is one of the givens that you must get used to.

Contract Language

We have always tried to be respectful of teacher contract language. This became an important factor when we started after-school programs. Some of our Title I reading teachers who wanted to supervise and facilitate the after-school reading club wondered if, instead of being paid extra for their after-school time, they could come in an hour late and then work an hour later after school. We developed an agreement with both the Board of Education and the Teacher's Association to make this work. This agreement allowed Title I reading teachers to use flexible scheduling (in at 9:00 a.m. and finished at 4:00 p.m.) if they chose.

Another question came up for teachers who chose to facilitate an after-school program. We had agreed to pay a set stipend to anyone who facilitated these programs: teachers, teaching assistants, parents, and community members. The question arose (though not from one of our staff), "Shouldn't teachers be paid the hourly rate that is in the contract?" Since teachers are not teaching academic subjects after school but are engaged in activities such as cooking and sports, we were able to continue with the set stipend. This could have become a major block because, over time, we could not have afforded to follow the contractual hourly rate and would have had to exclude the teachers who enjoyed staying after school to share a talent or skill with students.

Evaluation

Assessing progress and effectiveness of programs and activities that we provide to students and families is an ongoing process that takes much time and energy. Determining needs, finding out what is working that we might want to expand on, as well as what isn't working that we must change or let go of, are ongoing questions that we must continuously talk about. Now that we have begun to work with a researcher, we will be collecting the right data to see if we are making the impact we are aiming for.

The System

Probably one of our most difficult challenges has been fighting "the system." We have looked beyond the traditional role of schools to a more comprehensive solution to help children be more successful. Yet there continues to be a perception in our country that if we just teach them better, they will succeed—that providing social, emotional, and health support is not the job of a school. I believe we need to look more closely at what kinds of supports kids need to succeed. It isn't *just* good instruction that makes a difference; it's an array of experiences and opportunities from an early age that helps students be ready to absorb good instruction. We can't ignore the academic implications of social and health issues. I would venture to guess that those who think there isn't a relationship between the two have never held a kid trying to cope with a lousy life or sat with a parent whose life is in a continual crisis mode.

Sustainability

The challenge of sustainability elicits frequent questions, such as "What will happen when the money runs out?" and "What will happen when you move on?" These questions can't be answered in black-and-white statements. There are many unknowns, but not doing what's right at this moment because we are unsure of the future doesn't make sense. One of the greatest challenges is keeping the momentum. We know that there are no quick fixes for the consequences of poverty, and we know that if we are to make real change, we must set the same standards for poor kids as we do for their middle-class peers.

In May 2001, we made a difficult decision. We didn't have the human resources to offer a total summer program for our families. Many parents and staff were frustrated and upset, but discontinuing the program was a decision that had to be made. We had about 25 students at school during the morning for academic summer camp and served lunch free for those six weeks to any child 18 or younger who showed up. The challenge is this: If you spend too much time looking back and wondering if you made the right decision, you won't move forward. Some decisions are hard, but you have to believe that at that moment they were the right ones under the circumstances and move on from there.

The reality is that we can't get around many of the barriers we face without constant hard work. We continue to look at challenges as necessary steps toward innovation and change; meeting them is proof that we are facing the tough stuff so we can best serve children and families.

10

How Can These Schools and Programs Be Funded?

EXPLORATION OF RESOURCES

Just because we have put off the chapter about money until almost the end of the book doesn't mean we think it is not important. We thought we should lay out all the other issues first. Clearly, without financial support, full-service community schools could not exist. But the situation in each community, and even in each school, is so different that the amount of money needed can range from very little to a great deal. Probably the two most important variables are what specific goals are aimed for and what resources already exist to use for those purposes.

As she discusses later in the chapter, Sue was able in 2000–2001 to piece together support from 18 different sources for one-, two-, and three-year grants. That sounds like a bureaucratic nightmare, but it is not unusual for a school to deal with many sources of funds. And community schools actively seek relocation of existing services and the resources that come with them. In the case of Molly Stark, a major funding coup was the acquisition of a discrete, one-time grant from the state to actually erect a small building, the Family Center, to house early child care and family programs.

In this chapter, we review the status of funding for full-service community schools at the federal, state, and local levels.

Exploration of Major Federal Resources

In 2000, the Finance Project, a Washington-based nonprofit research group, reported 121 different federal sources of funding that could be used to support some aspect of full-service community schools (Reder, 2000). I comment on only a few of the most significant sources here but strongly advise interested program developers to examine the report. Note that of this plethora of programs, only 7 actually target community school or after-school activities.

When the Finance Project compiled this information in 2000, the only federal initiative with funds specifically focused on after-school activities (out-of-school time) was 21st Century Community Learning Centers (CCLC; described in Chapter 4). In 2001, the budget called for $845 million for this Department of Education effort. As Bill Alexander reported in *Youth Today* (2001), "While [the program] squeezes into a House-Senate conference committee with wildly disparate authorization levels, the fate of the nation's biggest pot of after-school funding hangs in the balance" (p. 14). A Senate bill called for $1.5 billion, and a House bill called for $900 million. Issues such as whether this money should go through state block grants or directly to communities and whether community-based organizations (CBOs), including faith-based organizations, could be direct grantees were widely discussed.

Testimony offered to the House Education and Workforce Committee as it considered the CCLC program was revealing. William S. White, president of the C. S. Mott Foundation, warned against merging CCLC funding with other programs. He also expressed concern about the idea of block-granting the federal funds to the states, because this would permit the states to decide who gets the grants at the local level rather than having the federal Department of Education award grants directly to local communities. In his testimony before the House Education and Workforce Committee, White (2001) stated,

> Aside from the danger that after-school funding could get lost in the blend of funding streams, I believe this would have a chilling effect on after-school initiatives generally, jeopardizing state and local funding and quelling the momentum of the field. Moving programs to the states raises other critical concerns. Accountability is best assured by having national oversight with a single set of standards and requirements, rather than 50 different programs [with] . . . 50 infrastructures and 50 administrative budgets.

White also supported extending the grant period from three to five years. He believes that a competitive federal program that provides direct funding to local entities for services to children and families is far more efficient than separate programs run by each state individually.

The 2002 DOE budget appears to contain $1 billion for the CCLC program; however, the money will go to the states, which will conduct their own competitive processes to award funds to schools eligible for Title I funds (based on the percentage of students eligible for free or reduced-cost lunches). The grant period will be extended to five years, and CBOs as well as school districts will be able to apply.

The Finance Project report (Reder, 2000) mentions six other programs that targeted funds in the 1999 budget specifically for after-school or community school efforts: (a) the Child Care and Development Fund of the Department of Health and Human Services, which subsidized child care for low-income families through state-administered grants (such as at Molly Stark); (b) the Child and Adult Care Food Program and the Summer Food Service Program run by the Department of Agriculture to subsidize free meals for eligible children and families; (c) the Juvenile Mentoring Program of the Department of Justice, which supported grants for violence prevention; (d) the Child Care Access Means Parents in Schools Program, a small program that assisted low-income students who were parents to place their children in preschool or child care; and (e) Boys and Girls Clubs of America, which received funds directly from the Department of Justice for prevention programs. But more than 100 other federal programs with broader targets can be tapped for resources to support community schools. States receive many different block grants to distribute to localities, such as Medicaid, Temporary Assistance for Needy Families (TANF, welfare funds), foster care, child welfare, community development, social services, law enforcement, and juvenile justice. Medicaid dollars are used in community schools with primary health care clinics or dental services. TANF is being used for after-school child care for welfare moms. About three-quarters of these federal sources of funding are categorical grants, or programs that address a specific problem or disease.

The Elementary and Secondary Education Act (ESEA) is the major source of funds to meet the needs of educationally disadvantaged children. Title I of this act is directed toward improving educational performance. An estimated 22 percent (nearly 22,000) of all public schools are eligible to receive these funds because more than half of their students are poor. Although in its earlier years Title I was used primarily to take disadvantaged children out of their classes and give them remediation, new regulations allow the use of these funds to upgrade an entire educational program by increasing the amount of learning time. A Title I plan must include these components: needs assessment, use of proven school reform strategies, access to counseling and mentoring along with college and job preparation, professional development for the staff, parental involvement and family literacy services, and strategies for an effective transition from pre-K (preschool) to kindergarten. This list puts Title I right in the community school ballpark. The CCLC appropriation is included under ESEA.

The total Title I appropriation is always a matter of contention. In 2000, almost $8 billion was granted to local education agencies for improving the educational outcomes for disadvantaged children. In recent years, under Title XI of ESEA, school districts could have used up to 5 percent of these funds for coordinated social and health services. Only a few systems took advantage of that flexible regulation; for example, the Dallas public schools used it to support an Office of Interagency Collaboration in the central administration and to provide oversight of nine Coordinated Service Centers throughout the school district. Many administrators are not aware that these funds can also be used for infants and toddlers, as well as pre-K children. In 2000, about 17 percent of school districts used Title I to serve children before they reached kindergarten (Jacobson, 2001, p. 1). The 2002 budget appropriates more than $12 billion for Title I services to disadvantaged students, a substantial increase over previous years.

The Safe and Drug-Free Schools Program (with $644 million in the 2002 budget) consists of state-administered federal grants that may be used to establish, operate, and improve local programs of school drug and violence prevention, early intervention, rehabilitation, referral, and education in elementary and secondary schools. The program also funds training, demonstration projects, evaluation, and supplementary services for the prevention of drug use and violence among students and youth. Both schools and CBOs can apply for these grants.

The Safe Schools/Healthy Students program (with $180 million in 2000) focuses on violence prevention. Local school systems receive grants to bring together many of the components of full-service schools, including school safety; alcohol, drug, and violence prevention; school and community mental health and treatment services; early child development; and education reform. This program had $180 million in 2000, but at this writing, it is not clear whether it can survive the current budget crunch.

Three Proposals for the Future

School and community people who come together to plan and implement community schools have the daunting task of searching through the maze of federal programs (as well as those at the state and local level) to try to identify grants that might help them put all the necessary pieces together. Of course, if there was one federal program that supported all the components, wide replication of these models would be more feasible. One central community school program would also give the concept visibility and credibility.

The Full-Service Community Schools Act of 2001

As we are writing this book, Congressman Steny Hoyer of Maryland, a long-time supporter of full-service community schools, is crafting legislation that would for the first time provide $200 million in federal funds for integrated full-service school-based programs. Much of the funding would go to "qualified local consortia"—community partnerships composed of qualified organizations and including a representative of the local education agency. A "qualified state consortium" would include the state education agency and at least two other state agencies related to the allowable services.

At the federal level, the Hoyer bill calls for the establishment of an Integrated School-Based Services Commission to make grants to qualified consortia that implemented a comprehensive approach to meeting the educational, health, social service, and other needs of children and their families. The commission would be established by the president and would include the attorney general and the secretaries of agriculture, labor, health and human services, housing and urban development, and education.

The act would appropriate $200 million to be administered by staff from each of the agencies and coordinated in the White House. Local grants would be $100,000 or more, which would have to be matched by the grantee. A qualified local consortium is defined as a group composed of any combination of qualified organizations or eligible governments, including representatives from a local school system or just one school and not less than two other organizations that could provide services, funds, and/or support in three of these areas:

- Early childhood learning
- Educational enhancement
- After-school programs
- Head Start
- Youth development programs
- Community service and learning
- Parent leadership development
- Parenting education
- Child care
- Family support and preservation
- Primary health and dental care
- Job training/career counseling
- Housing
- Nutrition
- Juvenile justice
- Drug abuse prevention and treatment
- Extension services
- Mental health

Priority would go to applicants with 50 percent or more of their students eligible for Title I. About 20 percent of the total funds would go for state consortia, 1 percent for evaluation, and another 1 percent to set up a technical assistance center.

The Child Opportunity Zone Family Center Act

Senator Jack Reed of Rhode Island, inspired by the example of Central Falls in his state (see Chapter 6), introduced in 2001 the Child Opportunity Zone Family Center Act to encourage communities to create school-based or school-linked family centers that would provide a seamless, integrated system of support to improve the education, health, mental health, safety, and economic well-being of children and families. Grants would be provided to partnerships consisting of a high-poverty (Title I–eligible) public school, a school district, public agencies such as health or social services, and a nonprofit CBO that includes a health care provider. These partnerships would provide children and families with links to existing community prevention and intervention services and would offer violence prevention education and training to help families and children.

The legislation mandates evaluation to ensure that the partnerships focus on improvements in student achievement, family participation, and access to health, mental health, child care, and support services and on reduction in violence-related problems and truancy, suspension, and dropout rates. An authorization of $100 million was called for in the first year. This program would be administered by the Department of Education as part of Title X of the ESEA.

Neither of these bills made it through Congress, but at least they have been introduced and a core of supporters is being created through the efforts of these congressional offices.

The Younger Americans Act

Another piece of legislation introduced in 2001 was the Younger Americans Act. Its purpose is "to provide assistance to mobilize and support United States communities in carrying out youth development programs that assure that youth have access to programs and services that build the competencies and character development needed to fully prepare the youth to become adults and effective citizens" (House Bill 17, 2001).

The act spells out a national youth policy to ensure access to caring adults, safe places, health and mental health services, work skills training, and community service opportunities. An Office of National Youth Policy would be located in the Executive Office of the President, and the work would be implemented by the Administration for Children, Youth, and Families in the Department of Health and Human Services. This program would provide noncategorical funding ($500 million in 2002) to agencies such as state and local youth bureaus, with priority to high-poverty, rural, and high-risk communities. This legislation had been referred to the appropriate committees and had not yet been taken up in Congress at the time of writing.

What States Do and Can Do

Initiatives in a number of states directly or indirectly support full-service community schools. We have referred to some of these programs in previous chapters.

- California: Healthy Start sites
- Florida: Full-Service Schools Program
- Kentucky: Family Resource and Youth Service Centers
- Maryland: Multi-Service Delivery Centers and Integrated Service Delivery Centers
- Minnesota: Youth Development and Family Services
- Missouri: Family and Community Trust, administering Caring Communities
- New Jersey and Iowa: School-Based Youth Services Programs
- New York: Community Schools Program
- Oregon: Community schools legislation

States can play a major role in the planning and implementation of programs to support school-community partnerships. An excellent example is Missouri, which was able to launch a three-level initiative: collaboration at the state level between seven public agencies and the private sector through a nonprofit trust; collaboration at the community level in the form of community partnerships; and collaboration at 100 sites at the school level with community-based agencies. This formalized approach was made possible by the pooling of funds at the state level, a sure indicator that the governor and state legislature were truly committed to partnering.

In Kentucky, almost every school now has a family resource or youth service center, a cornerstone of Kentucky's Education Reform Act of 1990 (Denton, n.d.). This program is managed from an office in the Cabinet for Families and Children rather than the Department of Education in an attempt to encourage collaboration between human services and education agencies. A measure of the centers' success and popularity came in 1999 when they were included as an element of required consolidated planning. In each school's plan for state and federally funded programs, the center's activities must be aligned with other school programs designed to improve student performance. This process has given the centers better information about what the schools are doing and has made school staff more aware of the centers.

States are major funders of school-based primary health centers; the money comes through direct grant programs from the state Department of Health, through funds from the Maternal and Child Health Block Grants, or by arranging for Medicaid fee-for-service reimbursement. A few states also directly fund family resource centers and other components of full-service community schools.

It should be noted here that as of November 2001, there are many uncertainties about state funding. For example, the $11 million Florida Full-Service Schools Program was cut out of the state budget along with many other services for poor families. We do not know whether these cuts will be restored later.

What Communities Do and Can Do

Several communities mentioned in this book are attempting to introduce changes across their whole school systems. In Buffalo, New York, the mayor originally took the lead in developing community schools, while in Hartford, Connecticut, and Plainfield, New Jersey, the superintendents have been organizing efforts to bring school and community agencies into partnerships to support the school systems. Community planning groups, community foundations, local education funds, and United Ways can initiate the process of introducing community school concepts by putting up seed money that will allow planning and data gathering to begin. Some local public funds are included in the budgets for full-service community schools.

The Schools Uniting Neighborhoods initiative in Portland, Oregon, pools dollars from many sources in the Multnomah County region. The first year's budget in 1999 was about $1 million, with grants ranging from $50,000 to $120,000 per school. Eight schools have been awarded full-service school grants, and two more received planning grants. By the second year, it was estimated that an elementary school would need $100,000 and a middle school $150,000, plus in-kind resources.

The 1999–2000 budget of a little more than $1 million showed the following collaborative financial arrangement:

- City of Portland: $300,000
- Multnomah County: $270,000
- Oregon Department of Human Services: $382,475
- Portland Public School District: $14,000
- Multnomah Education Service District: $25,000
- Foundations: small grants ranging from $4,500 to $10,000

Foundations

Foundations have been critically important in getting school-community partnerships off the ground. The C. S. Mott Foundation has been a major player in this field for the past half-century through its support of the community education/lifelong learning model that has been replicated in thousands of schools. More recently, the foundation has played a unique role in partnership with the U.S. Department of Education to launch the CCLC program. As William S. White described it, the C. S. Mott Foundation, with a commitment of over $100 million for a multiyear period, has been able to "do things the Department of Education couldn't do," including massive training, identification of promising practices, advocacy and policy work, supplementing federal evaluation dollars, convening meetings, and bringing other funders to the table (White, 2001).

We have mentioned a number of other foundations' projects, notably the Wallace-Reader's Digest Extended Services Schools Initiative that supported adaptations of four community school models in 80 sites around the country. The Polk Brothers Foundation in Chicago was instrumental in starting a full-service school program in three schools and then following up in collaboration with the Chicago Board of Education to adapt the model the foundation was evaluating in other schools. The Wilder Foundation in St. Paul brought together state and local resources with its own and initiated Achievement Plus in three schools. The Ewing Marion Kauffman, Carnegie Corporation, Wallace-Reader's Digest, and C. S. Mott foundations have made grants to the Coalition for Community Schools and support specific community school programs around the country.

More recently, the Eisenhower Foundation with support from the Department of Education selected three schools in Tukwila, Washington, Indian Head, Maryland, and Boston, Massachusetts, to replicate and evaluate full-service community schools. And in 2001, the Public Education Network, as part of a large-scale school improvement project with the Annenberg Foundation, launched the School and Community Initiative. Nine communities were awarded planning grants to come up with a scheme for building a seamless, coordinated, and comprehensive program, and supports for the high achievement of every child in and out of school. In the next phase, five of the sites will be awarded large grants to implement their plans.

Observations

I noted in the previous chapter that the Center for Mental Health in Schools (1999) advises deemphasizing the concept of moving existing community resources like social workers from a CBO to a school. They fear that the success of school-community partnerships has led some policymakers to the mistaken conclusion that community resources can effectively meet all the needs of schools in addressing barriers to learning.

> In turn, this has led some legislators to view the linking of community services to schools as a way to free up the dollars underwriting school-owned services. The reality is that even when one adds together community and school assets, the total set of services in impoverished locales is woefully inadequate. (p. ii)

In other words, the demands for supports are so enormous that even comprehensive community schools cannot meet them all. Community schools should not be used as an excuse for letting go of pupil personnel services supported by the school system, such as the school nurse, psychologist, social worker, or counselor.

Community school coordinators spend a great deal of time raising money. Although the number of sources is mind-boggling (and we have only touched on a few of them), each source has to be tracked down and "conquered" in a never-ending battle to stay funded. Each grant carries its own reporting requirements, eligibility restrictions, and regulations, requiring the administrator to keep track of a multitude of different forms, reporting periods, and other fiscal requirements.

How much do you need to start one of these things? Estimates range from $100 to $1,000 per student per year or even higher. Beacons are awarded about $400,000 a year, $50,000 of which goes to maintenance and security of the school building. The CCLC grants per school site in 1999 ranged from $35,000 to $200,000, depending on the number of students served, the array of activities, and the availability of additional resources. Martin Blank, director of the Coalition for Community Schools, believes that a minimum of $100,000 would give a school-community partnership sufficient funds to hire a community school coordinator and finance key services that will attract other partners to bring their services to the school.

The Finance Project has produced a worksheet for estimating the costs of after-school and community school initiatives (see Resources). Its purpose is to help program developers create an operating budget. The first step is to come up with some assumptions about the anticipated program: number of sites, types of services to be offered and to whom, and an operating schedule. All the costs are estimated in terms of both cash outlays and in-kind contributions, such as goods, services, volunteers, facilities, and equipment. One-time costs to get a program up and running include such items as planning, training, and needs assessments. Ongoing operating costs include staff salaries, equipment, space, maintenance, and administration. Other items might be food, furniture, utilities, transportation, and capital costs if new buildings are required. If a program encompasses multiple sites, systemwide costs could be associated with the infrastructure that runs the program. These might include coordination in such areas as referral activities, professional development systems, and licensing.

The one certainty in 2002 is uncertainty. It is hard to predict what will happen to the U.S. economy in the coming years; even if we knew, it is impossible to say how either its strengthening or weakening would affect public funding. I think we can have some confidence that in a few states, the momentum to fund school-community partnerships will protect the programs in the near future. Other states may move into the fold.

The prognosis for securing integrated federal funding for community schools, such as the passage of the Full-Service Community Schools Act, is probably dim, but the continuing support for the 21st Century Community Learning Centers is encouraging. Money for CCLC could exceed $1 billion in 2002. And the design of the centers is definitely broadening to include CBOs as lead agencies and perhaps in the future to allow the use of the funds throughout the school day rather just before and after school time.

MOLLY STARK'S RESOURCES

Like many other community schools across the country, we spend a great deal of time piecing together money from many sources to make things happen. I have learned two things about money: (a) There is a lot of it out there to be tapped, and (b) it takes a tremendous amount of time and energy to find it and fight for it. Each source has its own set of criteria and rules to adhere to.

In the 2000–2001 school year we needed just over $90,000 to pay all the Family Center employees and another $30,000 to $40,000 to fund the other programs and services. The money that is not local district money (which totals about $6,500 per child per year), but rather funds considered earmarked for full-service community school programs, averages less than $400 per student per year. Two significant ongoing sources of money to pay Family Center staff are Medicaid and child care subsidies.

There are two kinds of Medicaid. Our special education students each have a written plan (Individual Education Plan, or IEP) that must be followed to meet their needs. Medicaid money is available from the federal government to school districts, through the state's Department of Education, for Medicaid-eligible special education students who receive health-related services such as occupational therapy, speech services, physical therapy, counseling, case management, developmental therapy, three-year reevaluations, or other such services pursuant to their IEP. Money is given to school districts at different rates depending on the services they provide, and it must be used for prevention activities. For us to bill Medicaid for these services, special educators must obtain parental permission. In addition, the special education teachers must obtain parental permission to use Medicaid, must obtain authorization from a primary care physician or the school's physician, and must fill out monthly reports based on each eligible child's IEP, documenting the various hours of service that can be billed to Medicaid. This process demands a great deal of paperwork from our special educators but has definitely been worth the effort.

Early Periodic Screening Diagnosis and Treatment (EPSDT) funds, which are the other kind of Medicaid, are derived from a formula based on the number of hours the school nurse and the guidance counselor spend in EPSDT activities and the number of Medicaid-eligible students in the school. For example, the school nurse can log assessment and treatment hours and the guidance counselor can log one-to-one counseling hours with students and attendance at special education meetings. In addition, our consulting pediatrician, psychologist, and clinical social worker can log the hours they work with children and parents at Molly Stark, and a percentage of this money will come back to local schools for health promotion and prevention programs for children and families. Our school district has made the commitment to invest the EPSDT funds in early education opportunities.

As I mentioned in Chapter 3, because we are a licensed child care facility, we can use state child care subsidies as a continuous funding source. Families who use our Family Center go through an application process. Once eligibility has been determined, the subsidies are paid directly to the school and are reflective of the services provided (quarter, half, or full day). Eligibility is reviewed every four to six months. During a typical school year, we receive about $50,000 in child care subsidies.

IEP and EPSDT Medicaid funds and child care subsidies are the primary sources of ongoing funding that pay for a significant portion of the operating costs and ensure some degree of stability to our programs. This core funding provides enough to subsidize our site coordinator and some key staff positions. As shown in Table 10.1, it is supplemented by a variety of federal, state, and private funds, without which we could not sustain our programs. Since 1997, we have worked with a local grant writer, Chuck Putney, who is very familiar with a wide range of available grants. The usual steps are that Chuck and I (and sometimes our site coordinator, Judy Cohen) meet, we answer several questions

Table 10.1 Sources of Funding

Source	Amount	Use
Federal		
Title II, IV, VI	Approximately $5,000 per year	Support of schoolwide initiatives; technology, homework clubs, professional development
Medicaid special education funds	Approximately $15,000 per year (amount varies)	Consulting health service providers
Medicaid EPSDT* funds	Approximately $40,000 per year	Site coordinator
Comprehensive School Reform Demonstration Grant	$150,000 over three years	Family center staff
Juvenile Justice Grant	$95,000 over three years	Coordinator for mentoring program
Community Development Block Grant	$291,400 (one-time grant)	Family Center building
State		
Agency of Human Services	$36,000 over three years	Health initiatives
Community Foundation	$2,500 (one-time grant)	Parents-as-Teachers training
Council on the Humanities	$15,000 over three years	New baby books, homework clubs, parent literacy programs
Children's Trust Fund	$4,400 over two years	Kindercamp
Early Education Initiative	$15,000 per year	Preschool staff
Dental access grant	$45,000 (one-time grant)	Dental office
Child care subsidies	$45,000–$55,000 per year	Child care, preschool
Local		
Bennington School District funds	Approximately $15,000 per year	Utilities, telephone, cleaning, maintenance of Family Center

(continued)

Table 10.1 Continued

Private		
Windham Foundation	$10,000 (one-time grant)	Parents-as-Teachers startup
Turrell Fund	$12,000–14,000 per year for the last four years	After-school programs
Phoenix Grant	$3,000 (one-time grant)	After-school program equipment
MVP Health Insurance Co.	$2,000 (one-time grant)	Health initiatives

*Early Periodic Screening Diagnosis and Treatment

several times, and then Chuck writes the application. I can write the smaller grant applications myself because much of the information is the same for each. We pay Chuck hourly. He was instrumental in our receiving both the $291,400 Community Development Block Grant to build the Family Center and the $150,000 Comprehensive School Reform Demonstration Grant, which helps pay for Family Center staff.

Some of the funding we receive is obviously dependent on our population. Subsidies are available for low-income families and/or families with children with disabilities or other significant factors that may affect families or children. Other families pay fees on a sliding scale for preschool and child care. Title I is based on poverty. To receive the Community Development Block Grant, we had to meet benefit, which meant serving a percentage of low-income families. But many of the grants are not based on need. The Comprehensive School Reform Demonstration Grant is received from the state's Department of Education if a school can demonstrate that it will be implementing a research-based reform program. I do think that having poor children gives you a competitive edge in grants. But I also think that schools with a high population of poor children need the competitive edge.

Too often in education, we tend to just keep putting money into the same things, whether they have worked in the past or not. Using money wisely doesn't just mean receiving grants. It's also using what you already have in a better way. For example, with our goal of emphasizing our youngest and neediest, we shifted one of our Title I teachers to work part of the day in our preschool—no extra money, just a different use of it.

Funding our services and programs will be a continuing challenge until we have a permanent source of funds flowing from either the state or the federal government. When I hear that some states have taken on the challenge of funding and developing community schools or that at times there are major bills in Congress that would fund community schools, I am encouraged.

11

What Is the Prognosis?

SUSTAINABILITY ACROSS
THE COUNTRY

This book combines the day-to-day experience of a committed worker in the trenches—the principal of an emerging community school—and the observations of a long-time researcher, admittedly a strong advocate for these models. We started by exploring the need to change the way schools and community agencies operate and how these stakeholders could be brought together to envision a full-service community school. We showed the large number of diverse services and programs that might be carried out during the school day or during extended hours, particularly in after-school programs. Consideration was given to the problems of staffing for these complex models, mixing school and community-based organization (CBO) people, and how the design of the partnerships might influence the staffing patterns. We have placed a lot of emphasis on the "people factor"—the importance of committed individuals in these kinds of enterprises.

Parent involvement is another area we explored, trying to broaden our thinking on roles parents can play in schools. Evaluation research was cited to show evidence that the changes going on in the Molly Stark School and many others can positively affect educational, health, and social outcomes. In the discussion of barriers, we tried to emphasize that before a well-functioning, sustainable institution can be created, many issues must be resolved, including turf, space, and transportation. I hope we have made it clear that none of this is easy.

The financial picture is also complex. Molly Stark is typical of full-service community schools, relying on an array of federal, state, and local resources that must be combined to make good things happen under one roof. We can be somewhat optimistic about the future of community schools, given the existing resources that can be used and the growing movement to stimulate further development of community school concepts. We can temper our enthusiasm with the recognition that this movement is still largely invisible to the massive school reform action taking place in this country. The education establishment seems quite bogged down in an unending and often acrimonious debate over the efficacy of test scores and, at the same time, is unable to find a way to produce certified and able teachers and the classrooms to put them in.

This final chapter addresses several important questions about the outlook in each of the areas we have covered. It concludes with some ideas about who needs to do what at the national, state, and local levels to legitimatize community school principles and vastly expand the network.

Should Every School Be a Full-Service Community School?

Should universality be our goal? My answer is yes and no. Yes, all schools should be accessible to the community and serve as hubs for educational, social, and cultural enhancements. The constituents of the school—children, parents, staff—should all think of the school as community owned. And within almost every school, certain students need individualized attention that can be most effectively delivered through school-community partnerships. But no, not every school needs to be "full service," not all schools must have built-in health and social service centers to help families and children overcome the barriers to learning. These barriers are heavily influenced by social class. Poor communities obviously face more difficult barriers than middle-class communities.

Priorities have to be set based on volume and intensity of need. Every school already has an indicator: the percentage of children eligible for free or reduced-price lunches. Schools in which more than 50 percent of the students are eligible are deemed especially needy. It is estimated that about one in four of the 85,000 public schools in the United States meets that criterion. Thus nearly 22,000 schools should receive priority in planning for transformation into full-service community schools. Although we do not know how many fully realized community schools currently exist (probably a couple of thousand), the potential demand is enormous.

Are We Talking About Charter Schools?

No. We don't have to tear apart the public school system to come up with solutions. All the many programs cited in this book have been developed within the traditional framework of local boards of education that are fully responsible for the operation of the schools. Unquestionably, some charter schools are configured along the lines of the full-service community schools described here: open for extended hours, based on partnerships, parent friendly, community oriented, and so on. I would be delighted to see charter schools adopt these concepts. But it is important to show that public schools can be transformed into child- and family-responsive institutions without destroying public education.

Should Public School Systems Be Encouraged to Lengthen the School Day and/or the School Year?

In some parts of the country, schools are adding hours to instructional time to improve test scores. In other places, schools are changing class schedules to be open all year because of overcrowding. In my view, neither of these rationales is valid. We know that effective schools can teach children within traditional school hours, using extended hours for youth development and enrichment in voluntary programs. We also know that year-round scheduling is disruptive to family life, parental work plans, and teachers' contracts. Most important, it has no positive effect.

On the other hand, I am strongly supportive of having the doors of the school open all the time, including a rich summer program, though I have some concerns about laying the whole responsibility on the school system. The best approach seems to be combining the efforts of the school system with support from a well-run CBO that can take over the responsibility for "everything else" except excellent teaching. Work during before- and after-school hours, weekends, and summers can be assumed through creative partnerships.

What Is a "Quality Program"?

One of the more elusive subjects is the quality of programming. We have seen that some community schools can produce better results than their traditional peers. What is the quality outcome we are seeking? Is it just educational achievement, or is it more complex, including such goals as social competence, good behavior, or even community development? Most of the evolving financial support mechanisms for these efforts place a high premium on accountability. Programs will have to prove that they are meeting their goals, although the goals of an after-school program and those of a school-based primary health initiative may be vastly different.

The question of quality may be addressed through research. First, we must identify community school models that are effective in both improving educational outcomes and enhancing youth and family development. This work is already under way; for example, the Coalition for Community Schools is working on a study called *Linkages to Learning* (2002). Now the models have to be examined qualitatively to find out what aspects of the program influence the outcomes. What are the pieces that are absolutely necessary, and what are merely "add-ons" that sound interesting but have little effect?

What About Planning?

After looking at this diverse collection of community schools and school-community partnerships, I am convinced that a major component of successful implementation is careful attention to planning. Partnership is critical. Because so many relationships, policies, and regulations must be jointly addressed and issues about them resolved, the planning process sets the tone for the work that follows. Inclusiveness from the start will ensure broader participation in the long run; this means bringing together school and community agency people, parents, other interested stakeholders, and students. Careful gathering of the necessary data (needs, services, unmet needs) and creating an appropriate design that responds to those data are necessary steps.

If you are interested in pursuing the concepts of full-service community schools, be prepared to spend at least a year planning the program. Track down the many resources that can support this work, visit the various models, and take advantage of one or more of the sources of technical assistance.

What About Services?

In a school building, you can do almost anything that is required to promote a healthy and productive educational environment and reduce barriers to learning. In this book, you can find references to programs now being brought into schools that address health, mental health, social service, drug and violence prevention, educational enrichment, before- and after-school programming, juvenile justice, recreation, the arts, culture, business practice, and so on. A review of the list of services attached to the Hoyer bill (see Chapter 10) verifies the claim that almost any human service can be provided in a school building.

This is not a pitch to simply move every human service into school buildings. The important point is to find the appropriate intervention that will help solve the problems in a particular school. The program has to be needed (or it won't be used), and it has to be effective (or it won't make any difference). The program must not place additional burdens on the school system; rather, it should remove some of the burdens. As Sue has pointed out, flexibility is necessary. If a program doesn't seem to be working, discontinue it.

What About Staffing?

Without question, this work is labor intensive. No school principal or guidance counselor or interested teacher should imagine that he or she can do it alone. No community agency person or youth worker or child advocate should think that he or she can just go into a school and open up shop. I have stated repeatedly that community schools require the full-time attention of a coordinator or director, who may work for the school system, the lead community agency, or a consortium set up just for this purpose.

This is a relatively new category of labor. Although we have found many such people with various titles currently working in community schools, few universities have set up courses that might prepare people for this new profession. In my view, a community school coordinator is someone who understands both educational systems and human service systems, with knowledge that may come from combinations of graduate pursuits, such as education and community psychology or social work and public administration or even public health.

The same cross-disciplinary approach should be present in schools of education. Principals and teachers need to be exposed to ideas about child, youth, and family development as part of their training. They should learn about community school models and what's required to start one. At the same time, youth workers have to learn what goes on in schools and how they can play a role in creating new kinds of institutions.

Unions can play an important part in furthering the community school movement. Both major educational unions, the National Education Association (NEA) and the American Federation of Teachers (AFT), are already part of the Coalition for Community Schools and have indicated their support for these concepts, including keeping school buildings open for extended hours. As Joan Devlin, associate director of the AFT, stated, "Full-service schools require knowledge, collaboration . . . and the interest of political power brokers to marshal the resources needed . . . It takes a collective will and vision to think beyond traditional funding streams and power bases and focus on a single set of commonly agreed to goals" (e-mail, August 6, 2001). But many teachers in school systems around the country and youth workers employed by community agencies are not covered by union contracts and work at very low wages. In general, salary scales for youth workers are way below teachers' levels. And high turnover rates for all personnel are endemic.

What About Parent Involvement?

Despite the perceptions of many schools and community organizations that parents are hard to involve, we have shown numerous examples of very successful programs. The key here seems to be ensuring that the services and opportunities made available are ones that parents really want and need. They do not respond to invitations to attend professorial lectures in child development, especially if they have limited English proficiency or are otherwise alienated from the school; they do respond to small workshops on similar subjects held in parent resource rooms in which they feel comfortable. Home visiting reaches parents directly. Parents sign up in droves to volunteer in classrooms, cafeterias, site-based management teams, and playgrounds, and they are eager to enter training to become paid teacher's aides and to participate in adult education of all kinds.

What About Governance?

The design of the school-community partnership is basic to the discussion of full-service community schools. As you have seen, the number and diversity of the models are daunting. Molly Stark exemplifies the principal-run approach; Sue Maguire reorganized her school, invited a number of community agencies to help, and arranged for their funding. School principals also play a major role in the governance of Missouri's Caring Communities program, but integrated state grants go to established community partnerships—school and community collaboratives charged with achieving specific goals to improve the lives of children, families, and the community.

Some community schools are initiated not by a school but by a community organization. The Children's Aid Society partnership at the school level places a full-time coordinator next to the principal, with formal written agreements to guide the relationship. The community school district is also a partner in this collaboration through a Memorandum of Understanding, and so is the central school district by means of a formal resolution.

One might conclude that no two community schools have the same governance structure. All have some combination of school authority with outside community agency participation. Whether the lead agency should be the school or the CBO is a debatable issue and will probably not be resolved in the near future. The important point is that in each case, the responsibilities and roles have to be clearly established for such areas as keeping the school open and integrating the support services with the educational program.

What About Barriers to Implementation?

I hope potential community school developers are not turned off by our discussion of barriers. We have emphasized throughout that establishing a partnership and implementing a full-service community school is not an easy assignment. Knowing about the stumbling blocks in advance should help practitioners deal with problems of money, space, staff, transportation, turf, equity, and all the other items that appear in various studies and reports about implementing programs.

These kinds of issues are not found only in community schools; they are integral to any human endeavor that is built on relationships. The words that come up repeatedly are *communication, negotiation, patience,* and *fortitude.* Sometimes it helps to have outside facilitators who assist school and community people in working their way through these issues. I have noted throughout that technical assistance is available from a number of sources.

What About Accountability?

We are learning quite a lot from emerging school-community partnerships. The people in this work are vitally interested in research and accountability. Most of the community school initiatives have an evaluation component, particularly those that are foundation funded. The C. S. Mott Foundation's effort to support and track the success of the federal 21st Century Community Learning Centers (CCLC) has stimulated unprecedented evaluation projects in the after-school arena. As this research is completed, we will have access to considerable knowledge about how extending the hours a school is open can influence outcomes for students.

It is my view that after-school programs are a primary entry point for the development of full-service community schools. It is probable that some of the almost 7,000 schools that have received CCLC grants to open their schoolhouse doors and establish partnerships with community agencies will move on from after-school programs to other aspects of community schooling (for example, primary health clinics and family resource centers). An important area of research will be tracking the further development of these programs.

Evaluation of complex school-community programs is not a simple matter. The academic testing situation in this country is already in total chaos, and that covers only one piece of the community school action. Efforts are already under way to figure out how to capture the other pieces, such as tracking student and parent use of the various services and programs offered before, during, and after school. Surveys have been designed to measure behavioral outcomes and psychosocial attitudes. Some programs, such as California's Healthy Start, have excellent management information systems. The situation requires that universities actively seek partnerships with community school programs. As always, however this all comes together, it will be costly.

What About Financing?

So here we are, back to the bottom line. Our nation cannot embrace the concept of full-service community schools without a major commitment to funding them. If my figure of 22,000 schools with very needy populations has any validity, and if it costs around $100,000 a year to set up the infrastructure, we're talking about $2.2 billion for starters. And if it costs around $250,000 for a fully functioning program for 1,000 students ($250 per student per year, a minimum estimate), we're talking about $5.5 billion a year. Although that sounds like a lot, it is just about half of the Title I Elementary and Secondary Education Act appropriation for 2002, which was about $12 billion. And some of that money could come from existing resources, such as the CCLC after-school funds and others mentioned in Chapter 10.

Sustainability is the desirable goal. What happens to these community school programs when the five-year grants run out? Some of the CCLC after-school programs are already faced with this situation after three years. Perhaps the concept to pursue is "entitlement," meaning that every child is entitled to go to a school where he or she can gain access to the supports needed to overcome the barriers to learning. I do not know how this could be accomplished. But I would certainly encourage advocates for community schools to pursue this line of thinking.

States already play a major role in supporting community schools and after-school programs, as do foundations and local resources. Their potential roles are discussed later in the chapter.

What Can Be Done at the National Level to Promote Full-Service Community Schools?

A simple solution to all of this would be for the federal government to just write a big check for $5.5 billion, but of course that is not going to happen. And even if it did, the potential stakeholders are not quite ready to move forward. It would make a big difference, however, if there were legislation that moved in the direction of supporting coordinated school-community partnerships that go beyond after-school programs.

Two of the major bills introduced in the 2001 Congress, the Hoyer Full-Service Community Schools Act and the Reed Child Opportunity Zone Family Center Act (described in the previous chapter), didn't get very far, but at least the concepts have been introduced. A third bill, the Younger Americans Act, is still sitting in the appropriate committees awaiting action as we write. But Congress is so fixated on testing issues and negotiating the amount of money that will back up their proposals that it is unlikely they will take up youth development issues in the near future.

However, I can think of six actions that would be helpful at the national level, building on some of the ideas in the Hoyer bill.

1. *Community School Authority.*   In the federal government, create a community school authority, jointly administered by the Department of Education (DOE) and the Department of Health and Human Services (DHHS). The primary function of the authority would be to award five-year grants to school-community agency partnerships in high-need areas. Assuming about $100,000 for the first year to create a plan and $250,000 for each of the next four years to bring in services, the total grant would be $1.1 million per site for five years. The school-community group would have to deliver matching funds, such as for space rental, personnel, or equipment.

The community school authority would be backed up by a congressional working group on community schools. This group would bring together members of Congress to learn more about full-service community schools and would make sure that they visited model sites (in their districts).

2. *Technical Assistance and Capacity Building.* Technical assistance can be provided by both the public and the nonprofit sectors to help communities plan, implement, and sustain programs. The federal government could support a national center for community schools located in the DOE, with joint oversight from the DHHS as well as the departments of justice, labor, agriculture, and HUD, all of which have resources in community school programs. In the nonprofit sector, the Coalition for Community Schools could provide technical assistance and/or work with the many federally supported centers (such as the two Centers for Mental Health in Schools) and national intermediary organizations (such as Communities-in-Schools) that already have the capacity to do this work.

3. *Community Schools Awards Program.* Develop an awards program for effective school-community partnerships, recognizing the most effective coalitions. The program would have two components: (a) recognition and awards for a certain number of schools and (b) efforts to develop standards or criteria for what a community school is. The intent would be to raise the visibility of the movement. This could be jointly funded by foundations and the DOE.

4. *Expansion of 21st Century Community Learning Centers.* Support the expansion of 21st Century Community Learning Centers. Make sure that some of the grants go directly to community-based organizations. If states administer the program, they should be prepared to offer technical assistance, adequate funding, and training for coordinators and other staff. Monitor the process through which after-school programs are a first step in creating full-service community schools.

5. *Support for Research on Community Schools and After-School Programs.* Foundations can play a major role in conducting research on and evaluating community schools. Development of management information and student tracking systems can be furthered. Studies of implementation are important. Make sure that all federal grant programs include an appropriation for evaluation.

6. *Support for the Coalition for Community Schools.* As one of the founders and steering committee members of the Coalition for Community Schools, I would like to see it gain significant support for the essential role it plays. More than 170 national organizations have joined forces to work together and promote community schools. This is an avenue through which education and youth development people, administration and union representatives, and risk-reduction and asset-building experts communicate regularly. As Joan Devlin sees it, "The coalition . . . provides an opportunity to lay down the burden of protecting turf long enough to listen to the ideas and dreams of others. It helps to raise areas of

agreement and finds ways to make disagreements less volatile" (e-mail, August 6, 2001). The coalition can mobilize the voluntary sector to work with the public sector to see that these models are widely replicated and that the backup research and evaluation take place.

Martin Blank, director of the coalition, believes,

> The next several years represent a critical juncture for community schools. If the movement can build on its success and continue to engage people with its vision, educate policymakers, and make the case with educational leaders, leaders in other sectors, and the public, there is the potential to secure federal support for community schools in the next five or six years. Federal funding will remain a tough challenge, however. . . . In this era of high-stakes testing and accountability, where the success of students, teachers and principals often rides on a single test, [the challenge is] getting them to focus on anything other than academic performance. The community schools movement must continually demonstrate how a community school approach impacts student learning and helps to create the conditions for learning. (e-mail, August 7, 2001)

What Can States Do?

Some states have played major roles in initiating full-service community schools and school-community partnerships for after-school programs. As state administrations change, it is important to make sure that those programs continue and expand. In some states, new programs may be initiated. One approach for state governments might include the creation of a coordinating agency that draws in resources from education, health, and social services and awards grants directly to community coalitions (as in Missouri). States can develop a technical assistance capacity to work with communities in pulling together local groups, planning, implementation, and evaluation. State agencies, public and nonprofit, can sponsor conferences and workshops to spread the word and make these programs visible.

What Can Communities Do?

The movement for community schools originated at the local level. The first action was truly "bottom up," with the major models emerging one at a time from the hands of dedicated charismatic individuals or small groups. The next stage has been the emergence of intermediary organizations, the "parent" group for each of the models (such as the Children's Aid Society, the University of Pennsylvania, Beacons, the National Center for Community Education, and Schools of the 21st Century) with the capacity for providing technical assistance (see Resources). This has resulted in scattershot adaptations all over the country.

The next stage in the proliferation of community schools is to go systemwide. Boston may be the first city in the country to achieve this goal. School and community agency stakeholders are talking together about creating the Boston Full-Service Schools Roundtable as a vehicle for helping school and community agencies to jointly develop and expand Boston's supply of full-service community schools. Other cities attempting to influence a whole system are Buffalo, New York; Plainfield, New Jersey; Hartford, Connecticut; Portland, Oregon; Kansas City, Missouri; and Birmingham, Alabama.

The process for local change begins with planning. Any community agency can take the leadership role in calling together an inclusive group from one school or neighborhood, a cluster of schools, or the whole system. Local chapters of national organizations such as the United Way, Boys and Girls Clubs, the Public Education Network, and Communities-in-Schools have developed the capacity to initiate collaborative planning groups. Indigenous CBOs can do the same. A local school-community planning group may be brought together spontaneously, or it may be responsive to a call for proposals from a funding source.

Philip Nobel (2001), writing in the Education Life section of the *New York Times*, portrays a massive school-building boom across the country, and in every one, attention is being paid to community needs.

> An idea that first emerged in the late 1960s but didn't fly until the '90s, the concept is variously known as community schools, community learning centers, shared facilities or full-service schools. Where older buildings endeavored to create an icon to represent "education" within the community—but kept that community at bay by creating an insular world of learning within—these new schools are attempting to bring the life of the community into the building itself. (p. 22)

What Can You Do?

If these ideas interest you, you do not have to wait for the federal government to act or a state agency to offer you a grant to get started. The first step is to bring together a group of stakeholders and start moving toward envisioning what your local school could become if those concerned put their heads together. In this arena, one person can make a difference. One person cannot do this alone, but he or she can serve as a sentinel in a community to indicate that changes are both necessary and feasible. We dedicate this book to those sentinels all over the country who we know are out there ready to get to work.

THE FUTURE AT MOLLY STARK

So what's the prognosis for full-service community schools in our country, in the state of Vermont, in my community, at Molly Stark? I really can't answer that. When I am talking with my colleagues at school, with Joy, or with Doug Racine, Vermont's lieutenant governor, I quickly get into the mode of "We just have to do this in a bigger way!" But in the day-to-day whirlwind of running a full-service school, I don't take a lot of time to think about the bigger picture.

We may not have figured out all the answers or cured all the ills of our students and their families, but what I can say for certain is this: We have taken a risk to try to do the right thing. And speaking only for myself but being sure that it's true for those I work with each day, I can say that never has there been such a feeling of triumph, exhaustion, frustration, and pride all at the same time. We have created a community where kids can feel valued, parents can feel welcomed, and staff can feel proud. And whether or not it is the total answer isn't as important as that we have done, small step by small step, things that will in some way change many lives for the better.

Before I first presented our full-service school plan to the entire Molly Stark staff, I kept remembering the novel *Dominic*, by William Steig (1972), that I used to read to my fifth graders when I taught. The message became so clear to me that I printed it on top of the staff meeting agenda before my presentation of the journey that was about to begin. I'm sure some thought it was great, some thought it was corny, and some didn't have a clue what I was trying to say, but it didn't matter. I just *had* to give them this message from the alligator witch:

> I hope you don't mind if I tell you this much. . . . that road there on the right goes nowhere. There's not a bit of magic up that road, no adventure, no surprise, nothing to discover or wonder at. Even the scenery is humdrum. You'd soon grow much too introspective. You'd take to daydreaming and tail-twiddling, get absent-minded and lazy, forget where you are and what you're about, sleep more than one should, and be wretchedly bored. Furthermore, after a while, you'd reach a dead end and you'd have to come all that dreary way back to right here where we're standing now, only it wouldn't be now, it would be some woefully wasted time later.
>
> Now this road, the one on the left . . . this road keeps right on going as far as anyone cares to go, and if you take it, believe me, you'll never find yourself wondering what you might have missed by not taking the other. Up this road, which looks the same at the beginning, but is really ever so different, things will happen that you never could have guessed at—marvelous, unbelievable things. Up this way is where adventure is. I'm pretty sure I know which way you'll go. (pp. 7–8)

Ten Reasons Principals Should Think About Developing Full-Service Community Schools

1. Full-service community schools are a natural way to develop collaborations with community partners that will enhance services for kids and families.

2. Life for children and families is more complex than ever; the role of schools must shift to meet changing needs.

3. You can't do it alone. It makes sense to work together with others interested in helping children and families.

4. Lack of money is an ongoing issue. Working with others toward common goals maximizes your resources. In addition, taking a less traditional approach increases your chances of receiving funding.

5. All children need and deserve opportunities; these services may well be the only opportunity some children get.

6. It's more efficient *not* to be always in a crisis mode putting out fires, which is where many of us find ourselves much of the time. Although not a cure, more preventive services may lessen the crisis for the next generation.

7. Full-service community schools allow access to children and families who are already at the school, so providing services is more effective and efficient.

8. We must continuously look at what our schools are doing for children and families: Are we successful? Are our services and programs furthering our short- and long-term goals? If not, it's important to reflect and possibly use our resources differently.

9. If our commitment is to the success of children, assisting them in developing to their full potential, why begin our efforts at age five when we know through research that the years between birth and five are so critical?

10. It is important to feel that you are making a difference.

Appendix A

Strengthengin Partnerships:
Community School Assessment Checklist

In many communities, partnerships between schools and other community organizations and agencies are helping to create supports that enable chil dren and youth to learn and succeed and help families and communities to thrive. These partnerships bring together diverse individuals and groups, including principals, teachers, school superintendents, school boards, community-based organizations, youth development organizations, health and human services agencies, parents and other community leaders to expand opportunities for children, families, and communities.

Creating a successful community school partnership is a complex, challenging, and time-consuming task. To be effective, partnerships need to engage in a thoughtful process to define a vision and clear goals. Partnerships need to have effective governance and management structures to ensure that programs operate efficiently and the partnership is responsive to community needs. Community school partnerships also need to draw from a broad range of perspectives and expertise—from inside the school as well as from other organizations and individuals within the community. Finally, community school partnerships need to connect, coordinate, and leverage resources from a variety of sources to support and continue their work.

This tool contains a series of checklists to assist school and community leaders in creating and/or strengthening community school partnerships.

- The first checklist helps you to assess the development of your community school partnership.
- The second checklist helps you to take inventory of existing programs and services in or connected to your school that support children, youth, families, and other community residents.
- The third checklist helps you to catalogue the funding sources that support these programs and services.

Once completed, these checklists can serve as a planning tool to develop strategies to strengthen your partnership, improve coordination of existing programs and services, and/or expand current levels of support.

I. COMMUNITY SCHOOL PARTNERSHIP ASSESSMENT

Building and maintaining effective community school partnerships requires dedicated time and ongoing attention to the collaborative process. This checklist focuses on the *process* of bringing partners together and working to achieve desired results. This checklist can help partnerships to focus on, assess, and improve the quality of their collaborative efforts.

Our partnership has developed a clear vision.

    Disagree   1 . 2   3   4   5   Agree

Our partnership has collaboratively identified the results we want to achieve for children, youth, families, and our community.

    Disagree   1   2   3   4   5   Agree

Our partnership has developed strategies for coordinating and linking the array of supports and opportunities for children, youth, families, and community members that are available at or connected to the school.

    Disagree   1   2   3   4   5   Agree

Our partnership has established a clear organizational structure. Our partnership has agreed upon the roles that individual partners will play, and ensured that all partners understand and accept the responsibilities of those roles.

    Disagree   1   2   3   4   5   Agree

All partners involved in our community school have an understanding of who the other partners are, what organizations they come from, and what those organizations do.

    Disagree   1   2   3   4   5   Agree

Our partnership regularly communicates with all partners to keep them informed about its work.

    Disagree   1   2   3   4   5   Agree

Our partnership engages in activities to create awareness about and increase support for the work of the partnership.

    Disagree   1   2   3   4   5   Agree

Our partnership has identified and mobilized resources (financial and other) from partner organizations and other entities throughout the community.

    Disagree   1   2   3   4   5   Agree

II. COMMUNITY SCHOOL PROGRAM AND SERVICE CHECKLIST

An important first step for school and community leaders seeking to create or expand community school partnerships is to assess the broad range of resources that are currently available within or connected to their school. Some of these programs and services may be directly supported by the school; others may be supported by community organizations and agencies. This checklist helps you to take inventory of the programs and services already administered by the school and its partners. Once you know what programs and services exist, your challenge is to make sure these programs and services are strategically coordinated to achieve desired results and to identify new programs and services that may be needed.

Programs and Services	Program Administrator				If not run by school, list name of partner
	School or School District	Community-Based Organization	Local Public Agency	Other	
SUPPORTS FOR SCHOOL-AGE CHILDREN AND YOUTH					
Academic Enrichment/ Tutoring/Remedial Education					
Arts, Music, and Cultural Programs					
Before- and/or After-School Programs					
Community Service/ Service Learning					
Conflict Resolution					
Family Life/Personal Skills/Teen Parenting Programs					
Literacy					
Mentoring					
Recreation/Sports					
School Nurse					
Substance Abuse/ Violence Prevention Programs					
Other					
Other					

Programs and Services	Program Administrator				If not run by school, list name of partner
	School or School District	Community-Based Organization	Local Public Agency	Other	
COMMUNITY SUPPORTS					
Adult Education/ GED/Literacy					
Parenting Education					
Health Education					
Health Care and/or Dental Services					
Early Care and Education/Pre-K/ Head Start					
Job Training					
Substance Abuse Prevention					
Violence Prevention					
Mental Health Services					
Family Support Center					
Other					
Other					

III. COMMUNITY SCHOOL FUNDING SOURCE ASSESSMENT

Once you've taken inventory of the current programs and services operating in or connected to your school, the next step is to identify the sources of funding that support these services. In some cases, funding may come from federal, state, or local government agencies. In other cases, funding may come from private sources, such as community-based organizations or private foundations. This assessment can be used to catalogue existing funding sources that support a community school as well as to identify new funding sources to expand current programs and services.

SOURCES OF SUPPORT FOR COMMUNITY SCHOOL PROGRAMS AND SERVICES	
School and/or School District (e.g., Title I)	
Community-Based Organizations (e.g., YMCA, Boys & Girls Club, faith-based organizations)	
Universities and Colleges (e.g., work study or service learning students, professional development training)	
Federal Funds (e.g., food and nutrition funds, 21st Century Learning Centers, Community Learning Centers, VISTA, AmeriCorp)	
State Funds (e.g., funds from state departments of education, health and/or human services, parks and recreation, and juvenile justice)	
Private Foundations (e.g., local community foundations, national foundations)	
Private Businesses	
PTA	
Participation Fees	
Other	

SOURCE: Martin J. Blank and Barbara Hanson Langford, September 2000

Appendix B

Community Needs Assessment: Parent Survey

As we hope you have heard, we have received a grant from the state to build our Family Resource Center. The purpose of the Center will be to provide programs and support to families in the school district, including those with children not yet school age. Our current plans are to offer before-school and after-school child care, a preschool for 3- and 4-year-olds, play groups for infants and toddlers, expanded health and nutrition programs, and activities for families and adults. Right now, we need your help in identifying how many families will be needing some or all of these services. Please take a few minutes to fill out this questionnaire and return it to us by Monday, April 5.

1. Please fill in the grades and ages of your children under 12 years:

	Child 1	Child 2	Child 3	Child 4
Grade	___	___	___	___
Age	___	___	___	___
2. What does your child do after school?	___	___	___	___
a. Home with parent(s)	___	___	___	___
b. Home with adult relative (grandparent, aunt)	___	___	___	___
c. Home with adult babysitter	___	___	___	___
d. Home alone or with younger brothers/sisters	___	___	___	___
e. Home with older child (age of child ___)	___	___	___	___
f. Outside home in after-school child care (family day care home, sitter's home, center)	___	___	___	___
g. Other arrangements (lessons, sports)	___	___	___	___

3. How many hours does each child spend in child care?

   a. Before school   ____ ____ ____ ____

   b. After school   ____ ____ ____ ____

   c. Preschool child care   ____ ____ ____ ____

4. What do you currently pay per week for child care?

   a. Nothing   ____ ____ ____ ____

   b. $1–$15 per week   ____ ____ ____ ____

   c. $16–$35 per week   ____ ____ ____ ____

   d. $36–$45 or more per week   ____ ____ ____ ____

5. How often would you send your child/children to a supervised school-age child care program, if one were started at the school?

   a. Probably not at all   ____ ____ ____ ____

   b. Every school day   ____ ____ ____ ____

   c. Two to three times each week   ____ ____ ____ ____

   d. On an irregular basis   ____ ____ ____ ____

6. When would care be needed? (check all that apply)

   a. Before school   ____ ____ ____ ____

   b. After school   ____ ____ ____ ____

   c. Summer   ____ ____ ____ ____

   d. School holidays   ____ ____ ____ ____

   e. School vacations   ____ ____ ____ ____

   f. Before or after kindergarten   ____ ____ ____ ____

7. What is the *earliest* time you would need *before*-school care?

   a. 6:30 a.m.   ____ ____ ____ ____

   b. 7:00 a.m.   ____ ____ ____ ____

   c. 7:30 a.m.   ____ ____ ____ ____

8. What is the *latest* time you would need *after*-school care?

   a. 3:30 p.m.   ____ ____ ____ ____

   b. 4:00 p.m.   ____ ____ ____ ____

   c. 4:30 p.m.   ____ ____ ____ ____

   d. 5:00 p.m.   ____ ____ ____ ____

9. Would you send your children aged 3 or 4 to a preschool program if such a program was started at the school?

   ____ No children of preschool age

   ____ Yes (number of preschool-age children ____)

   ____ No

10. Many of our families will be eligible for child care subsidies based on monthly income and family size. These subsidies are based on federal poverty guidelines.

   a. Would you be willing to fill out the paperwork to apply for child care subsidies? ____ Yes ____ No

   b. If you do not qualify for child care subsidies, would you be willing to spend up to $2.50/hour for child care or preschool? ____ Yes ____ No

11. Has your child participated in after school enrichment programs at the school? ____ Yes ____ No

12. In addition to your child's enjoyment, do you use the enrichment program for child care? ____ Yes ____ No

13. If enrichment programs were available at the school during the summer, check the types of program that would most interest you:

   a. ___ 8:00–4:00 daily ___ 9:00–12:00 daily ___ 12:00–3:00 daily

   b. ___ 2-week sessions ___ 4-week sessions ___ 8-week sessions

   c. ___ Recreational ___ Educational ___ Combination

14. Would you be able to transport your child for child care or preschool? ____ Yes ____ No

15. Additional comments or suggestions:

   Name: _____

   Address: _____

   Phone: _____

Thank you for your information!

Appendix C

Child Care Programs Handbook

MOLLY STARK FAMILY CENTER CHILD CARE PROGRAMS Handbook

Information for Families

Fall 2000

CHILD CARE PROGRAMS HANDBOOK

MOLLY STARK FAMILY CENTER MISSION STATEMENT: to support children and families' ability to achieve sustainable academic and life success

PHILOSOPHY AND GOALS OF THE CHILD CARE PROGRAMS

The philosophy of the Molly Stark Child Care Programs is based on respect for the developing child within the context of the family and community. Our goal is to provide safe, healthy, developmentally appropriate preschool and school age child care that reflects current research and knowledge about children's physical, emotional, and cognitive growth and the ways in which growth is affected by school and home.

Because we recognize that students come from homes exhibiting a range of access to academically enriching activities and behavior models, our program will strive to provide students with ongoing experiences to increase their exposure to activities that promote literacy, numeracy, gross and fine motor development, and social and emotional development. However, we also believe that school-age child care should not simply be an extension of the school day but an additional program that serves to fulfill the continuing needs of childhood. A developmentally appropriate program for children of elementary school age acknowledges children's natural desire to re-create their surroundings into a personalized environment; it also recognizes the need for children in group care for long periods to be in "home like" surroundings. Therefore, an important aspect of our philosophy will be to include the children and families in the development of the program, the space, the routine, and the schedule. We will work at engaging both the families and children in the process of curriculum development because we believe that education comes from having the opportunity, materials, and time to explore thoughts, feelings, and concepts through meaningful activities.

Finally, we believe that children live in a world that is often complex and challenging for them. We will attempt to address the children's concerns and quest for understanding through our curriculum, our staff-child relationships, and our connections with parents and guardians. Because of our belief in the need to respect the child within the context of the family and community, we will strive to create a program that honors the diversity of all students, while developing a sense of acceptance and tolerance for one another. Ultimately, we will attempt to make our program a warm, welcoming place where children and families can feel good about themselves, can come for help and support, and can engage in experiences that will lead to present and continuing life success.

Based on this philosophy, our program goals include (but are not limited to):

1. Develop a safe and nurturing environment appropriate for a range of ages.

2. Always show respect for each child and each family.

3. Encourage active, hands-on exploration of equipment, materials, and ideas along with encouraging respect for materials and one another's ideas.

4. Emphasize process over product by offering open-ended creative activities and projects.

5. Promote tolerance and acceptance for one another, encourage group cooperation and problem solving, and work toward becoming a community of learners—both children and adults.

6. Work with other Molly Stark staff members to provide consistency of academic and behavioral growth.

7. Encourage parent involvement in all aspects of the program, including focusing some of our program priorities on the needs of parents themselves.

DAILY SCHEDULES

The following are approximate schedules for different groups. Children find security in a predictable series of events. Structure helps children emotionally and intellectually develop a sense of self-control and mastery of events and the environment. Within this structure, children have the freedom of individual choice of activities. Changes are made in the schedules throughout the year in response to the weather, the changing needs of the group, and other circumstances. A daily schedule is posted in each classroom as well as presented here:

BEFORE-SCHOOL CHILD CARE

7:00–8:00	Homework help
	Games and quiet activities
	(Depending on weather, staff, and enrollment, there may be some outside time)
7:45	Children participating in school breakfast program may leave to get breakfast
8:00	Time to go to regular classroom

MORNING PRESCHOOL (3- and 4-year-olds)

8:00–9:30	Breakfast/activity time, including gross motor and literacy options
9:30–9:50	Circle time
9:50–10:30	Outside time (in case of inclement weather, inside time in kindercare classroom)
10:30–11:20	Activity time, including snack, gross motor, and literacy options
1120–11:30	Clean-up
11:30–11:40	Story dramatization; group games
11:40–12:00	Lunch (as children get done eating, they go to listen to books)
12:00	Good-bye

MORNING KINDERCARE

8:00–8:30	Breakfast
8:30–8:45	Morning circle/meeting
8:45–9:45	Activity time
9:45–10:00	Clean-up
10:00–10:15	Snack
10:15–10:45	Outside time
10:45–11:15	Group activity time
11:15–11:45	Literacy circle time
11:45	Good-bye/lunch with other afternoon kindergarten students

AFTERNOON KINDERCARE

12:00–12:45	Outside time
12:45–1:00	Meeting at circle
1:00–2:00	Activity time, including snack option
*2:00–2:10	Clean-up
2:10–2:40	Rest/story time
2:40–3:00	Outside time/good-bye

*During winter months or inclement weather, activity time will go to 2:30, followed by clean-up and rest/story time

AFTER-SCHOOL CHILD CARE

3:00–3:20	Greeting, snack, and story
*3:30–4:45	Afternoon activity choice, including outside play, theme-related projects, homework help, art activities, dramatic play, gross motor activities
4:45–5:00	Clean-up
5:00–530	Quiet activity, individual reading until pick-up time

*After-school enrichment program classes for enrolled students from 3:15–4:15

FULL-DAY SCHEDULE

7:00–9:00	Arrival, breakfast, free choice of activities
9:00–9:15	Group greeting and story
9:15–10:00	Activity choice, including gym, computer, classroom play
10:00–10:30	Snack and story
10:30–11:00	Group walk
11:00–12:00	Activity choice, including gym, computer, classroom play
12:00–12:30	Lunch and story
12:30–3:00	Activity choice, including gym or outside, computer, cooking project, classroom play
3:00–3:30	Snack and story
3:00–4:45	Activity choice
4:45–5:00	Clean-up
5:00–5:30	Quiet activity, individual reading until pick up

CHILD CARE CALENDAR

The preschool will meet Monday–Thursday, from 8:00 a.m. to 12:00 p.m. It will follow the regular school calendar. The school-age child care program will operate on a regular basis following the school calendar. It will also operate full days over some school vacation days, in-service days, and school half-days. Children should bring a bag lunch and dress for outdoor and active activities for full-day child care. Snacks and drinks will be provided.

SNOW DAY POLICY

Although the school-age child care program will try to remain open on snow days, the coordinator and principal will decide whether to close it based on road conditions and the ability of the staff and families to travel safely. If it is able to remain open, the program will run from 8:00 a.m. to 5:00 p.m. If the weather conditions worsen, the coordinator will call parents to inform them of the closing. If the program is unable to open, the information will be announced on the

Bennington radio stations—WBTN (94.3 FM/1370 AM) and WZEC (97.5 FM). Parents may also call the Family Center at 802-447-7764.

Snacks and drinks will be provided, but children must bring their own lunches. As with all our child care programs, children must already be enrolled; we cannot accept drop-offs.

FEES AND PAYMENT PLAN

The Molly Stark Child Care Programs are fee based, with a sliding scale and child care subsidies available to eligible families. Full fee for the school-age program is $2.50/hour for the first child and $1.75/hour for any additional children. Full fee for the preschool is $30/week. Sliding scales will be based on parent/guardian income. In the case of the preschool, it will also be based on the developmental needs and requirements of the child. Families will be responsible for paying for all hours for which the children are enrolled. Molly Stark Family Center Child Care Programs will be open from 7:00 a.m. until 5:30 p.m. The preschool will run from 8:00 a.m. until 12:00 p.m., Monday through Thursday.

As a program licensed by the Agency of Human Services, Department of Social and Rehabilitation Services, Child Care Division, some of our families may qualify for state child care subsidies. Interested parties may call 802-447-6937, or write to Child Care Services, Bennington SRS Office, One Veterans Memorial Drive, Bennington, VT 05201.

Families may choose to be billed on a weekly or monthly basis. Some families receiving child care subsidies may be responsible for fees not covered by the subsidy.

GUIDANCE AND DISCIPLINE

The Molly Stark Child Care Programs believe discipline should be a positive and interactive process leading to growth. Discipline in terms of limits and controls adds reassuring structure to children's lives and helps them organize and stabilize their relationships with other people—both adults and peers. Our goal will be to help children develop self-control, self-esteem, and respect for others through the use of expectations and consequences appropriate to their age level and individual ability to process and understand information.

In the process of learning about the world, children need to understand which behaviors are acceptable and which are not and how to discriminate between the two. Drawing on developmentally appropriate practices, the Molly Stark community has developed a variety of strategies to help students develop good social skills. These include staff instruction, guidance services, and a schoolwide structure that uses a common language, procedures, and consistent consequences for challenging behaviors. Our staff will attempt to provide many daily opportunities for children to develop and practice social skills, such as helping, cooperating, negotiating, and talking through interpersonal problems. Where appropriate, the staff will endeavor to involve children in establishing clear and reasonable rules for group life and conflict resolution, and will also use such techniques as redirecting children to acceptable activities and encouraging children to mediate their own concerns with one another.

Recognizing that conflicts are a necessary part of growth, which is not to say that they should be encouraged, our staff will attempt to see conflicts as opportunities to teach children effective ways of developing social skills. We will work at giving children the message that although most feelings are acceptable, not all expressions of those feelings are acceptable. Taking into account each child's developmental age and previous experiences, we will set realistic expectations and consequences that help children see their actions in the context of other people's needs and reactions. These consequences may include reflecting on actions and completing a behavior plan with a supervising staff member, making appropriate and meaningful amends to any hurt parties, or occasionally a short time-out from the group. When consequences must be followed, they will be done with an understanding of each child's need for respect and a sensitivity to individual reactions. The use of consequences will also be communicated to parents, and the staff will attempt to engage parents in discussions about the ways in which home and school can work together in understanding each child's needs. If the staff feels that the child is regularly engaging in behavior that is unsafe to that child or to other children in the program, parents may be called in to discuss the child's removal from the program for a period.

In general, the Molly Stark Child Care Programs will view discipline as a process through which children learn to live together in an orderly way. The staff will encourage positive behavior by modeling good listening skills, negotiating skills, and respect for others.

SICK CHILD POLICY

If your child is home sick, please call the Family Center to inform the staff. If your child leaves school sick, please notify the program or ask the nurse to pass on the information. If your child becomes sick during child care hours, we will request that you pick up your child as soon as possible to ensure the well-being of all children in the program. Children who need to receive medication during the program must have a note indicating the child's name, date, time, and amount of medication to be administered.

In the event of a medical emergency or an accident, we will contact the child's parents and doctor. If it is impossible to reach either and if emergency treatment is required, the child will be taken to Southwest Vermont Medical Center. Parental authorization and signature will be part of the enrollment forms.

PARENT/GUARDIAN ACCESS TO PROGRAMS
AND RECORDS—CONFIDENTIALITY

Parents are always welcome to visit the Molly Stark Child Care Programs. Siblings of children participating in the programs are also welcome, but parents should call in advance and arrange the visit with the teacher. Parents are also welcome to join children for meals but should arrange this in advance so the teacher can make any additional plans.

The Molly Stark Child Care Programs do not release any information on a child to any institution or individual without written permission from a parent. Our records on children will be stored in the coordinator's office to ensure that they will be used only by those who have permission to do so. These records are available to parents on request. Parents who have any concerns about their children's records or progress are encouraged to discuss this with the teacher or the coordinator.

SAFE RELEASE OF CHILDREN

In the event that a child's parent, guardian, or emergency contact comes to the Family Center to pick up the child and appears to be under the influence of alcohol or drugs, we will not release the child. Our policy is:

1. To offer a ride to that person and the child.

2. To offer to call someone to come and pick them up.

3. If the person refuses the offered ride and insists on taking the child, we will make it clear to this person that a telephone call will be made to the Vermont State Police informing them of the apparent condition of the driver and the license plate number.

CHILD ABUSE AND NEGLECT POLICY

According to the regulations found in the revised statute regarding reporting and investigating child abuse and neglect, which was passed by the 1082 Vermont State General Assembly, Molly Stark Child Care Programs staff are mandated reporters of suspected physical and emotional abuse and neglect.

Once a staff person believes that abuse or neglect may have occurred, she or he is to convey this belief immediately to the coordinator of the program or the principal of the school. Once the coordinator has been notified, the staff person or the coordinator must contact the Department of Social and Rehabilitation Services (802-442-8138) and make a report of the suspected abuse or neglect.

It is also the program's policy to:

1. Ensure that all staff are informed of this policy and of their duty, as mandated reporters, to report abuse or neglect.

2. Question all staff at the time of initial employment as to whether the person has ever been convicted of abuse or neglect.

3. Provide staff with training as to the identification and prevention of abuse or neglect.

4. Cooperate with the Department of Social and Rehabilitation Services in any investigation involving the facility or its personnel.

5. Take immediate action to safeguard children, up to and including suspending the person from duty, should an allegation of abuse or neglect be made against a staff person or anyone having access to the children.

COMPLAINT PROCEDURES

According to school district procedures, parents are encouraged to discuss concerns they have regarding their children's educational program or a particular staff member with the individual staff member who is directly involved with the child or situation immediately. If this does not lead to a resolution of the matter, then it should be discussed with the coordinator of the Family Center or the principal of Molly Stark School. The individual employee involved will be given the opportunity to explain and comment. If the matter remains unresolved, parents can contact the assistant superintendent for special services or the superintendent of schools at 802-447-7501.

If these steps do not resolve the concerns, parents may request, in writing to the chairperson of the board, an executive session with the Southwest Vermont Supervisory Union (SVSU) board of directors for the purpose of the reviewing the superintendent's decision. The chairperson must arrange this meeting within thirty (30) days. All parties involved will be asked to attend this meeting. The board will conduct such a meeting in a fair and just manner.

In addition to the school district policies and resources regarding complaints, the state of Vermont also has a Child Care Consumer Concern Line, which is available toll free (800-540-7942). The Child Care Consumer Concern Line acts as a consumer education clearinghouse for information on regulations, becoming registered or licensed, and learning about substantiated child care complaints. Since the Molly Stark Preschool and Family Center is a licensed child care environment, this line will be an appropriate resource for the parents of children who attend our program when there are questions or concerns.

FINALLY

Molly Stark School and Family Center are pleased to be able to work with parents, families, and community agencies to provide a range of services and activities. If you have any concerns, suggestions, requests, or information, please feel free to communicate them to the Molly Stark principal or the Family Center coordinator. We look forward to continuing our work together.

Appendix D

Request for Consultation

Information form to be filled out by staff member requesting Mental or Physical Health Services for a student:

REQUEST FOR CONSULTATION

Student: D.O.B.:

Classroom Teacher: Grade:

Contact Person:

Parent(s):
Address: Phone:

Date of Parental Permission:

Reasons for Referral:

Services Presently Provided at School:

Services Presently Provided Outside School:

Specific Goals for This Student at School:

Possible Early Signs of Improvement:

Appendix E

After-School Program
Sample Forms

AFTER-SCHOOL ENRICHMENT PROGRAM

Dear Staff and Parents,

WE'D LIKE TO INVITE YOU TO JOIN THE PROGRAM BY TEACHING A CLASS! Session #2 dates are: weeks of 1/11, 1/18, 1/25, 2/1, 2/15, 3/1, 3/8, 3/15 (makeup week: 3/22). Classes run once a week, from 3:15 until 4:15 following the snack provided in the cafeteria. The facilitator's stipend for teaching an 8-week class is $90. There is also $25 per class available for materials.

Here is a list of some classes offered last year. Choose one of these, or design a new class. Class size averages can vary depending on the activity but usually run between 10 and 20 students. Some classes we have offered are Baking, Sign Language, Stenciling, Basketball, Spanish, Puppetry, Origami, Computer, Rock & Roll Band, Legomania, Tie Dye, Aerobics, Filmmaking, Baby-Sitting, Indoor Soccer, Arts & Crafts, Gardening, Chess, Field Hockey, Drawing, Astronomy, Karate.

Sign below and turn this in to the office by Friday, November 20.

AFTER-SCHOOL ENRICHMENT PROGRAM SIGN UP

Name: Phone Number:

Child's Classroom:

Day You Cannot Offer Class:

Class You Would Like to Offer (Name and Description):

Indicate MINIMUM and MAXIMUM number of students preferred and AGE of students (K–3 or 4–6)

_____ I can help with student check out (4:15–4:30) for an additional stipend on these days _____

(For Staff) You can use my room from 3:15–4:15 on these days for an after-school class: MON   TUES   WED   THURS   FRI

STUDENT REGISTRATION FORM

[Front – Initial Information / Invitation to After School Enrichment]

AFTER-SCHOOL ENRICHMENT PROGRAMS
Dates: weeks of 9/14, 9/28, 10/5, 10/12, 10/19, 10/28, 11/2, 11/9
(makeup week: 11/15)

Welcome to another year of popular after-school programs! We have many new classes and fun, qualified instructors as well as our quick-to-fill regulars on our roster this year. The program is set up as follows: each session runs for eight weeks, each class meets once a week, from 3:15 to 4:15, following the snack provided in the cafeteria. Don't hesitate to call with questions. We look forward to seeing your children participate in the program this year!!

Sincerely,

REGISTRATION PROCESS

Return the registration form to the office or to your child's classroom teacher by Tuesday, September 8, in a sealed, CLEARLY MARKED envelope with your child's name and registration fees included. Classes fill quickly. Class assignments are made in the order that they are received.

Tell us which days your child CANNOT participate after school so we will know in the event that we add additional sessions of popular classes.

If you are signing your child up for MORE than one class, indicate your 1st, 2nd, etc. choices.

A letter of confirmation will come home before classes begin.

FEES

$4.00 for each class. No fee for students already enrolled in child care. Checks should be made payable to _____.

[*Back – Registration Form*]

AFTER-SCHOOL ENRICHMENT PROGRAM REGISTRATION
Dates: weeks of 9/14, 9/28, 10/5, 10/12, 10/19, 10/26, 11/2, 11/9
(makeup week: 11/16)

STUDENT NAME_____ TEACHER _____ GRADE___

HOME ADDRESS _____ HOME PHONE _____

PARENT/GUARDIAN _____

Phone number an adult can be reached on afternoons in case of cancellation:

NAME _____ PHONE _____ DAY _____

Pick up is promptly at 4:15.

My child has permission to walk home _____
Will be picked up by _____ Phone _____

ALTERNATE DAYS: If we must add sessions of popular classes, circle days your child CANNOT participate after school.   MON TUES WED THURS FRI

Kindergarten–3rd Grade Offerings: 4th–6th Grade Offerings:

1. COOKING, K–3   10. SCRABBLEMANIA, 4–6

   Monday _____   Monday _____

2. BEGINNING CHINESE, 1–3   11. COMPUTER, 4–6

   Monday _____   Tuesday _____

3. LEGOMANIA, K–3   12. ROCK & ROLL BAND, 5–6

   Tuesday_____   Tuesday _____

4. JEWELRY MAKING, K–3   13. SIGN LANGUAGE, 4–6

   Tuesday _____   Wednesday _____

5. ARTS & CRAFTS, K–3   14. ULTIMATE FRISBEE, 4–6

   Wednesday _____   Wednesday _____

6. COMPUTER, K–3   15. PING-PONG, 4–6

   Wednesday _____   Thursday _____

7. RECREATIONAL GAMES, K–3   16. BABYSITTING, 5–6

   Thursday _____   Thursday _____

8. BEGINNING SPANISH, K–3   17. CHESS, 4–6

   Friday _____   Friday_____

9. PET CARE, K–3   18. QUILTING, 4–6

   Friday _____   Friday _____

Indicate your 1st, 2nd, etc. choices if signing up for more than one class.

[Facilitator's Evaluation Form for After-School Programs]

AFTER-SCHOOL PROGRAM FACILITATOR FEEDBACK SHEET

Thank you for helping make this year's after-school programs a success. We appreciate the time, care, and energy you put into your program and hope it was an enjoyable experience for you. Perhaps you will join us again next year.

To help us evaluate this year and plan for next year, please answer the questions below and drop this in the office.

Class Taught: Number Enrolled:

Instructor: Phone Number:

1. Overall experience: Excellent ___ Good ___ Satisfactory ___ Poor ___

2. Attendance: Consistently High ___ Satisfactory ___ Consistently Low ___

3. Interest exhibited by students: Number with sincere interest ___

    Number with satisfactory interest ___

    Number better served in another class ___

4. How much money did you spend on materials?

5. Was the room space adequate?

6. Would you recommend offering this class again?

7. Other comments:

8. Would you like to be contacted again next year to be a facilitator?

Appendix F

*Sample Communications with Parents
About After-School Programs*

AFTER-SCHOOL HOMEWORK CLUB

Dear Parents,

Your child has expressed an interest in becoming part of the *Molly Stark After-School Homework Club.* The goal of this club is to assist students in developing good study habits and organizational skills as well as accepting responsibility for their homework and successfully completing their assignments. The homework club is NOT remedial, a detention, or a punishment. It is a volunteer program designed to support those students who may simply lack homework strategies.

The club meets Tuesday, Wednesday, and Thursday ALL year long from 3:00–4:00 in Mrs. Johnson's room. The schedule includes time for a snack and individual homework time. There is NO charge for this program. As with any after school program, we expect appropriate behaviors.

The first Homework Club session starts Tuesday, October 5th. Students who join the homework club should come prepared to work for the ENTIRE TIME. It is not a time for games or casual conversation. It's a time to stay current with your work, get extra help, or catch up on work.

TRANSPORTATION HOME IS THE RESPONSIBILITY OF THE PARENT.

Mrs. Johnson has already met with your child and explained the program. We hope you will consider this opportunity for your child. Please complete the form below and return to Mrs. Johnson.

Sincerely,

- -

My child _____ will participate in the Homework Club on the following days: Tuesday   Wednesday   Thursday (circle as many as wanted)

Signature _____

AFTER-SCHOOL MATH PROGRAM

Dear Parents,

This year's first session of the After-School Math Program will be held during the following weeks: 10/4, 10/11, 10/25, 11/1, 11/8, 11/15, 11/29 and 12/6. The program will include group projects and math games. The program will be offered on Wednesday afternoons from 3:00 – 4:00.

The program is for students from 1st to 3rd grade. There is no cost to students. Snacks will be provided! Unfortunately, we cannot provide transportation home.

We look forward to exciting math adventures with your child. Please return the sign-up form as soon as possible.

Sincerely,

- -

My child _____ will participate in the After-School Math Program.

Check one:

_____ My child will be picked up at 4:00.

_____ I give permission for my child to walk home.

My after-school phone number in case of emergency is _____.

Classroom teacher _____ Grade _____

_____

(Parent Signature)

AFTER-SCHOOL READING PROGRAM

Dear Parents,

The last session of the After-School Reading Program will be held during the following weeks: 4/5, 4/12, 4/26, 5/3, 5/10, 5/17 and 5/24. The program will include supervised reading and reading computer games (on Mondays). The program will be offered on Monday, Tuesday, and Wednesday afternoons from 3:00–4:00.

There is no cost to students. Snacks will be provided!

Unfortunately, we cannot provide transportation home.

We look forward to exciting reading adventures with your child. Please return the sign-up form as soon as possible.

Sincerely,

- -

My child _____ will participate in the After-School Reading Program.

Please circle the days your child will attend:

Monday   Tuesday   Wednesday

Check one:

_____ My child will be picked up at 4:00.

_____ I give permission for my child to walk home.

My after-school phone number in case of emergency is _____.

Classroom teacher _____ Grade _____

_____

(Parent Signature)

Appendix G

Sample Job Descriptions for Family Center Employees

FAMILY/SCHOOL CLINICIAN

The Family Center Family/School Clinician will be a part-time, year-round position, including school vacations.

Responsibilities

- Provide individual, family, or group counseling services to parents and children in the home or at school, as needed.
- Make home visits to support families, as needed.
- Attend team meetings to plan and monitor services, including Individual Education Plan (IEP) meetings. Review cases regularly with involved agencies and Molly Stark personnel.
- Facilitate communication and support between agencies on behalf of parents and children.
- Provide consultation services to teachers and school personnel, as needed. Consultation can be educational or evaluative.
- Provide occasional in-service training for Molly Stark personnel on topics that the clinician and the Molly Stark Principal or Family Center Coordinator mutually agree on.
- Work with Molly Stark and Family Center staff to provide a parent support group and partake in community outreach.
- Perform related work as required.

Minimum Qualifications

- Master's degree in clinical social work
- Some experience in working with children, preschool through elementary school age

FAMILY OUTREACH WORKER

The Family Outreach Worker position will be a part-time, year-round position, including school vacations.

Responsibilities

- Work intensively with a small number of families living within the Molly Stark district, primarily within their homes at times convenient to them.
- Assess, plan, and help implement comprehensive services within a family context to address factors placing families in need, including the possibility of child out-of-home placement. These services include but are not limited to counseling, parent education, daily living skill instruction, assistance in securing concrete services, and advocacy.
- Plan, coordinate, and communicate with other community services involved with families.
- Work with the Family Center staff to provide and encourage literacy and healthy lifestyle activities for Molly Stark families, including some evening and weekend times.
- Participate in Family Center on-site activities, including but not restricted to play groups, parent classes, meetings with parents, meetings with Molly Stark and Family Center staff, for a minimum of two hours per week.
- Meet individually with the coordinator on a regular, mutually agreed on schedule as well as attending group staff meetings.
- Meet with the Family/School Clinician as needed to ensure provision of comprehensive services to families identified as needing those services.
- Keep up-to-date records of work with families and other information as required by the job and various grant sources.
- Maintain and enhance job skills through the use of professional development opportunities.
- Perform related work as required.

Minimum Qualifications

- Baccalaureate degree in a human services field, such as social work, psychology, or early childhood education
- Some experience working with children, parents, and/or families

PRESCHOOL HEAD TEACHER

The preschool program is generally based on the school calendar, with some adjustments made as necessary. Teachers will be given a specified number of sick and personal days. The preschool program will run four days in the classroom, with a fifth used for teacher-family home visits and consultation conferences.

Responsibilities

- Plan, supervise, and implement a developmentally appropriate curriculum for the particular group to be taught in conjunction with the overall philosophy and program of the Family Center.
- Supervise and help to train new classroom employees, student interns, and volunteer workers (including parents). This supervision will include regular, periodic meetings as well as regularly scheduled evaluations.
- Supervise and assist in activities encompassing personal health and safety, such as toileting, personal hygiene, rest and relaxation periods, meals, and outdoor play.
- Confer with parents on children's behavior and recommend methods of dealing with individual problems as well as general child development during daily encounters, twice annual parent-teacher conferences, and other times as necessary.
- Work with the Family Center staff to provide and encourage literacy activities for Molly Stark families, including some evening or other nonclass times.
- Provide an initial home visit before the beginning of the school year, and use one day per week to meet with families in their homes or at the school to provide individual child development information.
- Meet individually with the coordinator on a regular, mutually agreed on schedule as well as attending group staff meetings. Report to the coordinator any unusual behavior or problems observed in the children or with the parents.
- Be a member of IEP teams for children, meeting regularly with other members of the team as often as is necessary to ensure compliance with services and accommodations as written in the IEP.
- Write weekly plans and make them available to parents and the coordinator, and to the Family Center newsletter as required.
- Maintain developmental records on children and prepare a variety of related records and reports.
- Maintain and enhance teaching skills through the use of professional development opportunities.
- Perform related work as required.

Minimum Qualifications

- Baccalaureate degree in early childhood education, child development, or equivalent
- Some experience in teaching or working with young children
- Some experience working with children with special needs
- Course work or training in continuing education, especially in working with children with special needs, including emotional disabilities

KINDERCARE LEAD PROVIDER

The kindercare child care program is generally based on the school calendar, with some adjustments as necessary. Teachers will be given a specified number of sick and personal days.

Responsibilities

- Plan, supervise, and implement a developmentally appropriate curriculum for the kindergarten children in conjunction with the overall philosophy and program of the Family Center.
- Supervise and help to train new classroom employees, student interns, and volunteer workers (including parents). This supervision will include regular, periodic meetings as well as regularly scheduled evaluations.
- Assume responsibility for the safety of the children in the classroom and outdoors.
- Meet on an as-needed basis with Molly Stark teachers to develop complimentary curricula and share individual child and classroom information as necessary to provide consistent support for children enrolled in kindercare.
- Meet individually with the coordinator on a regular, mutually agreed upon schedule as well as attending group staff meetings. Report to the coordinator any unusual behavior or problems observed in the children or with the parents.
- Write weekly plans and make them available to parents and the coordinator, and to the Family Center newsletter as required.
- Maintain developmental records on children and prepare a variety of related records and reports.
- Maintain and enhance teaching skills through the use of professional development opportunities.
- Perform related work as required.

Minimum Qualifications

- High school diploma and some post–high school continuing education
- Some experience working with young children
- Course work or training in continuing education, especially in working with children with special needs, including emotional disabilities

TEACHING ASSISTANT (PRESCHOOL AND CHILD CARE)

The preschool and kindergarten child care programs follow the school calendar, with some adjustments. School-age child care runs during school vacations, including summer. Teaching assistants working in the school-age child care programs will be expected to work during school vacations, with a specified number of vacation, sick, and personal days.

Responsibilities

- Assist in planning, supervising, and implementing a developmentally appropriate curriculum for the particular group in which the assistant works in conjunction with the overall philosophy and program of the Family Center.
- Assist in activities encompassing personal health and safety, such as toileting, personal hygiene, rest and relaxation periods, and meals. Assume responsibility for the safety of the children in the classroom and outdoors and report any injuries or illnesses to the Head Teacher.
- Participate in staff meetings on a regular basis and attend other meetings or family conferences as required by the program for individual children.
- Assist in maintaining developmental records on children and preparing a variety of related records and reports.
- When the Head Teacher is absent, assume responsibility for more direct supervision in accordance with the needs of the substitute teacher. In some cases, this will mean assuming the role of Head Teacher.
- Maintain and enhance teaching skills through the use of professional development opportunities.
- Perform related work as required.

Minimum Qualifications

- High school diploma or GED certificate
- Some experience working with young children
- Course work or training in continuing education, especially in working with children with special needs, including emotional disabilities

Resources

We mention a number of organizations that provide technical assistance or other resources in this book. The following is a selected list of places where readers interested in additional information can go. Each Web site links to many more sites that contain valuable information. We have not included state and local sites, of which there are many.

Beacons Technical Assistance Center
Fund for the City of New York
121 Avenue of the Americas
New York, NY 10013
Telephone: 212-925-6675
Fax: 212-925-5675
E-mail: pkleinbard@fcny
Web site: http://www.fcny.org/

Center for Community Partnerships: University-Assisted
    Community Schools
University of Pennsylvania
133 South 36th Street, Suite 519
Philadelphia, PA 19104-3246
Telephone: 215-898-5351
Fax: 215-573-2096
E-mail: Harkavy@pobox.upenn.edu/
Web site: www.upenn.edu/ccp

Children's Aid Society Community School Technical Assistance
    Center
Salome Urena Middle Academies, IS 218
4600 Broadway at 196th Street
New York, NY 10040
Telephone: 212-569-2866 or 212-569-2882
E-mail: richardn@childrensaidsociety.org
Web site: http://www.childrensaidsociety.org/

Clearinghouse on Services in Schools
Center for Mental Health in Schools
Department of Psychology
University of California
Los Angeles, CA 90095-1563
Telephone: 310-825-3634
E-mail: smph@ucla.edu
Web site: http://smhp.psych.ucla.edu/

Coalition for Community Schools
Institute for Educational Leadership
1001 Connecticut Avenue NW, Suite 310
Washington, DC 20036
Telephone: 202-822-8405
Fax: 202-872-4050
E-mail: ccs@iel.org
Web site: http://www.communityschools.org/

Comer School Development Program
55 College Street
New Haven, CT 06511
Telephone: 203-737-1020
E-mail: schooldevelopmentprogram@yale.edu
Web site: http://www.schooldevelopmentprogram.org/

Communities in Schools
277 S. Washington Avenue, Suite 210
Alexandria, VA 22314
Telephone: 703-519-8999
E-mail: smithm@cisnet.org
Web site: http://www.cisnet.org/

**ERIC Clearinghouse on Elementary and Early Childhood
    Education**
University of Illinois at Urbana, Champaign
Children's Research Center
51 Gerity Drive
Champaign, IL 61820-7469
Telephone: 800-583-4135 (voice/TTY) or 217-333-1386
E-mail: ericeece@uicu.edu
Web site: http://www.ericeece.org/

The Finance Project: Funding for Community Schools
100 Vermont Avenue NW, Suite 600
Washington, DC 20005
Telephone: 202-628-4200
Fax: 202-628-4205
E-mail: sdeich@ financeproject.org
Web site: http://www.financeproject.org/

National Association for the Education of Young Children
1509 16th Street NW
Washington, DC 20036
Telephone: 202-232-8777 or 800-424-2460
E-mail: naeyc@naeyc.org
Web site: http://www.naeyc.org/

National Center for Community Education
1017 Avon Street
Flint, MI 48503
Telephone: 810-238-0463
Fax: 810-238-9211
E-mail: pedwards@earthlink.net
Web site: http://www.nccenet.org/

National Institute on Early Childhood Development and Education
555 New Jersey Avenue NW
Washington, DC 20208
Telephone: 202-219-1935
E-mail: eci@inet.ed.gov
Web site: http://www.ed.gov/offices/OERI/ECI/

National Institute on Out-of-School Time
Wellesley College
106 Central Street
Wellesley, MA 02481
Telephone: 781-283-2547
E-mail: niost@wellesley.edu
Web site: http://www.niost.org/

National Mentoring Center
Northwest Regional Educational Laboratory
101 S. W. Main Street, Suite 500
Portland, OR 97204
Telephone: 503-275-9500
E-mail: fulopm@nwrel.org
Web site: http://www.nwrel.org/mentoring/

National Network for Child Care
Cooperative Extension Systems Resource
E-mail: kidcare@extension.umn.edu
Web site: http://www.nncc.org/

National Network of Partnership Schools
Johns Hopkins University
3003 N. Charles Street, Suite 200
Baltimore, MD 21218
Telephone: 410-516-8800
E-mail: nnps@csos.juh.edu
Web site: http://www.csos.jhu.edu/p2000/

National Assembly on School-Based Health Care
666 11th Street NW, Suite 735
Washington, DC 20001
Telephone: 202-638-5872
E-mail: jschlitt@nasbhc.org
Web site: http://www.nasbhc.org/

Schools of the 21st Century
The Yale University Bush Center in Child Development and Social Policy
310 Prospect Street
New Haven, CT 06511
Telephone: 203-432-9944
E-mail: jennifer.heath@yale.edu
Web site: http://www.yale.edu/bushcenter/21C/

Thirteen Ed Online/Disney Learning Partnership
Workshop Month 11: After School Programs—From Vision to Reality
Web site: http://www.thirteen.org/edonline/concept2class/month11/
   index.html

**21st Century Community Learning Centers After-School
   Programs**
U.S. Department of Education
400 Maryland Avenue, SW
Washington, DC 20202-6175
Telephone: 202-260-0919
E-mail: 21stcclc@e.gov
Web sites: http://www.ed.gov/21stcclc/; http://www.afterschool.gov/
   (links to 47 agencies); http://www.afterschoolalliance.org/

United Way of America Bridges to Success
701 North Fairfax Street
Alexandria, VA 22314-2045
Telephone: 703-836-7112
Fax: 703-549-9152
E-mail: mobilization@unitedway.org
Web site: http://national.unitedway.org/mobilization/mob_b2s.cfm

References

Abidin, R. (1995). *The parenting stress index* (3rd ed.). Lutz, FL: Psychological Assessment Resources.

Achenbach System of Empirically Based Assessment. (1991). *The behavior checklist.* Burlington, VT: Author.

Achenbach System of Empirically Based Assessment. (1997). *Caregiver-teacher report form.* Burlington, VT: Author.

Alexander, B. (2001, July/August). CBO access to funds is key in education bill. *Youth Today,* 14.

American Association of School Administrators. (2000). *An educator's guide to schoolwide reform.* Retrieved December 17, 2001, from http://www.aasa. org/Reform/overview.htm

Anyon, J. (1997). *Ghetto schools: A political economy of urban educational reform.* New York: Teachers College Press.

Blank, M., & Langford, B. (2000, September). *Strengthening partnerships: Community school assessment checklist.* Washington, DC: Coalition for Community Schools. Retrieved December 17, 2001, from http://www. communityschools .org/assessmentnew.pdf

Blank, M., & Melaville, A. (1999). Creating family-supportive schools: Taking the first steps. *Family Support Journal, 18*(3), 37-38.

Blank, M., & Samberg, L. (2000, October). *Strengthening schools, families and communities: Community school models* [Working draft]. Washington, DC: Coalition for Community Schools. Retrieved December 17, 2001, http:// www.communityschools.org/Models.pdf

Blue Ribbon Schools Application, 2000–2001. McCoy Elementary School, Kansas City, MO.

Building strong full-service and community schools. (2000, May). Report of the Conference of the Collaborative for Integrated School Services. Cambridge, MA: Harvard University Graduate School of Education.

Burns, C., & Gorman, K. (1999). *Kindergarten teacher questionnaire.* Unpublished manuscript, University of Vermont at Burlington.

Calfee, C., Wittwer, F., & Meredith, M. (1998). *Building a full-service school: A step-by-step guide.* San Francisco: Jossey-Bass.

Canada, G. (1996, Spring). The Beacons: Building healthy communities. *Community Education Journal,* 16–18.

Center for Mental Health in Schools. (1999, October). *Expanding educational reform to address barriers to learning: Restructuring student support services and enhancing school-community partnerships.* Los Angeles: UCLA, Department of Psychology.

Center for Mental Health in Schools. (2000). *Pioneer initiatives to reform education support programs.* Los Angeles: UCLA, Department of Psychology.

Center for Mental Health in Schools. (n.d.). *School-community partnerships: A guide.* Los Angeles: UCLA, Department of Psychology.

Coalition for Community Schools. (2001). *School-community partnerships in support of student learning.* Washington, DC: Author.

Coalition for Community Schools. (2002). *Linkages to learning.* Washington, DC: Author.

Council of Chief State School Officers. (2000, May). *Extended learning initiatives: Opportunities and implementation challenges.* Washington, DC: Author.

Denton, D. (n.d.). *Helping families to help students: Kentucky's family resource and youth service centers.* Atlanta, GA: Southern Regional Education Board. Retrieved December 17, 2001, from http://www.sreb.org/programs/srr/pubs/Helping_Families.pdf

Dryfoos, J. (1994). *Full-service schools: A revolution in health and social services for children, youth, and families.* San Francisco: Jossey-Bass.

Dryfoos, J. (1998). *Safe passage: Making it through adolescence in a risky society.* New York: Oxford University Press.

Dryfoos, J. (2000, July 11). *Evaluation of community schools: Findings to date.* Retrieved December 17, 2001, from http://www.communityschools.org/evaluation/evalcontents.html. Also available by request from author at jdryf65322@aol.com.

Edwards, P. (1996, Spring). The challenge to community educators. *Community Education Journal,* 33.

Epstein's six types of parent involvement. (n.d.). Retrieved December 17, 2001, from http://www.northstar.k12.ak.us/parent/pacifour.html

Fashola, O. (1998, October). *Review of extended-day and after-school programs and their effectiveness* (Report No. 24). Baltimore, MD: Johns Hopkins University, Center for Research on the Education of Students Placed at Risk.

Fletcher, A. (n.d.). *After-school learning and safe neighborhood partnerships.* Sacramento, CA: California Wellness Foundation & The Foundation Consortium.

Florida Department of Health and Rehabilitative Services & Florida Department of Education. (1991). *Request for program designs for supplemental school health programs, Feb. 1–June 30, 1991. Instructions.* Tallahassee, FL: Author.

Fullan, M. (1993). *Change forces: Probing the depths of education reform.* New York: Taylor & Francis.

Gray, L. (2000, November 17–23). Working together: Not-for-profit organizations in Kansas City thrive thanks to active businesses and community participation. *Focus: Nonprofit.*

Grossman, J., Walker, K., & Raley, R. (2001). *Challenges and opportunities in after-school programs: Lessons for policymakers and funders.* Philadelphia: Public/Private Ventures.

Halpern, R., Deich, S., & Cohen, C. (2000). *Financing after-school programs.* Washington, DC: The Finance Project.

Harvey, B., & Shortt, J. (2001). *Working together for children and families: A community's guide to making the most of out of school time.* Wellesley, MA: The MOST Initiative at the National Institute on Out-of-School Time.

House Bill 17 (2001, January 3) and Senate Bill 1005 (2001, June 7). The Younger Americans Act. Introduced in the 107th Congress and referred to committees.

Ireton, H. (1992). *Child development inventory.* Minneapolis, MN: Behavioral Science Systems.

Jacobson, L. (2001, February 14). Districts utilize Title I flexibility to prepare little ones for school. *Education Week,* 1.

McLeod, B. (n.d.). Parent involvement. *School reform and student diversity: Educating students from diverse linguistic and cultural backgrounds.* Retrieved December 17, 2001, from http://www.ncbe.gwu.edu/miscpubs/ncrcdsll/3r3d/parcnt3.htm

McMahon, T., Ward, N., Pruett, M., Davidson, L., & Griffith, E. (2000). Building full-service schools: Lessons learned in the development of interagency collaboratives. *Journal of Educational and Psychological Consultation, 11*(1), 65–92.

Melaville, T., & Blank, M. (1998, September). *Learning together: The developing field of school-community initiatives.* Flint, MI: Charles S. Mott Foundation.

Miller, B. (2001, April). The promise of after-school programs. *Educational Leadership, 58*(7), 6–12.

Moving forward: Making the grade becomes the center for health and health care in schools. (2000, Winter). *Access,* 4. Washington, DC: George Washington University.

National Assembly on School-Based Health Care. (2000, June). *Creating access to care for children and youth: School-based health center census, 1998–1999.* Washington, DC: Author.

National Association of Elementary School Principals. (2001). *Principals and after-school programs: A survey of pre-K–8 principals* (Executive summary). Arlington, VA: Author.

National Institute on Out-of-School Time (NIOST). (2001). *The MOST initiative: Making the most of out-of-school time.* Retrieved December 17, 2001, from http://www.niost.org/most.html

National Network of Partnership Schools. (2000). *Schools report five elements for successful partnership programs* (Type 2 research brief). Retrieved December 17, 2001, from http://www.csos.jhu.edu/p2000/

Nobel, P. (2001, August 5). Community schools: The gang's all here. *New York Times,* Education Life Supplement, p. 22.

Olsen, L., & Sharf, A. (2000). *Realizing the opportunity of after-school programs in a diverse state.* San Francisco: California Tomorrow and the Foundation Consortium.

Pardini, P. (2001, August). School-community partnering. *The School Administrator.* Retrieved December 17, 2001, from http://www.aasa.org/publications/sa/2001_08/pardini1.htm

Public/Private Ventures. (1995). *Making a difference: An impact study of Big Brother/Big Sister.* Philadelphia: Author.

Reder, N. (2000). *Finding funding: Guide to federal sources for out-of-school time and community school initiatives.* Washington, DC: The Finance Project.

Ringers, J., & Decker, L. (1995). *School community centers: Guidelines for inter-agency planners.* Charlottesville, VA: University of Virginia, Mid-Atlantic Center for Community Education.

Rusk, B., Shaw, J., & Joong, P. (1994). *The full-service school.* Toronto: Ontario Secondary School Teachers' Federation, Educational Services Committee.

Santiago, E. (2000, December). The real successes of partnerships. *Collaborative for Integrated School Services Newsletter, 6*(2), 3.

Sarason, S. (1995, March). *Parental involvement and the political principle: Why the existing governance structure of schools should be abolished.* San Francisco: Jossey-Bass.

Schorr, L., & Yankelovich, D. (2000, February 16). What works to better society can't always be measured. *Los Angeles Times,* p. 7.

Schweinhart, L., & Weikart, D. (Eds.). (1993). *Significant benefits: The High/Scope Perry Preschool Study through age 27.* Ypsilanti, MI: High/Scope Press.

Sparks, P. (1996, Spring). Community schools the Birmingham way. *Community Education Journal,* 19–22.

Steig, W. (1972). *Dominic.* New York: Farrar, Straus & Giroux.

Sylvester, K., & Reich, K. (2000, November). *After-school programs: Issues and ideas.* Los Altos, CA: David and Lucile Packard Foundation.

Testa, K. (2000, May). *Development of joint-use educational facility agreements between California public school districts and community entities.* Unpublished doctoral dissertation, University of La Verne, CA.

Thirteen Ed Online & Disney Learning Partnership. (n.d.). *After-school programs: From vision to reality.* Retrieved December 17, 2001, from http://www.thirteen.org/edonline/concept2class/month11/index.html

Tierney, J., & Grossman, J. B., with N. L. Resch. (2000). *Making a difference: An impact study of Big Brothers/Big Sisters.* Philadelphia: Public/Private Ventures.

Toch, T. (2001 January 7). The plight of the PTA. Education Life Supplement, *New York Times,* p. 14.

U.S. Department of Education. (1996, May). *Putting the pieces together: Comprehensive school-linked strategies for children and families.* Washington, DC: Author.

U.S. Department of Education. (2000a, April). *Schools as centers of community: A citizens' guide for planning and design.* Washington, DC: Author.

U.S. Department of Education. (2000b, June). *After-school programs: Keeping children safe and smart.* Washington, DC: Author.

U.S. Department of Education. (2000c, September). *21st Century Community Learning Centers: Providing quality after-school learning opportunities for America's families.* Washington, DC: Author.

U.S. Department of Education, Office of Elementary and Secondary Education. (2001). *21st Century Community Learning Centers program: Application for grants.* Washington, DC: Author.

U. S. Department of Justice. (2000, November). *Comprehensive responses to youth at risk: Interim findings from the Safe Futures initiative.* Washington, DC: Author.

Veale, J., Morley, R., & Erickson, C. (2002). *Practical evaluation for collaborative services: Goals, processes, tools, and reporting systems for school-based programs.* Thousand Oaks, CA: Corwin.

Walker, K., Grossman, J., & Raley, R. (with Holton, G., & Fellerath, V.). (2000, December). *Extended services schools: Putting programming in place.* Philadelphia: Public/Private Ventures.

Warren, C. (1999, January 27). *Lessons from the evaluation of New Jersey's School-Based Youth Services Program.* Paper presented at the National Invitational Conference on Improving Results for Children and Families by Connecting Collaborative Services with School Reform Efforts, Temple University Center for Research in Human Development and Education, Philadelphia.

White, W. (2001, March 29). Testimony before the House Education and Workforce Committee.

Index

National Association for the Education of
Young Children, 62, 217
National Association of Elementary School
Principals, 70
National Center for Community Education
(NCCE), 18, 113, 182, 218
National Coalition for Parent Involvement in
Education (NCPIE), 122
National Collaboration for Youth, 72
National Education Association (NEA), 177
National Institute on Early Childhood Devel-
opment and Education, 218
National Institute on Out-of-School Time
(NIOST), 70, 89, 92, 218
National Mentoring Center, 93, 218
National Network for Child Care, 218
National Network of Partnership Schools,
218
  collaborating with community, 123
  decision making, 123
  home learning, 123
  parental involvement and, 122-124
  parent education, 122
  parent volunteers, 123
  school/home communication, 123
National School-Age Care Alliance, 92
Needs assessment, conducting, 23-24
Negron, R., 101-102
Nemeth, J., 57
New American Schools Development
Corporation, 51
New American Schools initiative, 3
Newark (NJ):
  CAS adaptation site, 91
  Newark School District, 153
New Jersey Department of Human
Services, 2
New York City School District 6 super-
intendent, CAS director of
community schools and, 102
New York State:
  Community Schools Program, 166
Nobel, P., 183

Olsen, L., 151, 152
Open Society Institute, 75
Oregon:
  collaborative children's services/programs,
111-112
  community learning centers, 111
  community schools legislation, 166

Papitto, M., 107
Pardini, P., 102
Parent programs, 119, 124-125
  exemplary, 119-121
  family-school compacts, 121
  family-school contract, 121
  Feinberg-Fisher Elementary School, 119

Florida Full-Service Schools program, 120-
121, 166
home visits, 122
Quitman Street Community School, 120
special components, 121-122
Wake County Education Partnership, 121
See also National Network of Partnership
Schools, parental involvement and;
PTA
Partnerships, developing effective, 100-101.
See also Governance structures; Lead
agencies
Payzant, T., 26
Plainfield (NJ), systemwide planning in, 89, 167
Planning process, full-service community
school, 18, 21-24, 27-28, 176
  components, 22
  conducting needs assessment, 23-24
  convening a planning group, 22
  goal setting, 24-25
  identifying leaders/governance structure,
25-26
  inclusiveness, 21
  systemwide, 26-27
  visioning, 18
  See also Full-service community schools,
models of
Portland (OR):
  collaborative financial arrangements, 167
  systemwide planning in, 27, 89
  See also Schools Uniting Neighborhoods
(SUN)
Prentiss, A., 105
Preschool programs, 50
Professional development, 42-43
Pruett, M., 147, 153
PS 5 (New York City), achievement outcomes
at, 132
PTA, 121, 124
Public Education Network, 168
Public/Private Ventures, 84, 147, 150
Putney, C., 58, 170, 172

Quitman Street Community School (Newark,
NJ), 5, 76-77, 124
  Comer concepts and, 56
  family resource center, 120
  Health Place, 48
  leadership, 87
  Parent Academy, 48
  parent program, 120, 121
  preschool program, 50
  summer camp, 77
  transportation, 151

Racine, D., 44, 183
Raley, R., 78, 88, 91, 147, 150
Reder, N., 161, 162
Reed, J., 165